SHAKESPEARE AND AMATEUR
PERFORMA

CW00816199

From the *Hamlet* acted on a galleon
outdoor productions of *A Midsummer 1*
each English summer, *Shakespeare and A*
the unsung achievements of those outs
who have been determined to do Shakespeare themselves. Based on
extensive research in previously unexplored archives, this generously
illustrated and lively work of theatre history enriches our understanding of how and why Shakespeare's plays have mattered
to generations of rude mechanicals and aristocratic dilettantes
alike: from the days of the Theatres Royal to those of the Little
Theatre Movement, from the pioneering *Winter's Tale* performed in
eighteenth-century Salisbury to the *Merchant of Venice* performed by
Allied prisoners for their Nazi captors, and from the how-to book
which transforms Mercutio into Yankee Doodle to the Napoleonic
counter-spy who used *Richard III* as a tool of surveillance.

MICHAEL DOBSON is Professor of Shakespeare Studies at Birkbeck College, University of London. He comments regularly on
Shakespeare for the BBC, the *London Review of Books* and other
publications, and he has written programme notes for the RSC,
Shakespeare's Globe, the Old Vic, the Sheffield Crucible and Peter
Stein. His books include *The Making of the National Poet* (1992), *The
Oxford Companion to Shakespeare* (with Stanley Wells, 2001, winner
of the Bainton Prize in 2002), *England's Elizabeth: An Afterlife
in Fame and Fantasy* (with Nicola Watson, 2002) and *Performing
Shakespeare's Tragedies Today* (2006). Between 1999 and 2007 he
reviewed every major English production of a Shakespeare play for
Shakespeare Survey.

SHAKESPEARE AND AMATEUR PERFORMANCE

PERFORMANCE

A Cultural History

MICHAEL DOBSON

CAMBRIDGE
UNIVERSITY PRESS

CAMBRIDGE UNIVERSITY PRESS
Cambridge, New York, Melbourne, Madrid, Cape Town,
Singapore, São Paulo, Delhi, Mexico City

Cambridge University Press
The Edinburgh Building, Cambridge CB2 8RU, UK

Published in the United States of America by Cambridge University Press, New York

www.cambridge.org
Information on this title: www.cambridge.org/9781107613201

First published 2011
First paperback edition 2013

A catalogue record for this publication is available from the British Library

Library of Congress Cataloging-in-Publication Data
Dobson, Michael, 1960–
Shakespeare and amateur performance : a cultural history / Michael Dobson.
p. cm.
Includes index.
ISBN 978-0-521-86234-9 (Hardback)
1. Shakespeare, William, 1564–1616–Dramatic production. 2. Shakespeare, William,
1564–1616–Stage history. I. Title.
PR3091.D63 2011
822.303–dc22
2010050042

ISBN 978-0-521-86234-9 Hardback
ISBN 978-1-107-61320-1 Paperback

Contents

Illustrations

Acknowledgements

Much of the research for this book was carried out with the support of a Leverhulme major research fellowship in 2005–7, for which I am profoundly grateful. I am happy to have the opportunity to acknowledge an older financial debt too; I first became interested in the Kilkenny private theatricals of 1802–19 when I came across and identified a cache of the company's part-books in the Bodleian Library while I was still a postgraduate student, and in 1985 the Society for Theatre Research awarded me a small grant towards visiting Ireland in order to find out more. A quarter of a century later I am pleased to have this occasion to share some of what I found.

I am particularly grateful to those in the voluntary sector who have given of their own free time to allow me to study the archives of amateur groups: in particular, Chris Metcalfe at the Middlesbrough Little Theatre; Phil Jackson at the Minack; Robin Griffin at the Stockport Garrick; Elizabeth Tatman at the Bolton Little Theatre; the archivists of the Brownsea Open Air Theatre and the Bournemouth Shakespeare Players; the members of the York Shakespeare Project who took me to a pub in York; the secretaries and other representatives of the expatriate amateur groups mentioned in my conclusion who were kind enough to correspond about their activities and send programmes and other records; and Mary Venny of the St Peter's Players in Upper Wolvercote, a group which celebrated its fiftieth birthday in 2007 by performing the mechanicals' scenes from *A Midsummer Night's Dream*. (I am proud to be the keeper of the punctured, brick-decorated duvet cover worn by Wall on that occasion.) Abigail Rokison very kindly checked some details in the Loder papers in Cambridge. Among professional archivists who have looked into otherwise rarely disturbed corners of their holdings I particularly wish to thank Walter Zvonchenko at the Library of Congress; Róisín McQuillan at the Rothe House Museum in Kilkenny; and the staffs of the Folger Shakespeare Library, the New York Historical Society, the New

York Public Library for the Performing Arts, the Special Collections Library of the University of Michigan, Ann Arbor, the Bodleian Library, the National Army Museum, and the Imperial War Museum.

I have presented work towards this book at a number of conferences and other fora, including the European Shakespeare Research Association, the Shakespeare Association of America, the British Shakespeare Association, the British Graduate Shakespeare Conference, the Swiss Association of University Teachers of English, the Renaissance group at York University, the London Shakespeare Seminar at Senate House, and the Birkbeck Eighteenth-Century Studies Group; some material towards Chapter 3 was originally presented at the Stanford conference 'Stephen Orgel: a celebration', which I would not have missed for anything. I am very grateful to my hosts, audiences and fellow seminarians on all these occasions. I must particularly thank Clara Calvo and Ton Hoenselaars for welcoming me not only to their seminar on Shakespeares exiled and imprisoned at the 2009 ESRA conference in Pisa, but also to their seminar on Shakespeare and commemoration at the 2010 SAA Conference in Chicago. Conversation with each of them has been both illuminating and delightful. I have benefited, too, from conversations with the following: Tom Betteridge; Gordon and Biddy Brown of the Lymington Players; Mark Thornton Burnett; Luisa Calè; Lisa Dillon; Lukas Erne; Lisa Freeman; Andrew J. Hartley; Peter Holland; Russell Jackson; Ros King; Tina Krontiris; Kiki Lindell; Katy Ling; Joyce Green MacDonald; Kevan Mayor; Kate McLuskie; Jane Moody; Marion O'Connor; my beloved aunt Margaret Opie-Smith; Stephen Orgel; Lois Potter; Abigail Rokison; Beaty Rubens; Prunella Scales; Richard Schoch; Isabelle Schwartz-Gastine; Robert Shaughnessy; Sir Donald Sinden; Neil Taylor; Paul Taylor; Ann Thompson; Liz Watson; Stanley Wells; Samuel West; Wendy Williams; Kathleen Wilson; and my colleagues in Theatre Studies at Birkbeck, Helen Freshwater, Andrew Mackinnon, Aoife Monks and Rob Swain.

Embryonic sections of individual chapters have appeared in *GRAMMA*, in *Swiss Papers in English Language and Literature*, in *Shakespeare, Memory and Performance*, ed.Peter Holland (Cambridge, 2006) and in *Playwrights, Players, and Playhouses: Investigating Performance, 1660–1800*, ed. Peter Holland and Michael Cordner (Palgrave, 2007); I am grateful to the editors of all these publications. In 2007 I made two short radio programmes about outdoor Shakespeare, based on research towards Chapter 4, for BBC Radio 3; their producer, Beaty Rubens, has been enormously helpful and a pleasure to work with.

At Cambridge University Press, Sarah Stanton has been a model of expertise, patience and understanding, and she made a terrific fairy in *A Midsummer Night's Dream*. I am grateful to her mother, too, who loaned me a copy of the videotape of a splendid 1981 Bath Drama Club production of the same play. Rebecca Taylor and Abigail MacDonald have been invaluable, and David Watson has been an exemplary copy editor.

Of the nine full-length books and two doctoral theses that have so far shared our household since we married, not to mention all the editions, chapters and articles, this one has probably been the most recalcitrant and the most awkward finally to see off the premises, and to describe Nicola Watson's roles in the processes of thinking it up, researching it, writing it and rewriting it as 'helping' would be a ludicrous understatement. As always, she has my awed gratitude and love. Our daughters, Elizabeth and Rosalind, meanwhile, have been a continual source of encouragement, and their willingness to accompany me to Shakespearean productions both amateur and professional, coupled with their aptitude and enthusiasm for many forms of dramatic and musical performance, suggest, I am glad to say, that the family tradition of amateur Shakespeare to which this book bears witness is not extinct yet.

UPPER WOLVERCOTE, OXFORDSHIRE,
SEPTEMBER 2010

Introduction: Shakespeare in culture

Let but a Briton step upon the stage,
Whence will he draw the glass for every age?
To one lov'd fount of magic he will go;
With one lov'd name his head and heart will glow;
One only volume will his hand unroll;
SHAKESPEARE, the mighty master of the soul!
  (Samuel Egerton Brydges, 'Prologue for Shakespeare's Henry IV', 1830)[1]

This is a book about one of the most widespread and significant ways in which the plays of William Shakespeare have participated in English-speaking culture over the four centuries since they were written. It offers the first ever sustained examination of the contexts and styles in which people who are not theatrical professionals have chosen to perform Shakespeare's plays for themselves and their immediate communities, in locations ranging from aristocratic drawing rooms to village halls, and from military encampments to rain-swept cliffsides. This is an area which earlier studies of Shakespeare's reception and dissemination – including my own – have substantially overlooked, and they have been mistaken in doing so. While amateur productions generally have shorter runs than professional ones, over time they have been far more numerous, and at several important points in theatrical history the geographical scope and social inclusiveness of the amateur theatre have dwarfed those of the commercial and subsidized playhouses. In the immediate post-war years, for example, some provincial English cities had as many as fifty competing amateur dramatic societies, and even the small York-shire town of Mirfield, birthplace of Patrick Stewart, was home to six: once asked by an American interviewer whether his working-class parents had been surprised that he had become interested in the classical theatre, Stewart replied that given his home town's investment in drama they would have been more surprised if he had not.[2] The word 'invest-ment' is crucial here: the long history of how Shakespeare has been performed by amateurs is a story of how successive groups of people have committed themselves to incorporating these plays into their own lives and their own immediate societies, and it makes visible a whole range of responses to the national drama which other reception histories have missed. This is not another book about the societies which Shakespeare's plays depict, then, but a study of the ones which they have helped to convene. Within the changing modes of amateur production, I will be arguing, the place and meaning of Shakespeare's work for successive generations of Anglophones has been continually renegotiated between his time and our own, and this book represents a first attempt at outlining the cultural history of this pervasive and enduring response to his canon and to his canonicity.

AMATEUR AND PROFESSIONAL

That history begins, as far as surviving written records are concerned, on a single date back in Shakespeare's own lifetime, namely 5 September 1607. In London that season the King's Men were performing Shakespeare's *Pericles*, during which the stage of the Globe had to imitate the deck of a ship, but some thousands of miles to the south the deck of a ship was instead imitating the stage of the Globe. 5 September 1607 was a memorable day all round for the crews of the *Red Dragon* and the *Hector*. Bound for the East Indies on the third-ever voyage organized by the East India Company, the galleons had already had an eventful journey. Separated from the third ship that had sailed with them, they had been blown off course towards Brazil, and they had then been becalmed for so long in the doldrums that their supplies had run dangerously low. Now, replenishing their stores along the coast of West Africa so as not to have to turn back towards England, they were moored at the mouth of the Mitombo river, in what has since become Freetown harbour in Sierra Leone. The overall commander of the expedition and captain of *Red Dragon*, William Keeling, had on 4 September received the brother-in-law of the local king, Buré, together with three followers, onto his ship. This African royal emissary, christened Lucas Fernandez, was a former resident of the Portuguese-governed Cape Verde islands, where he had been brought up as a Catholic and educated in European languages; Keeling refers to him in his journal simply as 'the interpreter'. He would soon encounter a major challenge to his skills as such, the task of providing, for his three companions, the first-ever simultaneous translation of a Shakespearean performance, quite possibly into both Portugese and the local African language, Temne:

> September 5. I sent the interpreter, according to his desire, aboard the *Hector*, where he broke fast, and after came aboard me, where we gave the tragedy of Hamlet; and in the afternoon we all went ashore together, to see if we could shoot an elephant; we shot seven or eight bullets into him, and made him bleed exceedingly, as appeared by his track, but being near night we were constrained aboard, without effecting our purposes on him.[3]

Three diplomatic presents: a meal, a bloody but inconclusive elephant hunt and, in the interim, *The Tragedy of Hamlet, Prince of Denmark*. The first-ever recorded production of a Shakespeare play outside Europe was not performed by professional actors in a commercial playhouse, but as part of an exchange of gifts, so that 5 September 1607 saw the beginning not only of the history of Shakespeare in Africa but of the recorded history of Shakespeare in non-professional performance. As if determined to underline his crew's historic status as the first honorary amateur dramatic society ever to play the work of William Shakespeare, Captain Keeling had his men perform another script by the same author to entertain his colleague, the master of the *Hector*, on 29 September – 'Captain Hawkins dined with me, when my company acted King Richard the Second' – and half a year later, on 31 March 1608, they repeated *Hamlet*. Recording this event, Keeling noted his reasons for allowing it, echoing some of the East India Company's standard instructions for the maintenance of discipline: 'I invited Captain Hawkins to a fish dinner, and had Hamlet acted aboard me; which I permit, to keep my people from idleness and unlawful games, or sleep.'[4]

However odd *Richard II* may look as a play chosen to keep mariners too busy to think about mutiny (the main potential danger which might make any captain fear 'idleness'), there were good reasons why *Hamlet* might recommend itself to a sea-captain in quest of material for shipboard performance by his crew, quite apart from those which might make it suitable for professional command performances at court back home. Quite apart from his salty offstage adventures encountering pirates in the North Sea, the Prince himself recognizes drama, and especially tragedy, as something which ought at very least to keep the discerning awake, as he makes clear in his derisive comment on Polonius' theatrical tastes – 'he's for a jig, or a tale of bawdry, or he sleeps' (2.2.503–4).[5] But in the world of *Hamlet* drama has social uses far beyond this, and they are

not confined to the professional Players. Even the supposedly undiscriminating Polonius is a veteran of the amateur stage, having played Julius
Caesar while at university, and Hamlet, with the possible exception only
of Nick Bottom the weaver, is the most passionate exponent of amateur
theatricals in the Shakespeare canon, serving as actor, director and even
playwright. He insists on performing most of Aeneas' account of the
killing of Pyrrhus when the players arrive at Elsinore, gives them detailed
notes before the performance he arranges before the court and contributes
his own speech of some dozen or sixteen lines to *The Murder of Gonzago*,
a.k.a. *The Mousetrap*. It is not entirely surprising that this level of enthusiasm, like so much else within *Hamlet*, should have spilled over from the
play into the culture at large and inspired generations of readers to give
their associates a taste of their own quality by treating *Hamlet* just as its
protagonist treats the death of Pyrrhus. It is true that the Players are
themselves full-time, and that Hamlet's discussion of the rivalry with
child-actors in the city which has forced them to go on tour reveals a
shrewd sense of the economics of the public stage. But here, as elsewhere,
Shakespeare – unlike contemporaries such as Beaumont and Fletcher –
refrains from depicting either commercial playwrights or purpose-built
theatres. Participation in dramatic performance within the Shakespeare
canon is not primarily a business matter for professionals.

In fact, just like the 1607 shipboard *Hamlet*, theatrical events depicted
by Shakespeare take place not on a solely commercial basis but within a
gift economy. The Pageant of the Nine Worthies in *Love's Labour's Lost*,
'Pyramus and Thisbe' in *A Midsummer Night's Dream* and the morris-
dance in *The Two Noble Kinsmen* are subordinated to the surviving codes
and practices of feudalism, presented strictly as the dutiful offerings of
commoners to their social superiors, and even the troupes who arrive at
the Lord's house in the induction to *The Taming of the Shrew* and at
Elsinore in *Hamlet* offer 'service' to individual patrons rather than services
to all paying comers. While doing so they are not treated as independent
contractors working solely for a cash fee, moreover, but are adopted as
temporary members of these respective households. The Lord in *The
Taming of the Shrew*, hearing the actors' trumpet, at first expects 'some
noble gentleman that means, / Travelling some journey, to repose him
here', and even when he discovers that it is merely the actors (offering
what they describe as their 'duty') he provides a similar sort of feudal
hospitality: '. . . give them friendly welcome every one. / Let them want
nothing that my house affords' (Ind, 73–4, 101–2). Hamlet too welcomes
actors as members of his household, requesting that Polonius should see

them 'well bestowed' (2.2.524–5). Acting, in Shakespeare's plays, is primarily a food gig, whether you do it for a living or not. It is striking in this connection that Shakespeare's most elevated vision of the theatre – his brief glimpse of a Platonic super-drama able to do full justice to human history – does not feature professionals at all:

> O for a Muse of fire, that would ascend
> The brightest heaven of invention:
> A kingdom for a stage, princes to act,
> And monarchs to behold the swelling scene. (*Henry V*, Prol, 1–4).

However one reads the metaphor here, no one, presumably, would be paid for any of this, or have to do it for a living. What is being imagined seems much closer to the court theatricals which King James would patronize a few years later, when princes really did act before monarchs, albeit with some incidental help from more experienced players such as the in-house royal servants, Shakespeare's troupe, the King's Men. This arrangement has an even closer corollary within the Shakespeare canon, in that Prospero, like James, uses his own resident servants – Ariel and his fellow spirits – when he wants to host a theatrical entertainment in act 4 of *The Tempest*. As at court, at the very top of the social pyramid of favours and obligations, theatre in Shakespeare's time, even commercial theatre, takes place under the sign of gift and patronage. In fact Shakespeare's company, the Lord Chamberlain's Men, probably became the King's Men on the accession of James as a gift themselves, their services passed on to the new monarch from the old Chamberlain as a display of loyalty to the new regime and in hope of future preferment.[6] William Shakespeare was not what we would call an amateur, certainly, but as the liveried nominal servant of an aristocrat and then a king he was not exactly what we would now describe as professional either, and it should not be too surprising that in performance his plays have gone on appearing on both sides of the boundary between those who do it for love (to spell out the etymology of the word 'amateur') and those who do it for money.

Back-dating a modern sense of where that boundary lies and what it means into Shakespeare's own time is of course an unhistorical thing to do, and to describe the crew of the *Red Dragon* as an 'honorary amateur dramatic society' is consciously to misapply nomenclature which did not exist until the nineteenth century to a group of performers from the early seventeenth. Self-identified amateur companies could not come into being until other groups of actors had codified their working practices and financial arrangements into regulatory patterns, common to other skilled occupations, to which the word 'professional' would only be applied in the later eighteenth and early nineteenth centuries, and in practice the terms 'amateur dramatic society' and 'amateur dramatic club' were only widely used from the Victorian period onwards. Back in the sixteenth and seventeenth centuries, since there was no designated guild for full-time actors (and the social status of players admitted to the membership of existing guilds was at best ambiguous), there was no correspondingly clear non-guild status for occasional performers. If this means that strictly speaking it would be anachronistic to describe any part-time performers in Shakespeare's time as amateurs, it also implies that it would be equally misleading to describe early modern full-time performers as professionals. Although the received history of the English stage has usually wished to identify Shakespeare's period as the era which saw the emergence of the theatrical profession as such (what in 1962 Muriel Bradbrook influentially called *The Rise of the Common Player*), the desire to represent Shakespeare and his colleagues as thoroughgoing self-established professionals may reflect not so much the state of the Elizabethan stage as that of twentieth-century universities, where the first generations of full-time academic theatre historians were perennially anxious to distinguish themselves from the mere dilettantes and enthusiasts who had hitherto chronicled the development of English drama.

Indeed, the more one examines the categories of 'professional' and 'amateur' across theatrical history the more precarious and complicated they appear to be, even without tracing modern Western drama back to its pre-professional religious roots in ancient Athens or medieval Europe. Any study of amateur drama is therefore confronted at its outset with the vexed problem of how to define it. Before the 'amateur dramatics' of the nineteenth and twentieth centuries, for instance, there were 'private theatricals'. These were typically performances staged at aristocratic country houses before invited audiences, but given by casts which might well include London professionals hired for the occasion alongside high-born volunteers, and the question of exactly how the professional status of famous and experienced actors was to be negotiated against the social status of their inexperienced but often titled colleagues was never a simple one. The attempt to distinguish amateur performance from professional simply by noting whether hard cash changes hands, either at a box office or between managers and players, usually fails. It is not true that professionals are simply those who make theatre for money, as opposed to those who make theatre for love alone: today plenty of professional companies are run on a not-for-profit basis, and plenty more which intend to make profits do not but are in practice lovingly subsidized out of the savings of their personnel. ('I have never been able to understand why anybody should think that those who devote their entire lives to the most insecure and heartbreaking profession in the world,' wrote an exasperated Norman Marshall in 1947, 'should be considered less sincere than those to whom acting is merely a pastime for the winter evenings.')[7] Some mainstream amateur companies raise more money from ticket sales than do many nominally professional fringe companies, and a high percentage of aspiring actors whose CVs describe them as professional can in fact make ends meet only by holding day-jobs outside the theatre even while appearing in productions. Without the benefit of hindsight, it has never been easy to distinguish between a young waiter with a serious amateur interest in the theatre and an apprentice actor with a part-time job in catering. Although the line between gentlemen and players is as fiercely policed today around the edges of the modern theatrical profession as it ever was in Victorian cricket, with the majority of career actors condescending nervously to their amateur colleagues as a pool of unqualified blackleg labour willing at a moment's notice to do their work for no pay, most professional actors have performed as amateurs in their youth, and even the major metropolitan playhouses have at different times been willing to violate the supposedly sacred distinction between professional and amateur – as in the case of anonymous unpaid try-outs ('The Part of Hamlet will be played by a Gentleman, making his first appearance on any Stage!', as eighteenth- and nineteenth-century London playbills routinely declared), or the nineteenth-century vogue for members of Society appearing as amateurs with professional companies (pioneered by the rakish Colonel William Berkeley, of whom more in my second chapter).

Nominally amateur productions, meanwhile, have often employed full-time professional personnel, whether as principal actors (as in the case of some Augustan private theatricals, in a pattern which survives in the semi-professional American 'summer stock' system, whereby professional actors arrive in provincial towns to perform summer seasons with supporting casts of local volunteers), as musicians, or as directors. In one standard practice for the classic English amateur dramatic society of the first half of the twentieth century, a practice which in many instances persisted as late as the 1960s, the subscriptions of the members who took acting roles in the society's productions were used to pay the salary of a full-time professional 'producer', a figure who supervised the rehearsal and mise-en-scène of every single show the society mounted, and who occupied much the same position as the resident 'professional' within a golf club. These societies had often evolved from groups which originally confined themselves to private play readings, and whose members turned to acting in public themselves only after a period of instead either commissioning benefit performances at a local professional theatre or buying in professional performers to act their chosen plays on their own premises. What we would now recognize as amateur dramatic societies in many instances emerged only from semi-public theatrical activity associated with local literary societies (such as the Manchester Athenaeum), and the question of whether such performances – given by professional actors hired by a private patron or club – would count as amateur or professional remains moot (as is that as to which of the two designations would give them more prestige or respectability). Even performances given by a self-sustaining professional company in a professional theatre, but given for charity rather than gain, are also only questionably 'commercial', as are any number of subsidized 'community theatre' projects into which local volunteer performers may be organized by paid professional administrators and directors.[8] Once one starts examining the permeable boundaries of what might count as non-professional performance, it is surprising what a high percentage of theatrical activity over the last four centuries might fall within them.

The category 'amateur' being as unstable as it is, and perpetually defined against the changing and equally shaky category of 'professional', there can be no seamless unitary history of amateur performance, let alone an exhaustive one, and this book does not purport to offer such a thing. Teleological stories about the seemingly inevitable chronological 'evolution' of British and American drama, which are precarious enough when applied to the metropolitan professional stage, look even more so when applied to the comparatively intermittent activities of different amateur groups. Whereas Olivier knew about Irving, and Irving about Garrick, for instance, most of the non-professional casts I will be writing about knew little if anything of their amateur predecessors' existence or styles of playing, but produced the performances they did largely in imitation of or reaction against the professional productions of their own times and places and the recent repertories of their own local groups. Equally, while the history of professional performance has left detailed records, many of which have by now been laboriously and usefully catalogued and sometimes even interpreted by generations of theatre historians, amateur performance (although some societies do possess rich and excellently preserved archives) leaves more diffuse and scattered traces: blandly approving reviews in local newspapers mainly anxious to mention all the people involved who would wish to be thanked; letters; diary entries; collections of programmes in sheds; folders of fading and sometimes unlabelled photographs; passing references in volumes of otherwise untheatrical memoirs. It has also given rise to very little published history and criticism as such, instead inspiring how-to books, official and semi-official reports, compilations of amusing stories about embarrassing onstage accidents, enthusiasts' magazines (often short-lived), and privately published accounts of individual clubs. Revealing as this evidence can be, it does not add up to the unbroken chronicle of a single continuous phenomenon, and it lends itself best not to any one totalizing perspective but to the detailed investigation of discrete incidents, contextualized by reference to contemporary professional productions, to other contemporary non-professional performances and to social and cultural history more generally. The surviving visual records of amateur performance, I should add, are also of very variable quality, so that the case histories I will be exploring are illustrated here with pictures whose technical accomplishment is not to be compared with those found in the biographies of professional thespians famous enough to have been painted by Zoffany or photographed by Angus McBean.

Faced with the large and complicated field of amateur theatre, of which no single history has been published since the 1960s,[9] I have chosen to address only the amateur performance of Shakespeare. Despite the centrality of Shakespeare to the amateur repertory asserted by my epigraph, it should be recognized that this decision produces a necessarily skewed and partial view of the non-professional stage, since many important amateur theatres have never produced his work, much preferring more recent and newly commissioned material.[10] I have further confined myself, reluctantly, to amateur performances given in English, and although I devote the whole of my third chapter and part of my conclusion to the expatriate amateur players, civilian and military, who have followed the example of the *Red Dragon*, my focus is primarily on Britain and Ireland and, to a lesser extent, North America. This is in part simply a pragmatic decision aimed at producing a manageable-sized study of a long period of cultural history. It is also prompted, however, by divergences between different national traditions of amateur theatre. It would evidently make good sense, for example, to write a pan-European history of the enthusiasm for private theatres displayed by internationally connected aristocrats right across the Continent from the mid-seventeenth century onwards, often seen as part of a general withdrawal of the upper classes from the public sphere, which peaked in France, Switzerland, Italy and parts of what is now Germany as well as in Britain during the 1770s and 1780s. But once the more parochial middle classes started to get in on the act in the nineteenth and twentieth centuries, distinct national cultures of non-professional performance evolved, and among them those of Great Britain and its former transatlantic colonies are more than sufficiently varied, complex and conspicuous to be going on with.[11]

What has motivated me to write this book has been less a paucity of extant historical and analytical accounts of amateur drama in general (lamentable though this is) than a persistent inattention among scholars to the importance of non-professional activity within the reception of Shakespeare in particular. The sole major exception which proves this rule has been the admission that the amateur casts directed by William Poel and Nugent Monck carried out important late Victorian and early twentieth-century experiments in the recreation of Elizabethan staging practices.[12] My guiding interest through the case-histories presented here, then, is less the importance of Shakespeare in the history of the amateur theatre since the early modern period, great though it is, than the importance of the amateur stage within the history of Shakespeare more broadly over the same period. The chapters which follow, though arranged in a broadly chronological fashion, are really extended semi-independent essays on different traditions within the amateur performance of Shakespeare, namely the domestic, the civic, the expatriate and the outdoor. The book's structure shares a pattern of departure and return with Shakespearean comedy: from looking at how Shakespeare's plays operated within the dynamics of families in country houses, it moves outwards to examine the roles they have played in articulating the public life of towns and cities, and then explores how they have served to dramatize national identity outside Britain entirely, before coming back to the English countryside to see how issues of heritage and collective history continue to inflect the plays' amateur performance today.

Despite their diversity and their historical and geographical scope, these chapters are bound together by a number of recurring questions. How has the ever-changing status of the Shakespeare canon stimulated and enabled different groups of people to mount their own non-commercial performances across time? What has this enormous range and variety of theatrical activity carried out in Shakespeare's name meant to its participants and its spectators, and what issues of gender, class and status have the plays helped them to articulate? With what other kinds of drama have Shakespeare's plays been equated or contrasted in non-professional repertories? How have different instances of amateur performance negotiated between Shakespeare's plays as expressions of high or at least national culture and the lived everyday local cultures in which they have been mounted?

I am interested in amateur performance, in short, as one of the ways in which the Shakespeare canon has been not just read but lived out over the last four hundred years. To that extent this study takes its place in a line of critical works interested in Shakespeare's participation in cultures subsequent to his own. The history of Shakespeare's reputation, and of the ever-increasing range of activities through which his fame and influence have been promulgated, has been an object of scholarly inquiry since as early as the 1930s, when Ivor Brown and George Fearon published *Amazing Monument: A Short History of the Shakespeare Industry* (1939). This self-reflexive subset of that industry greatly expanded in the 1980s and 1990s, which saw the publication of Terence Hawkes' *That Shakespeherian Rag* (1986) and *Meaning by Shakespeare* (1992), Jonathan Bate's *Shakespearean Constitutions* (1989), Gary Taylor's *Reinventing Shakespeare* (1990), Hugh Grady's *The Modernist Shakespeare* (1995), Michael Bristol's *Big Time Shakespeare* (1996) and my own *The Making of the National Poet* (1992). Between them, these studies established something like a consensus about how Shakespeare became the global phenomenon and cultural brand-name that he is today.

In outline, these accounts of the history of Shakespeare since Shakespeare have customarily told a tale of two enduring and often lucrative businesses, sometimes opposed, sometimes collusive: namely the making of shows out of Shakespeare (at an ever-growing number of venues worldwide and across an ever-widening range of media), and the making of books out of Shakespeare – at first just editions, but then biographies, dictionaries of quotations, historical novels, academic criticism, and so on. To summarize this received account of the posthumous participation of Shakespeare in Anglophone culture at speed, singling out only five dates between Keeling's shipboard *Hamlet* in 1607 and the present, one could do a lot worse than pick 1623, 1774, 1843, 1904 and 1932.[13]

In 1623 the First Folio, the first collected edition of the plays, made Shakespeare for the first time into a large up-market book, its publishers buying up copyright in the earlier quartos so that its appearance had the paradoxical effect in the short term of making some of the plays less accessible rather than more so. The Folio also declared Shakespeare's art, for the first time, to be a matter of national import: 'Triumph, my Britain,' urges Jonson's prefatory elegy. Despite its status as a piece of cultural nationalist library furniture, however, the Folio's conflicted identity as at once a new literary product and the funerary monument to a seven-years-dead man of the theatre is also visible throughout these preliminary materials. John Heminges and Henry Condell commend the volume 'To the great variety of readers', famously calling the Shakespeare canon's consumer readership into being as such with the words 'But whatever you do, buy', but the 'readers' their dedicatory letter imagines are in fact long-experienced playgoers who have already approved in performance the plays they are now revisiting in print. Ben Jonson's elegy at first consigns Shakespeare to his now past lifetime – calling him the 'Soul of the age', whose plays 'so did take Eliza, and our James' – but changes its mind at the end to bequeath the writer to an indefinite future – 'He was not of an age, but for all time!'

The more distant the age of Eliza and our James became, however, the more work it took to allow Shakespeare to participate in that imagined future, and hence the parallel and opposed development of the two businesses I have already mentioned over the century and a half that followed the Folio's publication. In the theatre, Shakespeare's texts needed adaptation (to bring them up to date, for potentially uncomprehending and unwilling present-day performers and audiences), while in print they needed annotation (to explain them, in terms of the social and linguistic usages of their own time). These apparently contradictory practices happily cooperated in the elevation of Shakespeare to his status as Britain's premier literary and theatrical icon – the more cultural work he occasioned, the more he must be worth – and they often co-existed in a single career: Lewis Theobald, for example, was at once the greatest textual editor of the early eighteenth century and the author of a distressingly sentimental rewrite of *Richard II* (1719). By the time of our next key date, 1774, both the modernizing and the historicizing of Shakespeare were well established. In the theatre, cultivated playgoers could see the ageing David Garrick performing his rewritten *Hamlet*, decorously rid of the Gravediggers, while at home in their libraries they could weigh up the rival attempts to date the original text(s) of the play, identify its sources and gloss its phraseology recorded in the accumulated footnotes to the Samuel Johnson/George Steevens variorum edition, published the previous year. Garrick's authority to rewrite *Hamlet*, however, was in part based on precisely the same claims to antiquarian expertise as the edition. He could and did boast that he had amassed the largest collection of Elizabethan and Jacobean playbooks then in existence, guaranteeing that his onstage liberties with Shakespeare's words were based on a thorough understanding of their now defunct original contexts, and it was this body of textual evidence about Shakespeare's vanished culture which Garrick shared with Johnson and Steevens so that they could use it when preparing their editions.

The official great first of 1774, though, was the publication of the first academic monograph about Shakespeare, a book which helped get interpretation onto a par with adaptation and annotation, and which indicated what is still the chief terrain where the exploration of Shakespeare in the theatre and in the study has converged. This was *A Philosophical Analysis and Illustration of Some of Shakespeare's Remarkable Characters*, by William Richardson, Professor of Humanity at Glasgow University.[14] Because he could claim to understand Shakespeare's period thoroughly as an authorized historian and philologist, Richardson felt qualified to treat the manners of Shakespeare's now two-centuries past time as mere incidentals, and its linguistic particularities as the mere 'dress' of Shakespeare's thought, just as had stage adaptors such as Garrick before him. His book identified the domain of character, the treatment of the speaking subject-positions who people Shakespearean drama as ethical and psychological case-histories equally applicable to all periods, as the natural home of Shakespearean criticism, and hence literary criticism could now discuss both theatrical performance and textual scholarship, while professing a sort of moral superiority to them both. *A Philosophical Analysis ...* paved the way for the centrality of this sort of treatment of Shakespeare in print, and, furthermore, in the development of professional English studies south of the Border a hundred years later.

With this shift towards character in criticism, the impulse to historicize Shakespeare, paradoxically, now spread from criticism into the theatre. Once the likes of Richardson and his successor Maurice Morgann had granted Shakespeare's dramatis personae an honorary freedom from history, in the theatre they could be consigned back into it, forbidden to wear modern dress for the best part of the ensuing century. The writing was already on the pasteboard castle wall just before Richardson's book appeared, when Charles Macklin first mounted his controversial 'Old Scottish'-look *Macbeth* at Covent Garden (1773), but the insistence that even live Shakespeare should look and feel like a reanimation of a lost feudal past, a living monument to the loyal chivalric heart of the British constitution, would become *de rigueur* after Planché's post-Sir Walter Scott mise-en-scène for Charles Kemble's *King John* in 1823.[15] Whether via adaptation (now turning the plays into fashionably spectacular and illusionistic costume drama), or via annotation (producing ever larger variorums), or via interpretation (reading the characters as embodiments of perennial types or ruling passions), Shakespeare was now definitely part of a national heritage, a shared past that needed moralizing and curating by professional experts in order to serve and secure a shared present. When in 1843 the duopoly by which the Theatres Royal of Drury Lane and Covent Garden had enjoyed exclusive rights to play 'straight' drama in London was abolished, many called for the establishment of a National Theatre, with the Shakespeare canon at the centre of its repertory. This did not (yet) happen, but a popular, inexpensive historical-style Shakespeare was provided from 1843 onwards nonetheless when Samuel Phelps took over the management of Sadlers' Wells theatre in Islington, where over the next eighteen years he would mount thirty-two of Shakespeare's plays. Even live Shakespeare was now felt to be vitally important to the improvement of the masses, and sixty years later the centrality of Shakespeare to a burgeoning system of vernacular education was powerfully asserted when A. C. Bradley, Professor of Poetry at Oxford, published his *Shakespearean Tragedy* (1904). This successor to William Richardson's *Philosophical Analysis . . .* is still 'probably the most influential book of Shakespeare criticism ever published', and it has been central to many recent accounts of the modern interpretation of Shakespeare. Although Bradley has regularly been criticized for being insufficiently theatrical, treating Shakespeare's tragic protagonists as novelistic rather than stage fictions, it is this very interest in the apparently real offstage lives of Shakespeare's characters which continues to endear Bradley's book to Stanislavskyan actors, and the partly psychological approach it exemplifies continues to be the chief meeting-point between literary critics and theatrical practitioners.[16]

Cut from 1904 to 1932, and adaptation, annotation and interpretation are all still thriving, albeit with slightly different interrelations. The official Shakespearean novelties of 1932, the Folger Shakespeare Library and the second Shakespeare Memorial Theatre, are still very much with us, though one has by now had most of its original foundations dug out to make room for more books and the other has recently been all-but demolished save its façade in order to undergo a comprehensive internal remodelling. By 1932 Shakespeare was so national that he had not only come to occupy the core of the new school and university discipline of

English, but he had also become American, supplying cultural legitimacy for the next Anglophone world empire in the queue. Hence the overwhelming majority of surviving copies of the First Folio were now housed in the first of these two new buildings, the Folger Shakespeare Library in Washington, DC.[17] With resources like this at its disposal and a growing number of universities to subsidize and support it and produce a demand for its products on both sides of the Atlantic, textual scholarship was in 1932 enjoying something of a renaissance in the quasi-scientific form of the New Bibliography. Historical criticism, too, was alive and well, with modern critics such as the young E. M. Tillyard considering T. S. Eliot's recent claim that Shakespeare's was the last golden period of English culture before 'a dissociation of sensibility set in, from which we have never recovered'.[18] This blend of the nostalgic and the modern was visible in the theatre too. In 1932 the new Shakespeare Memorial Theatre opened in Stratford, with all the national and imperial pomp its name implies. In overall configuration it resembled any Victorian proscenium-arch theatre, and there were colourful pictures of medieval kings and queens on its carpets; but it was also notoriously reminiscent of a more modern cultural icon, the Odeon cinema, and among its first productions were several with highly stylized modernist designs by Komisarjevsky. Renamed the Royal Shakespeare Theatre, this building would in 1960 be declared the headquarters of a new entity, the state-sponsored Royal Shakespeare Company, and even in its remodelled, proscenium-free shape it remains as fitting an emblem as any of the uneasy truce and collusion between professional performance and professional scholarship which we still inherit. School parties fill the cheap seats, in the hope that watching performances will help them write Bradleyan essays about the plays' characters at the behest of the GCSE boards; the shop in the foyer is well stocked with academic editions, as well as with audio recordings and DVDs; and in the RSC's programmes the musings of Shakespearean critics continue to vie for space with the biographies of the actors (biographies which, placing the performance side of the present-day Shakespeare industry in its full commercial and institutional context, continue to detail each player's seemingly inevitable progress from RADA to *The Bill* and then onwards via Stratford to that final accolade, a cameo in *Midsomer Murders*).

Shakespeare's interpreters both onstage and off, in this familiar account, have all been co-opted by the state into the grand business of managing its cultural capital. The plays, which as some of the first products of early modern cultural entrepreneurship got in on the ground floor of the Western economy's spiralling growth, have been enabled to maintain their value through the cumulative and ever-renewed efforts of their adaptors, curators and vendors, and have been deployed as a useful resource not just for the making of shows and books but for the making of subjects. Despite this allegedly commodified status of Shakespeare's works, the continuing presence of Bardolatry within post-Renaissance culture is nonetheless often taken as a sign of the persistence of the feudal within bourgeois commercial society, a special space in the cultural sphere where the lingering emotional tug of absolute monarchy and the dynastic family can be at once cherished and made safe for an otherwise democratic age.[19] The persistence of the Bard's work over the last four centuries remains at the same time hopelessly implicated in Western imperialism, with Shakespeare peddled by showmen and scholars alike as the universal export, Britain's insidious undercover cultural agent par excellence, still on her majesty Eliza's secret service after all these years. As ever around the topic of established Shakespeare, in short, it is hard to get very far away from Dame Judi Dench.

<h3 style="text-align:center">THE RECEPTION OF SHAKESPEARE:
THE UNTOLD (AMATEUR) STORY</h3>

But the posthumous history of the Shakespeare canon might look very different if it were to take into account some of the other, more voluntary ways in which different groups and individuals have sought to use and make sense of the plays across time: supposing Dame Judi, for example, were to be invoked not as a figurehead for the professional, metropolitan and international Shakespeare business, but as an enthusiastic ex-amateur from York who is currently a patron of the most ambitious amateur Shakespearean venture in the country, the York Shakespeare Project?[20] The story I have just outlined concentrates entirely on the Shakespeare of the professionals: the narrative I have summarized is that of the Shakespeare of the Tonson publishing monopoly, the Shakespeare of the Theatres Royal, the Shakespeare of the National Curriculum, a creature of large-scale commerce and of big institutions. The participants in this story, accordingly, have generally been cast either as manipulative oligarchs, cynical profiteers or naive and passive consumers. But how would the posthumous history of the canon look if we were for once to concede that for an enormous proportion of Shakespeare's readers and playgoers over the last four centuries his work has represented neither an opportunity for profit, nor a field for the devising of public examinations, nor an instance of social oppression? After all, the Folio contains many other phrases than 'whatever you do, buy', and the authority it began to confer on Shakespeare has often been one in which his readers have been able to share, frequently as performers, rather than one exerted solely at their expense. What I will be examining over the course of this book, then, are some hitherto neglected aspects of Shakespeare's reception which at the very least complicate this received story about his canonization; moments at which Shakespeare's audiences, instead of merely being inert recipients of his works giving credulous assent to their official significance, have got up on stage themselves.[21] Just as the emergence of the World Wide Web has enabled the revolutionary nineteenth-century technology of the telegraph to be retrospectively understood as the 'Victorian internet', so perhaps in the era of YouTube it may be possible for us to revalue and re-examine the long history of amateur Shakespeare as an important theatrical instance of user-created content. YouTube, incidentally, has made it possible for film clips of countless recent amateur performances of Shakespeare to be inspected online, and elsewhere the internet has spawned what is probably the most post-modern instance of amateur Shakespearean performance to date, the virtual *Hamlet* enacted in a virtual Globe Theatre by the avatars of paying subscribers to the digital fantasy world of Second Life.[22] If only Captain Keeling could have known what he was starting.

On whatever virtual plane it may now have reached its *reductio ad absurdum*, the practice of non-professional Shakespeare began early, and it has paralleled and intersected with the narrative I have just outlined from the time of the *Red Dragon* to the present day. A counter-history that revisited just the five dates I used above – 1623, 1774, 1843, 1904 and 1932 – might start by noting that when the First Folio appeared in 1623 one of its first buyers was Sir Edward Dering. Dering, however, was no passive consumer. As my first chapter, 'Shakespeare in private', will show, by the time he bought his Folio he had already earned the distinction of being responsible for the first recorded non-professional production of Shakespeare to be performed on English soil, a conflation of both parts of *Henry IV*. This was only the earliest of many productions of Shakespeare performed not on a public stage but as an instance of private theatricals, in the bosom of that institution which crucially mediates between the individual and the state, namely the household or family. It would be followed by other neglected firsts in the same sphere. The chapter goes on to examine, for example, a hitherto unsung Shakespearean breakthrough of 1774, that year which saw the publication of Richardson's pioneering academic monograph, namely the first recorded all-female production of a Shakespearean play. This was an adapted version of *The Winter's Tale* produced by the Harris sisters and their friends in the Cathedral Close in Salisbury, and its circumstances and context can tell us at least as much about the educational cultures within which Shakespeare was by then taking root as can Richardson's better-known book. Despite the emphasis on public institutions and professional playhouses shared by existing accounts of Shakespeare's reception, the transmission of an enthusiasm for the reading and performance of the plays has been promulgated within families at least as importantly as within schools and colleges.

As my second chapter, 'Shakespeare in public', shows, if existing histories of Shakespeare's reception have remembered the 1840s primarily for the abolition of the patent-holders' monopoly, it is perhaps time to record alongside it the establishment of the oldest surviving amateur dramatic society in Britain, the Canterbury Old Stagers (est. 1842), which started life as the entertainments mounted by sporting gentlemen during a cricket tournament. The definitive emergence of the civic amateur dramatic society represented the confluence of two distinct tendencies in recreational theatre: a mid-Victorian upper-middle-class tradition of often all-male drawing room theatricals such as these, generally happier with Shakespearean burlesques than with Shakespeare proper; and the more radical heritage of the early nineteenth-century 'spouting clubs' and their politicized Chartist descendants. Coupled with the organizational models provided by nineteenth-century literary societies, and the high-minded theatre-for-theatre's-sake commitment of those activists and philanthropists who in the later nineteenth century became convinced that the commercial stage could no longer be trusted to produce the best and most demanding plays, these traditions combined at an extraordinary cultural moment in which Shakespeare shared an alternative theatrical repertory with the likes of Ibsen and Strindberg.

The resulting Little Theatre Clubs, by placing Shakespeare in the same oppositionally highbrow repertoire as George Bernard Shaw, profoundly affected the cultural status of his work in the era of high modernism, and in 1904, when A. C. Bradley was explicating the mainsprings of Shakespearean tragedy to ever larger constituencies of students, new theatrical societies, especially in the industrial North, were starting to promulgate a popular engagement with Shakespeare's work in a local public sphere far from that of the old universities. By the time *Shakespearean Tragedy* appeared, an enthusiasm for Shakespeare had already galvanized the Stockport Garrick Society, which in between organizing public lectures on

Wagner had in 1902 mounted *The Merchant of Venice* as its first-ever production, at the Stockport Mechanics' Institute. Such amateur societies as the Stockport Garrick defined the cultural space that after the Second World War would be taken over in Britain by the subsidized professional theatre, but in their sense of the role that might be played in local communities by Shakespeare and his more recent fellow playwrights, the Little Theatres went well beyond their state-sponsored successors.

Nor was this kind of activity confined to Britain. As my third chapter, 'Shakespeare in exile', shows, by the 1840s the tradition of military and expatriate amateur performance that stretches back to the *Red Dragon* had long been using Shakespeare as a vehicle for the maintenance and assertion of British cultural identity. In 1842, for instance, it gave rise to the first recorded performance of a Shakespeare play in the Windward Islands in the Caribbean: appropriately enough, given Falstaff's desire that Mistresses Page and Ford should become his 'East and West Indies' (1.3.64), this was a production of *The Merry Wives of Windsor*, given by 'the Amateurs of the Garrison and Island' at the Theatre Royal, Kingstown, St Vincent. At venues like these around the empire, from the rebellious American colonies to the hill-stations of British India, voluntary live Shakespeare, often preserving the single-sexed performance conventions of the Renaissance, provided a social activity which could at once interrogate and endorse the entitlement of expatriate communities to native British culture. In continental Europe it could also provide a forum in which British visitors and residents might display their island heritage to their host societies, and the chapter will accordingly examine the Shakespearean activities of English-speaking theatre groups run by exiles and diplomats, including Richard Aldworth Neville in Voltaire's Geneva and Constantine Phipps, Marquis of Normanby, in Byron's Tuscany. These two aspects of expatriate amateur Shakespeare – the military and the diplomatic – converge on the sometimes troubling case of Shakespearean performances given by Allied prisoners-of-war during the Second World War, where the active patronage and support of the Nazi authorities may call into question the simple identification of live military Shakespeare with British national self-assertion.

If the claiming of Shakespeare by the subsidized companies since that war has made his plays less of a staple than they once were on the proscenium-arch stages of British amateur dramatic societies – now more often occupied by the work of Alan Ayckbourn – the post-war period has nonetheless seen a boom in non-commercial productions staged under very different conditions. Although histories of Shakespeare's reception to

date have singled out 1932 primarily as the year which saw the opening of
the Folger Shakespeare Library and the Royal Shakespeare Theatre, it is
just as significant for marking the inauguration of another purpose-built
Shakespearean venue, still the most celebrated non-professional theatre in
the British Isles, namely the roofless Minack in Cornwall. As my fourth
chapter, 'Shakespeare in the open', will show, outdoor performance has
over the last century become the dominant mode of amateur Shakespearean performance in Britain, and indeed as a mode of theatre it is
now associated almost exclusively with productions of Shakespeare's
plays, customarily given in some semblance of Elizabethan costume.
The activities of founder Rowena Cade at Minack, I shall argue,
which were themselves profoundly influenced by the Edwardian actor-
manager Ben Greet and the traditions of the historical pageant, were
a necessary precondition for the phenomenon that is 'Shakespeare's
Globe' in London, now the most commercially successful non-subsidized
Shakespearean theatre in the United Kingdom and itself more open-air
than indoor.

I should probably acknowledge openly here that, as the observant may
already have noticed, one aspect of amateur Shakespeare around which
I have not based a whole chapter is the performance of Shakespeare by
students, whether at schools or at universities. Although school teachers of
English and Drama and their more favoured pupils have undoubtedly
played a disproportionately large role in amateur dramatic groups over the
last century, and although more people over the same period have acted
Shakespeare in school and college productions than anywhere else, the
large subject of Shakespeare and education has been discussed so extensively elsewhere that I have chosen to touch on it here only as one factor
determining or helping to reveal the shape of other kinds of amateur
performance.[23] (The decision of Oxford University to permit the establishment of a dramatic society in 1885 only on condition that it confined
itself to performing Greek tragedy and Shakespeare, for example, will be
noticed here primarily in relation to its consequences for the nature and
status of subsequent amateur Shakespeares, rather than in its own already
well-charted right.)[24] School productions of Shakespeare – like the organized educational and quasi-therapeutic performances of the plays now
mounted with increasing frequency in prisons, which have already given
rise to an extensive literature of their own[25] – are of their very nature
much less voluntary than other forms of non-commercial performance,
and as such they can readily be assimilated to the established history of
Shakespeare's co-option by the State to which I have already alluded.

This book, as should already be clear, is not an anthology of touching and amusing anecdotes about amateur dramatic societies, nor an assemblage of detailed eyewitness accounts of notably worthy amateur performances, but a work of academic cultural history. But if I have not come uncritically to praise or champion amateur Shakespeare, I have not come to bury it or sneer at it either. Widely regarded as a definitively middlebrow activity, nowadays associated above all with the aspiring lower middle classes, the non-professional performance of Shakespeare has hitherto been at best ignored and at worst traduced by cultural critics of both right and left, for whom it has seemed either inadequately avant-garde, or inadequately populist, or both. The depiction of amateur Shakespeare in the culture at large – which purports to take its cue from Shakespeare's own most famous depiction of non-professional theatre, the mechanicals' scenes of *A Midsummer Night's Dream*, around which my conclusion is structured – has been almost uniformly satirical. The best-known account of amateur Shakespeare extant remains that provided by Michael Green in his classic mock how-to book *The Art of Coarse Acting* (1964), an affectionate but fairly scathing account of an amateur dramatic milieu of which ever fewer readers now have first-hand experience. I should probably admit (or even boast) here that I myself do, and that in seeking to open amateur Shakespeare to historical and analytical scrutiny I do not mean to distance myself superciliously from it. My grandfather was a founder member and long-serving officer of one of the great Northern civic societies founded during the inter-war years, the Middlesbrough Little Theatre, which boasted Tyrone Guthrie as its honorary patron, and which continues to include Shakespeare prominently in its repertory; my parents met as members of the local society which he subsequently organized in the nearby market town of Stokesley. (Hence, in common with some other academics and scholars of the drama, I can claim to be not just a veteran of the non-professional theatre but a product of it.)[26] This book's attempt to find wider contexts in which to understand that devotion to the practice of live local Shakespeare is devoted to their memory.

CHAPTER I

Shakespeare in private: domestic performance

SIR JOHN ... Hostess, clap to the doors. – Watch tonight, pray
tomorrow. Gallants, lads, boys, hearts of gold, all the titles of
good fellowship come to you! What, shall we be merry, shall we
have a play extempore? ... Well, thou wilt be horribly chid
tomorrow when thou comest to thy father. If thou love me,
practise an answer.
PRINCE HARRY Do thou stand for my father, and examine me
upon the particulars of my life.
SIR JOHN Shall I? Content. This chair shall be my state, this dagger
my sceptre, and this cushion my crown.
PRINCE HARRY Thy state is taken for a joint-stool, thy golden
sceptre for a leaden dagger, and thy precious rich crown for a
pitiful bald crown.
SIR JOHN Well, an the fire of grace be not quite out of thee, now
shalt thou be moved. Give me a cup of sack to make my eyes
look red, that it may be thought I have wept; for I must speak
in passion, and I will do it in King Cambyses' vein.
PRINCE HARRY Well, here is my leg.
SIR JOHN And here is my speech. Stand aside, nobility.
HOSTESS O Jesu, this is excellent sport, i' faith.
SIR JOHN Weep not, sweet queen; for trickling tears are vain.
HOSTESS O the Father, how he holds his countenance!
SIR JOHN For God's sake, lords, convey my tristful Queen,
        For tears do stop the floodgates of her eyes.
HOSTESS O Jesu, he doth it as like one of these harlotry players as
ever I see!

(*Henry IV part 1*, 2.5, 282–3, 376–400).

Before there were 'amateur dramatics', there were 'private theatricals'.
This term was first adopted in the eighteenth century, to designate a wide
range of non-commercial theatrical activities, carried out in venues
ranging from full-scale purpose-built auditoriums at aristocratic country
mansions to improvised stages in urban drawing rooms.[1] However they

may vary in budget or expertise, though, all private theatricals are defined as such by a taxonomy of dramatic endeavour which distinguishes rigorously between the public, national world of the commercial stage and the domestic, familial realm of the household. If there is a representation of 'private theatricals' within the Shakespeare canon, then, it is not exactly provided by *A Midsummer Night's Dream*. The mechanicals' wedding-present to Duke Theseus, though rehearsed in private (most obscenely and courageously), expresses the public dutifulness of a team of representative artisans, a troupe, furthermore, who expect their star actor to be rewarded with sixpence a day for life. The tradition of private theatricals that evolved in Britain and Ireland in the seventeenth and eighteenth centuries is more closely analogous to the play extempore in *Henry IV part 1*, quoted in part above. Mounted at the Boar's Head by Prince Harry's alternative Eastcheap household, the improvised playlet in which Falstaff and the Prince role-play as the Prince and his father offers at once an explicit burlesquing of the public theatre (performed as it is in 'King Cambyses' vein') and an explicit defiance of the Prince's public duties (which are urged on him in vain between Falstaff's initial suggestion and the performance itself by the offstage arrival of Sir John Bracy with news of impending rebellion, lines 287–366). Although the play extempore deals with matters of state, in the form of the succession crisis seemingly constituted by Prince Harry's truancy from the court, it does so strictly in private, behind doors which are not just closed but clapped-to.

What happens to *Henry IV*, though, when the whole play takes place behind closed doors, and when the entire cast are recreational, part-time performers rather than the professional 'harlotry players' disparagingly mentioned by the actor playing Mistress Quickly? The play extempore appears to have provided an enabling precedent for non-professional performers wishing to make use of Shakespeare's scripts in their own private spaces from very early in the canon's afterlife. As my introduction pointed out, the first recorded non-professional production of a Shakespeare play to take place on British soil was the conflation of both parts of *Henry IV* staged by Sir Edward Dering at his country house at Surrenden in Kent in 1623; and Shakespeare's account of Prince Harry's youth, the fortunes of Falstaff and the rebellion of the Percies and their allies would remain a favourite of private theatres for many years thereafter. *Henry IV part 1* was the most popular Shakespeare play among non-professional performers during the great boom in aristocratic and gentry performance experienced in the later eighteenth century throughout Britain and Ireland, appearing at venues which included Castletown

House in Kildare, Wynnstay House in Denbighshire, and one building actually mentioned in the play, Berkeley Castle in Gloucestershire.[2] It featured prominently, too, in one of the largest-scale and most long-lived of these private theatrical enterprises, the impressive seasons of charitable performances mounted at Kilkenny in Ireland from 1802 to 1819.

Whether all of these early instances of non-professional Shakespeare should be categorized solely under the potentially dismissive heading of 'private theatricals', however, will be a running concern both of this chapter and the next. In the seventeenth and eighteenth centuries, for those of Prince Harry's rank and for several of the gradations below it there was arguably no such thing as a private sphere, and no matter how many doors were closed before their in-house theatrical performances began or how strictly invitation-only such events remained, these aristocratic amusements might still be regarded as matters of legitimate public concern – not least by the participants themselves. Sir Edward Dering for one seems to have regarded the staging of *Henry IV* as part of a general engagement with matters of state rather than primarily as the aesthetic self-indulgence of an embarrassing host. Certainly he would have resented the derision implied when subsequent commentators described such performances as, for example, 'Private theatricals, when many of the first personages in the land choose to make themselves fools for the good of a large company.'[3]

Ridiculed or not, the country-house tradition of non-professional drama enjoyed a hegemony among non-commercial forms of performance during the two centuries following Shakespeare's death: although a compilation of just the mechanicals' scenes from *A Midsummer Night's Dream*, called *The Merry Conceited Humours of Bottom the Weaver*, was performed by apprentices around 1660,[4] most amateur performers of Shakespeare for years afterwards were of considerably higher rank. This chapter will consider three principal examples of private theatricals, which between them canvass most of the different opportunities and risks which the amateur performance of Shakespeare offered to members of the seventeenth- and eighteenth-century landed élite. At Surrenden in the 1620s, *Henry IV* provided the occasion for what might easily look like an instance of political conspiracy, when an all-male cast of courtly allies, neighbouring gentry and servants gathered away from any metropolitan centre of political debate to perform a play concerned with controversial issues of loyalty, prerogative and national unity. As well as thereby pioneering the domestic performance of potentially topical Shakespeare plays, Dering also initiated a tradition of juvenile performance within the family, which would come to dominate private theatricals a century later.

In the years following the disappearance of the boy-player from the public stage, children reappeared on the private, often showcased by their parents in the most prestigious roles available – among them, leading parts in the plays of Shakespeare. If the reading of Shakespeare became a private activity suitable for women and children over the course of the Enlightenment, as has frequently been pointed out,[5] then so too did the performance of Shakespeare. Such domestic Shakespearean performances, however, depended crucially on parental consent and encouragement, and that might not always be forthcoming – especially when the performers in question were not ambitious, unruly sons (like Prince Harry) but potentially amorous and disobedient daughters (like Juliet). Even more insistently than in the public playhouses – where female performers were usually felt to have no reputations to lose anyway – acting by women was subjected to stringent codes of propriety and decorum, which greatly restricted what uses mixed-sex or all-female casts might make of Shakespeare. Those daughters who were permitted to display themselves in private theatricals were more frequently cast as the suffering, punished protagonists of Restoration and eighteenth-century 'she-tragedies' by the likes of Thomas Otway and Nicholas Rowe than they were as Shakespeare's often transgressive and exploratory heroines. As my second principal example will show, however, the Shakespeare canon did provide one counter-example to the play extempore in *Henry IV* that was enabling for female performers. In the fourth act of *The Winter's Tale*, instead of a son performing in defiance of his father, a daughter obediently dresses up and shows off only at the insistence of her (step-)father, and in the Cathedral Close in Salisbury in the 1770s this scene provided the occasion for one of the most revealing and intimately documented of all eighteenth-century instances of private theatricals.

One last Shakespearean precedent for amateur acting taken up by eighteenth-century private theatricals was that of Hamlet's performance of the death of Pyrrhus (*Hamlet*, 2.2.416–70), a scene in which the prince both tries on the role of revenger and offers his views on the superiority of a private audience of connoisseurs over a public crowd of undiscriminating groundlings. At the most artistically ambitious and generously funded end of the private theatrical spectrum, a group of Ascendancy landowners cooperated in Kilkenny during the first two decades of the nineteenth century to mount whole seasons of amateur drama for just such a groundling-free audience as Hamlet imagined. Their leader cast himself as the Prince of Denmark to the extent of having his portrait painted in character, and for all of this company the business of dressing up as Shakespeare's kings, lords and conspirators in front of a select audience of insiders, as well as producing political resonances akin to those of the Surrenden *Henry IV,* clearly constituted an important means of asserting their own real-life status.

In each of the three major instances this chapter will be exploring, then, the special power of non-professional performance within a closed community – whether a single private household, or an extended network of aristocratic connections – lay in the close comparison and synergy that it enabled between the personal identities of the players and those of the characters they represented. In front of any audience as intimately acquainted with the actors as with the characters they portray, casting is all. Within an influential family, fathers cast as political rebels might be persuasive beyond the boundaries of the play as well as within it; young sons cast as invincibly valiant adults might be charmingly incongruous; young children cast as young children might be charmingly and unaffectedly themselves; and older daughters cast as Juliet might be positively alarming. This perennial aspect of amateur drama, whereby players may be powerfully and perhaps disturbingly identified with their onstage roles, is also anticipated in *Henry IV.* The play extempore ends, after all, when Prince Harry's performance as his own reprimanding father becomes indistinguishable from his own sentiments and intentions:

SIR JOHN (as PRINCE HARRY) ... Banish plump Jack, and banish all the world.
PRINCE HARRY I do; I will. (2.5.485–6)

SHAKESPEARE IN SURRENDEN

Sir Edward Dering's first son, Anthony, was only two or three at the time of his father's production of *Henry IV* and thus could not be cast as the Prince or as anything else, but he does make sporadic appearances in his father's detailed account book alongside expenses associated with drama and literature. Items for which Dering paid good money in March 1621, for instance, soon after his son's birth, include 'A yellow Coate and petticoates for Anthony', 'a Cradle', 'Shoes for Anthony', '2 per of stockins for Anthony' and 'sweete meates at ye Christeninge', though the following month Dering was once again pursuing his interests in more public affairs, buying 'Two smalle bookes viz: one call-d Hispanus reformatus' (by Juan de Nicolas, an important work of ecclesiastical controversy, which had only just been published) 'and ye other, ye polonians speech' (*A true copy of the Latine oration of the excellent Lord George Ossolinski*, 1621, a translation of the Polish ambassador's speech to King James concerning one of the major foreign policy concerns of the time, the Turkish threat to eastern Europe).[6] Knighted in 1619, at around the time of his twenty-first birthday, married soon afterwards to the daughter of the future earl of Thanet, and now the father of an heir, Dering was in the early 1620s a follower of the King's favourite the Duke of Buckingham and an aspiring courtier in his own right. During his frequent visits to London he not only bought works of courtly literature, political theory and international affairs appropriate to this status (among them Thomas Gainsford's *The Glory of England*, Philip Sidney's *Arcadia*, Jurius' *Brutus Vindiciae, contra tyrannos: or, Concerning the Legitimate Power of a Prince over the People, and of the People over a Prince*, George Barclay's *De Regno et Regali Potestate*, and the works of Machiavelli),[7] but he made regular visits to the playhouses, some of them associated with his networking activities (he spent 3 shillings and 6d in October 1622, for instance, 'Seeinge a play for my selfe and others').[8]

Dering also bought large numbers of 'play bookes' (164 in total), which must have included the 1613 fifth quarto of *Henry IV part 1* and the 1600 1st quarto of *Henry IV part 2*, since verbal details of the manuscript which is the principal remaining trace of the one Shakespearean production which he mounted in the hall of his house at Surrenden, near Pluckley, in Kent (among performances of a number of non-Shakespearean plays) show that it was prepared from those editions.[9] More unusually, he also paid the substantial sum of 17 shillings and 6d on 18 February 1623 'ffor heads of haire and beards',[10] as clear a symptom of impending amateur theatrical activity as Bottom's mental running-through of his catalogue of available false beards before he embarks on the role of Pyramus (*A Midsummer Night's Dream*, 1.2.86–9). Beyond the cue for amateur performance supplied by the play extempore, we do not know why Dering should have chosen *Henry IV* in particular (though his alterations to the script reveal very clearly which aspects of the play he found most interesting), but over the previous two decades his social superiors had already shown a predilection for commissioning private performances of *Henry IV part 1*, albeit mounted by professional players. The patron of Shakespeare's company, Lord Hunsdon, had shown the play off at a dinner given in honour of the Flemish ambassador in 1600, while his successor in this role, King James himself, had seen the play at Whitehall Palace during the celebrations of his daughter Elizabeth's marriage to the Elector Palatine in 1612–13, and would do so again on New Year's Eve

1624–5. In putting on this play at Surrenden with a non-professional cast, Sir Edward may have felt that he was trying to emulate his betters, making such shift as a mere knight could given that he had no professional acting company of his own at his disposal.

He may even have felt that he was going one better, given that his production would not just show off his theatrical taste but would demonstrate both his own thespian skills and his own abilities as a dramaturg. Dering's private performance of *Henry IV* improves on those hosted by his superiors by supplying part 1 with a proper ending, condensed from part 2, which follows the Percies' rebellion and Bolingbroke's reign to their ultimate conclusions. The laconic entry concerning its script which appears in his account book for 27 February 1623 – just over a week after the purchase of the wigs and the beards – does not really do justice to the extent of the adaptations which Dering made to Shakespeare's two plays: 'paid master Carington for writing out the play of K Henry the fourth att 1d ob' per sheete and given him more 00 04 00 [4 shillings]'.[11] In Dering's hands the play of K Henry the fourth had in fact lost about 25 per cent of part 1 and almost 90 per cent of part 2, to leave a composite of both parts which is shorter than either. It is not clear from the manuscript that Carrington (who was the rector of a nearby village) really earned what appears to be a tip, since at a number of points in the manuscript Dering has had to make corrections in his own hand, a few of which represent editorial afterthoughts but which more often simply restore words mistranscribed from the quartos (at one point in the play extempore scene, for instance, Dering adds the marginal note 'vide printed booke').[12]

The result of their shared endeavours, however, is a highly actable script, which takes matters of theatrical practicability very seriously. Its intelligent reassignments of speeches and the judiciousness of its cuts mean that it can be performed by fewer players than its original, among them, probably, some of the same neighbours, acquaintances and servants listed as possible cast members for a subsequent performance of John Fletcher's *The Spanish Curate* on a slip of paper preserved with the manuscript: Dering himself, his brother John Dering, Sir Thomas Wotton, Sir Warham St Leger, Robert Heywood, Thomas Slender, Mr Donne, Mr Kemp, John Carlisle, Frances Manouch, and 'Jack of the buttery'.[13] John of Lancaster disappears from the opening scene, for instance, as do the Vintner from 2.5 and Lady Mortimer from 3.1; the carriers' scene, 2.1, is omitted from the highway robbery sequence; and only a fragment of Rumour's induction survives, reallocated to

Northumberland and prefaced by a new stage direction which, economizing nicely on messengers, makes the first scene of part 2 (Act: 4^{ti}. Scaen: 9na of Dering's conflation) begin in soliloquy:

> *Enter* NORTHUMBERLAND: *alone in his garden*
> *and Night-Cappe:*
> NORTHUM: Tis Noys'd abroad that Harry Monmuth fell
> Under the wrath of Noble Hottspur's sword
> And that the kinge: under the Dowglas Rage
> Stoopt his anoynted head: as Low as death . . .[14]

With the whole of part 2 reduced to the final act-and-a-bit of the Surrenden conflation, it is from here onwards that Dering's cutting becomes most drastic and most revealing. All of *Henry IV* becomes more plot-driven in Dering's hands, and, with fewer cuts made to the King's role than to those of his subjects, that plot is much more squarely about the monarchy. In the Surrenden text, what survives of part 2 focuses almost entirely on the court: while the King's soliloquy on insomnia, Prince Harry's taking of the crown from his bedside, their reconciliation and the Jerusalem chamber survive more or less intact, the defeat and capture of the surviving rebels is reported rather than shown, with no excursion to the Forest of Gaultres: and there is no excursion to Gloucestershire either. Although the highway robbery, the play extempore, the soliloquy on honour and Falstaff's feigned death on the battlefield at Shrewsbury continue to adorn the section of Dering's redaction drawn from *Henry IV part 1*, the fat knight's role in *Henry IV part 2* dwindles to a short-lived row with Mistress Quickly – drastically condensed from 2.1, here shorn of Fang, Snare and the Lord Chief Justice – and two short speeches during Harry's coronation procession. As in Dering's handling of part 1, characters below the social rank of those performing them suffer worse than those of gentry status and above (hence the recruiting expedition disappears like the carriers' scene, and Pistol and Doll Tearsheet go the way of the Vintner), though Colevile is cut too, and so is the supper in the orchard with Shallow and Silence, who are never mentioned. After Shrewsbury, Falstaff survives in Dering's version of the play principally to be banished at its close. The banishment itself is conducted as swiftly and efficiently as the reductions to the play's cast mandate, with none of Falstaff's associates present and no Lord Chief Justice, though it is given some added force by the fact that the new King's speech rejecting his former companion becomes the last in the play. Taking over in his own hand from Carrington, Dering rounds off his adaptation with a foretaste

of *Henry V* which, borrowing from 1.2.224–5,[15] reveals him to have been
intimately familiar with that play too:

> We will according to yowr strength and qualityes
> Give yow advancement: as you shall deserve itt:
> Now change our thoughtes for honour and renowne.
> And since the royalty and crowne of Fraunce,
> Is due to us wee'll bring itt to our awe,
> Or breake itt all to peeces. Vanityes farewell
> Wee'll now act deedes for Chronicles to tell.[16]

The Surrenden version of *Henry IV parts 1 and 2*, in fact, offers just the
sort of private performance of Shakespeare one might expect from a man
who was born in the Tower of London and would in 1644 end his life,
after several agonized changes of allegiance, as a conscientious but conflicted member of the Long Parliament: as Peter Holland points out,
Dering's *Henry IV* is not 'a family drama of princely education nor a
subversive drama of the comic commentary on political ambition', but 'a
political drama of rule and rebellion'.[17] In Dering's conflation, performed
by Kentish gentry and perhaps a loyal servant or two during continuing
anxieties about the extent of King James' prerogatives and his high-
handed dealings with Parliament, *Henry IV* usefully dramatizes exactly
the concerns of the political tracts Dering was buying at the same time.
This 1623 production at Surrenden, like the play extempore, may have
taken place in private, but it dealt with very public issues.

SHAKESPEARE IN SALISBURY

If the play extempore takes place very much behind Prince Harry's
father's back and in defiance of his authority, one model of private theatre
which would become dominant over the ensuing two centuries would
instead take place under the aegis of a flaunted parental blessing. In
Salisbury in 1774 the practice of using private theatricals as a vehicle for
staging parental approval would give rise to an important first in the stage
history of the Shakespeare canon, the first recorded all-female production
of any Shakespearean play. In order to understand this event it is necessary
to look first at the pre-history of putting children into private theatricals,
which goes all the way back to the Dering household.

   Although too young to participate in his father's *Henry IV* in 1623,
Anthony Dering may have taken part in subsequent private theatricals at
Surrenden, since he is listed as one of two possible takers for the minor

role of the 'Assistant' (a judge) in the cast-lists for John Fletcher's *The Spanish Curate* preserved with its manuscript. This performance cannot have taken place after 1630 (when Sir Thomas Wootton, noted down as a possible Leandro, died), so it may well have concluded with a boy no older than ten coming onto the stage in judicial robes and solemnly distributing punishments and moral lessons among the older members of the cast:

> Curat, and Sexton,
> I have heard of you too, let me heare no more,
> And what's past, is forgotten; For this woman,
> Though her intent were bloody, yet our Law
> Calls it not death: yet that her punishment
> May deter others from such bad attempts,
> The Dowry she brought with her, shall be emploi'd
> To build a Nunnery, where she shall spend
> The remnant of her life … The strict discipline
> Of the Church, will teach you better thoughts. And Signiors,
> You that are Batchelours, if you ever marry,
> In *Bartolus*, you may behold the issue
> Of Covetousnesse, and Jealousie; And of dotage.
> And falshood in *Don Henrique*, keep a meane then;
> > *For be assur'd that weake man meets all ill,*
> > *That gives himselfe up to a womans will.*[18]

In thus bringing on his son and heir for the finale of this performance, Dering was only following the more expensive example of the masques in which James I had presented his own children to the royal court, while the trial of memory and elocution hereby set to young Anthony is as nothing compared to those faced by Alice Egerton (15), John Egerton, Viscount Bracly (11) and Thomas Egerton (10) when they found themselves cast as the Lady and her brothers in John Milton's *Maske Presented at Ludlow Castle* (1634). What differentiates Anthony Dering's appearance in *The Spanish Curate* from other such performances by well-born children in contemporary domestic theatricals, however, is the element of burlesque it knowingly and perhaps sentimentally introduces into the production. The only child in the cast, Anthony's premature attempt at simulating stern and authoritative adult behaviour is clearly expected to look comically incongruous. His real identity as the son of the house supplies Anthony with a presence and importance which do not depend either on his acting abilities or on the significance of the part he has been given in Fletcher's play, and the audience of friends and neighbours assembled by his father are invited to enjoy the spectacle of his being placed on the stage to speak this manly summing-up as an ingenious and proper reflection of paternal pride, equally pleasing whether the child's performance is impressively precocious or ridiculously juvenile. With the exception of the in-jokes available around professional actors sufficiently famous to have established what Joseph Roach has termed a 'public intimacy' with their audiences,[19] this is a kind of dramatic effect unique to private theatricals, and one which should warn us against dismissing Dering's enterprise and its successors as mere imitations of the public stage.

With this piece of casting Dering anticipates a major strain in private theatricals which, over the following two centuries, forms a kind of amateur missing link between the professional all-boy companies of Jacobean London, whose popularity Shakespeare had decried in *Hamlet,* and the vogue for seeing infants performing professionally in *Hamlet* and other Shakespearean tragedies experienced in the time of Master Betty and his Regency peers. (In fact among Dering's heirs we might also number those Victorian children who gave miniature cardboard cut-out performances of Shakespeare in toy theatres in their nurseries, or the early twentieth-century children encouraged by the likes of Ben Greet to perform *A Midsummer Night's Dream* in their parents' gardens.)[20] After the Civil Wars, a fashion developed for mounting domestic performances which exploited the effect produced by the appearance of Anthony Dering as the Assistant throughout their duration, showing off entire casts of children in roles deliberately and comically chosen to be as mismatched as possible to their physical size.[21] These performances were often of Restoration heroic tragedies, plays which had teetered on the edge of self-parody from the outset, and whose idiom remained the standard starting-point for stage burlesques from Buckingham's *The Rehearsal* (1671) right through to the time of William Barnes Rhodes' *Bombastes Furioso* (1810). Later, however, this fashion for exhibiting young children in roles for which they were comically inappropriate gave place to a quest for characters whose sentiments older children might safely articulate with a minimum of indecorum.

In its time, the most famous private performance by a family's rising generation was probably the double bill of John Dryden's *All for Love* and Nicholas Rowe's *Tamerlane* staged in the Bow Window Room of Blenheim Palace as a vehicle for the Duke of Marlborough's grandchildren in 1718, which was so talked-about that the prologue to *All for Love,* spoken by the sixteen-year-old Lady Anne Spencer (who played Octavia) was still of sufficient interest to be printed in the *Gentleman's Magazine* in February 1774. *All for Love* offers a heavily sanitized version of *Antony and Cleopatra* at the best of times, but in this setting its dramatis personae were on even better behaviour than usual. As the young Miss Cairnes, who was co-opted to play Serapion, the high priest, recalled years later, both Dryden's text and the cast's body language were carefully censored to keep them within the bounds of drawing-room etiquette: 'The duchess scratched out some of the most amorous speeches, and there was no embrace allowed &c. In short no offence to the company.'[22] The best-remembered of such productions now, however, is probably the performance of another Dryden play mounted at a town-house in Hanover Square early in 1732, if only because it had the good fortune to be commemorated by William Hogarth, as *The Indian Emperor, Or the Conquest of Mexico, Act 4, Scene 4, As performed in the year 1731* [sic], *at Mr Conduit's, Master of the Mint, before the Duke of Cumberland &c.* (Figure 1). This image beautifully exhibits the social functions such domestic performances served. Ludicrously small in their heroic roles (so that the bust of Dryden placed over the mantelpiece seems to be smiling), the children have their own dynastic importance and relative status at once underlined and affectionately mocked. The non-professional child performer makes visible the para-doxical blend of authority and powerlessness that characterizes any actor: while commanding the stage and insisting on the attention of their parental audience, these children are also obediently performing their duty, their accuracy carefully monitored by the onstage adult prompter in the corner behind them.

Hogarth would himself take part in private theatricals in later years as both performer and designer, and his painting (reproduced here in the form of the popular engraving produced by Robert Dodd) depicts with admiration a drawing room expensively and convincingly got up to incorporate almost as impressive a stage as that shown in Hogarth's equally famous image of the original production of John Gay's *The Beggar's Opera* at the Lincoln's Inn Fields theatre in 1728.[23] The two images resemble each other in part because, though one depicts an infant cast and the other an adult, both depict prison scenes in which two female characters vie for a captive male: at the opening of act 4 scene 4 of Dryden's play, Cortez is 'discovered bound', and the bulk of the scene (written, like the rest of the play, in sonorous rhyming couplets) consists of his captor Montezuma's daughter Cydaria con-tending for his love against her rival, Cortez's jealous beloved, Almeria. With such an under-aged Cortez at the focus of the onstage action, and such under-aged princesses declaring their undying passions for

Figure 1. William Hogarth, *The Indian Emperor, Or the Conquest of Mexico, Act 4, Scene 4, As performed in the year 1731, at Mr Conduit's, Master of the Mint, before the Duke of Cumberland &c.*

him (Georgiana Lennox, who played Cydaria, was eight at the time, Catherine Conduit, in the dark dress behind her, twelve), this scene would clearly have been a comic highlight for the adults in the audience, and indeed the grown-ups at the left of the picture (who include Sir John himself) look adequately amused. Just in front of the fireplace, though, is a more important cluster of spectators. In an improvised royal box are the king's son William, Duke of Cumberland (10, in a red military coat and sash and with a rigid military bearing appropriate to the future victor of Culloden), and his two sisters, the Princesses Mary (9) and Louise (7). Endearingly, these two English princesses are taking the action at least as seriously as are the nominally Aztec ones on the stage, their level of attention and engagement contrasted with that of the young commoner in front of them, who is being sternly reprimanded by a governess for dropping her fan. This is amateur drama as conversation piece, an occasion both for showing off one's own children on the stage and for showing off the importance of the patrons whose children one is entertaining (or not) in the audience. Its nearest analogue to have used a Shakespeare play was probably the *Julius Caesar* staged in 1728 at the Haymarket Theatre by 'the young Noblemen of the Westminster School', which was in part sponsored by George II (one of its performances, on Friday 16 February, was 'bespoke by the King and Queen' and attended by 'the Queen, his Royal Highness the Duke, and the Princesses Amelia and Carolina').[24] Lord Lansdowne's niece Mary Pendarves attended twice, partly because she found its seventeen-year-old Cassius, played by Lord Middlesex, 'a handsome creature'.[25] Portia and Octavius were played by his brothers John (14) and George (12), Caesar by Lord Danby (14). The hire of the theatre is most likely to have been paid for by the cast's parents, who once more were advertising both their dynastic ambitions and the statesmanlike futures they envisaged for these promising if still under-sized choice and master spirits of the age.

The Hanoverians' involvement in such performances was not limited to occasional appearances in the audience at *Julius Caesar* or *The Indian Emperor* either. In 1749 and 1750, years after the now much more heavily studied court theatricals of the early Stuarts had been largely forgotten, Frederick, the Prince of Wales, arranged for several of his children, the future George III (10), his brother Edward (9) and their sisters the Princesses Augusta (11) and Elizabeth (8), to appear in productions of Joseph Addison's high-minded *Cato* and Nicholas Rowe's *Lady Jane Grey* at Leicester House, under the tutelage of the veteran actor James Quin.

The prologue composed for *Cato* by David Mallet, spoken by Prince George, concisely summarizes one rationale for this kind of performance:

> To speak with freedom, dignity, and ease,
> To learn those arts which may hereafter please,
> Wise authors say – let youth in earliest age,
> Rehearse the poet's labours on the stage.[26]

(Years later Quin, hearing George III's first speech from the throne, is reported to have exclaimed with satisfaction 'Ah! I taught the boy to speak.')[27]

The casting of the young Princess Elizabeth as Jane Grey, presumably, both was and was not intended as an exercise in burlesque: her age may have safely and amusingly distanced her from Lady Jane's adult miseries, but her royal status meant that one aspect of the role at least required no acting at all. What she was presumably supposed to learn from the play nonetheless, however, in addition to the rhetorical confidence appropriate to her brothers, was that for women political ambition and sexual desire were equally liable to prove fatal. She-tragedies like this one were the plays of choice for eighteenth-century parents prepared to allow their daughters to appear in private theatricals, and despite the opportunities which they might offer for conscious self-display the idea was that those playing their heroines, even if more mature than the young Princess Elizabeth, should look just as artlessly self-identical.[28] One of the great double-binds of eighteenth-century sexual ideology was that, in order successfully to play the role of the perfect eligible young woman, a young woman had to appear not to be playing a role at all, and this might simultaneously sabotage and intensify the dramatic effects produced when any such officially modest and self-effacing young woman was given the opportunity to take centre stage as a doomed heroine of sensibility. In private theatricals, she-tragedy offered respectable heiresses the tricky social challenge of impersonating women salutarily victimized for attempting to shape their economic and marital destinies, while still looking as though such thoughts would never cross their own minds.

In a sense, such genteel female performers could not lose – if they acted badly, they could be praised for being properly incapable of dissimulation – but she-tragedy still carried definite risks when its performers were a little older than Princess Elizabeth. The trouble with casting women of marriageable age as heroines like Rowe's was that they might treat such characters not as awful warnings but as potential role models. It was one thing for Georgiana Lennox to appear as an amorous princess at the age of eight. It was quite another when, a generation later, her husband Henry Fox's niece Lady Susannah Fox-Strangways, a performer in the family productions of Rowe's *Jane Shore*, Ambrose Philips' *The Distressed Mother*, Edward Young's *The Revenge* and William Whitehead's *Creusa* which Georgiana and her husband encouraged at Holland House between 1761 and 1764, eloped with the professional actor they had hired to help, William O'Brien.[29] Performances by younger children thrived on a discrepancy between player and role, as does 'Pyramus and Thisbe', in which the amateur actors insist, comically, on reminding their audience of their real names. Older children, however, might be identified much too readily with the amorous sentiments they voiced. Hence where nubile daughters were concerned a different approach to casting might be adopted. In June 1774, for instance, a specially constructed summer house in a garden in Lymington in Hampshire was the venue for a performance of Arthur Murphy's *Zenobia*, followed by Henry Carey's burlesque *Chrononhotonthologos*, given by a company consisting entirely of young women.[30] Sadly, we know little of this event beyond the contents of a polite notice in the *Salisbury Journal*, but a directly contemporary all-female production in Salisbury, with much to say about the place of Shakespeare in the evolving domestic repertoire, is one of the best-documented of all amateur theatrical ventures of its time. This was a double bill of David Mallet's *Elvira* – another classic specimen of she-tragedy – and Macnamara Morgan's *The Sheep-Shearing: or, Florizel and Perdita*, an adaptation of *The Winter's Tale*, mounted in 1774 at a house in the Cathedral Close.[31]

Despite its rich surviving traces, this event remains strangely unknown, compared even to Dering's *Henry IV*. If anyone had left evidence that a provincial group had staged a play based on *The Winter's Tale* before the early modern playhouses were closed in 1642 rather than a century and a half afterwards, it seems likely that by now it would all have been minutely assembled and reproduced and indexed, and it would be the subject of several books. Such has been the emphasis on the professional Theatres Royal among theatre historians of the succeeding period, however, that the evidence that a provincial group actually did stage *The Sheep-Shearing* in 1774 was only brought together in a single work as recently as 2002, and it is primarily a work of musicology, interested in the Harrises because of their connections with London musicians such as Thomas Arne and Charles Burney.[32]

The story this evidence tells is largely one, again, of parental patronage, appropriately enough given the model of domestic performance

offered in act 4 of the *The Winter's Tale* itself, when the nominated
hostess Perdita, in her 'borrowed flaunts', plays as she has seen them do
in Whitsun pastorals only at the prompting of her presumed father, the
Old Shepherd: 'Come, quench your blushes, and present yourself / That
which you are, mistress o'th' feast' (4.4.66–7). In 1769, at around the
time of David Garrick's Shakespeare Jubilee, Mr James Harris, MP, of
Salisbury (known as 'Hermes' Harris since 1751, when he had published
Hermes, a philosophical inquiry concerning universal grammar), together
with his wife Elizabeth, encouraged his two daughters Gertrude (then
19) and Louisa (then 16) to expand the dramatic parlour-games in
which they engaged with family friends into a full-scale theatrical
performance.[33] Harris was an enthusiastic student and reader-aloud of
Shakespeare, and in 1749 he had put up a sundial on the wall of his
house in the Close, still visible today, which despite its proximity to the
Cathedral bears a motto taken, shockingly, not from the Bible but from
Macbeth: 'LIFE'S BUT A WALKING SHADOW'.[34] His daughters did
not begin with Shakespeare, however: instead as their first effort they
produced William Whitehead's tragedy *Creusa* (adapted from Euripides'
Ion), with Harris' own pastoral *Daphnis and Amaryllis* (which had already
been performed professionally in London) as an afterpiece. Harris had
almost certainly attended the private performances of Dryden's *All for
Love* and Aaron Hill's *Zara* which were given, in 1766 and 1768 respectively, in a handsomely converted barn at nearby Winterslow House, home
of the Hon. Stephen Fox (son of Henry Fox and Georgiana Lennox, and
co-star earlier in the decade of his disgraced cousin Susannah Fox-Strangways). The series of occasional domestic productions which Harris sponsored in Salisbury between 1770 and 1782 may well have been prompted
by a desire to emulate the Foxes' theatrical enterprise (which itself revived
in the 1770s). Like other, grander private theatricals of the time, for
instance, including those of the Foxes, the Harrises' productions always
included a sort of semi-public dress rehearsal or preview given to the
servants of the house, before the performance proper in front of invited
guests and neighbours. In private theatricals, the lower classes were
displaced from the upper not spatially, as in the commercial playhouses,
but temporally.

The Salisbury performances differed from those offered by the
Foxes, however, in two important respects. Firstly, as befitted the
relative status and means of the Harrises at this time, they did not
use a full-scale theatre building but only the Chapel Room, above
St Anne's Gate in the Cathedral Close, fitted up with a three-foot

high stage, a small orchestra pit and sufficient benches and chairs to seat about forty people.[35] Secondly, instead of displaying the sons of the family as well as the daughters, and serving as part of their training in rhetoric, the Harris family performances, with the eldest son James already away on government service abroad (pursuing the diplomatic career which would later result in his being made the 1st Earl of Malmesbury), featured only the daughters of the house, their cousin Laetitia Wyndham and female friends. The cast of *Creusa*, performed in January 1770, was all-female, though a number of men assisted in different capacities. Harris himself was active behind the scenes, a Cathedral canon called Dr Stevens conducted the band for the after-piece, and the chorus for *Daphnis and Amaryllis* was swelled by one Mr Parry (bass) and two borrowed cathedral choristers (trebles). (Mrs Harris took the view that in music at the very least the artistic efforts of amateurs could easily excel those of mere theatrical profes-sionals: 'the orchestra consists of a proper band for the Pastorall of Daphnis & Amaryllis that I have heard rehear[s]'d,' she wrote to her son, '& I will say they do infinitely better than it was performd at Drury Lane'.)[36] Male help was accepted with aspects of the design too: the dress worn by Gertrude Harris as the Priestess of Apollo, was, as her mother boasted, 'not design'd by either milleners or mantua makers but by herself assisted by Dr [Thomas] Warton and Mr Harris'.[37] (This was probably the future Poet Laureate Warton's only foray into costume design.) The dress was 'taken from the antique . . . white sattin, quite simple & elegant, only fasten'd by a row of large pearls round the wast[;] on her head she wears a white kind of veil & round it a row of Alexandrian laurel'.[38]

Costumes, indeed, feature heavily in all accounts of the Salisbury theatricals, and they must have played their part in the choice of plays. The classical setting of *Creusa* helped to keep the girls playing male roles within the bounds of modesty, saving them from the brazenness of breeches – 'all the *lady gentlemen*,' explained Mrs Harris, 'act in Eastern dresses with long robes'.[39] This did not exempt the production from some mildly titillated comments about its cross-dressing: one Mr Tobin, for example, sent the family a poem 'On Miss Louisa Margaret Harris in the Character of Ilyssus', which runs

> In her own beauteous form Louisa can
> Secure the heart of each admiring man[,]
> But anxious still fresh conquests to persue
> Lovely Ilyssus charms the women too.[40]

However the resulting effects were interpreted, the same considerations of modesty probably influenced the Lymington women's choice of the exotic *Zenobia* in June 1774, when, reported the *Salisbury Journal,* '[t]heir dresses, scenes and decorations were very good; those of Zenobia and Zelmira, exceedingly rich and elegant'.[41] It was a fairly radical decision, then, when the Harrises' next production, again all-female, opted not for ancient Greece but for medieval Spain, choosing as main-piece Mallet's *Elvira.* Their performance of this agonized tale of clan-destine love – the story of a lady-in-waiting secretly married to a prince and already a mother, who conveniently if tragically dies after her husband is put under pressure to marry a princess – attracted a good deal of attention, and in some quarters a definite *frisson* of scandal. The participants, however, seemed at the time blissfully oblivious to any hint of perceived immodesty, largely taken up with the intensity of Mallet's pathos: the young Misses Gross, who played Elvira's children, cried so much in their scene that the older performers too would regularly break down in tears during rehearsals, and Elizabeth Harris found the spec-tacle too affecting to watch.[42] The sorrows of the story were counterbal-anced, however, by the pleasures of dressing up. A letter from Elizabeth to her son is again usefully informative about the women's dresses, and makes it quite clear that the girls' outfits were seen primarily as clothes rather than as costumes, affording the opportunity to display jewels and possessions which were not felt to be signifying the status of fictitious characters alone. One accessory, indeed, retained an obstinate life of its own:

[Salisbury, 13 November 1774]. I have but little to send from hence[,] we are so tottaly taken up with our own theatrical business that nothing else is thought on. The ladies acted last night in their dresses to all their servants[:] a most crouded house they had[.] Though I was not admitted to the performance, I saw all the ladies[:] their dresses are fine and elegant[.] Miss Trenchard makes an excellent Spanish Ambassadeur, a fine figure and richly drest. She had a prodigious large sword, and not be[ing] accostom'd to wear it, she contriv'd, as she walk'd, to run it through a scene and damag'd it greatly.[43]

This is so much what an eighteenth-century young lady ought to do when equipped to her surprise with a masculine sword and placed on a stage, especially a young lady who is not a member of the family, that one can hardly believe it; it is as if Miss Trenchard has modelled her behaviour on that of Hippolito, the naive principal boy in the Restoration version of *The Tempest,* who turns out to be equally inept with an unaccustomed sword.[44] The real insiders, however, made no such blunders, expertly deploying and displaying props which in part derived from (and now advertised) the son's recent period as a diplomat in Madrid:

Louisa has taken a sword you left here, and she manages it right[.] She is very fine in a purple Spanish dress, all the buttons Irish diamonds, a fine button and loop to her hatt, and your King of Spains picture hanging from her neck[.] The Queen (Miss Hussey) is blue and silver with a number of diamonds[;] Miss Wyndham[,] who is Elvira[,] white trim'd with pearls[.] Gertrude (the Princess), is a black Spanish trim'd with red and silver, and a great quantity of diamonds[;] it becomes her much.[45]

In thus stressing the display of family jewels and real weapons, Mrs Harris sounds a little like Miss Cairnes on the comparable, if more lavish, Blenheim *All for Love* sixty years earlier: 'I suppose we made a very grand appearance ... Jewels you may believe in plenty; and Mark Anthony wore the sword that the emperor gave the Duke of Marlborough.'[46] It is a pity Mrs Harris is so comparatively vague about the costumes worn by those who played male roles, commenting only on their swords, though in all probability it was the swords as much as anything else which distinguished nominally male outfits from female. The most important norms to be maintained in this setting were not those of theatrical mimesis, in which male characters are supposed to look like men, but those of polite society, in which young ladies might just be allowed dress up in such a way as to signal that their characters were supposed to be men, but without showing the contours of their legs in the process. However they were addressed in *Elvira*, however, the problems of cross-dressing without indelicacy had been solved for its afterpiece *The Sheep-Shearing* by Morgan's decision to follow the editor Thomas Hanmer in calling Polixenes' kingdom not Bohemia but Bithynia: as a result the girls playing masculine parts could once more fall back on vaguely classical robes, or long smocks for the shepherds, as they had in *Daphnis and Amaryllis*. One beneficiary was the tireless Gertrude Harris, described in family correspondence as the 'impresario' of the whole event, who combined her directorial activities not just with the small role of the Princess in *Elvira* but with that of the Young Shepherd in *The Sheep-Shearing*.[47] As she wrote to her brother, 'I have of late been so engaged between the Spanish princess & the Bithynian clown, that I have had no leisure to act the part of Gertrude Harris which perhaps I should perform more naturally than either of the aforementioned.'[48]

If Gertrude thus felt distanced from her onstage roles, however, her younger sister Louisa did not, at least once she had metamorphosed from a prince in the mainpiece to a princess in the afterpiece. Cast as Perdita,

Louisa Harris seized the occasion to display one of her own most prized
social accomplishments, her mastery of a musical instrument destined to
remain a conspicuous vehicle for the social display of young women's
sensibilities for many years to come: 'I intend introducing the harp at the
drawing up of the curtain which I think will have a good effect,' she wrote
during the rehearsal period,[49] and she sang to her own accompaniment
too, probably taking the smug added pastoral lyric which Morgan's script
assigns to Dorcas: 'Our sheep timely shorn, enriching the swain, / As fresh
as the morn, frisk over the plain. / So the generous mind, that with
bounty o'erflows, / Feels the heart grows more light, for the good he
bestows.'[50] (Louisa presumably joined in with Morgan's choral finale, too,
'Sing high, sing down, sing ding-dong bell, / For Perdita and Florizel.')[51]
This added musical content clearly went over well with the family
friends in the audience: Gertrude subsequently reported that 'Louisa acted
well; & in the farce gained much applause by her harp which was very well
introduced.'[52]

   In appearing simultaneously as herself, accomplished co-hostess of this
refined social occasion, and as Perdita, rustic but delicate mistress of the
shepherds' feast, Louisa was perfectly in accord with Morgan's prologue,
which offered *The Sheep-Shearing* as an afterpiece designed for the more
discriminating and genteel guest:

> ... Princess, and milkmaid, and a prince's bride,
> A subject for [Shakespeare's] *Winter's Tale* supply'd;
> In which, the master-poet has interwove
> The virgin innocence of past'ral love.
> At ev'ry feast, to crown the rich repast,
> The choicest fruits are always serv'd the last:
> Stage cooks, indeed, reverse the bill of fare,
> And ribaldry and farce, bring up the rear.
> But for such guests as you, in whom we find
> Judgment so clear, and taste so well refin'd,
> A treat more delicate we wish to lay,
> And *Shakespear*'s wit shall send you pleas'd away.[53]

The use of Shakespeare's wit by this particular cast, moreover, harmon-
ized with one widespread contemporary perception of the playwright,
who since the time of the Shakespeare Ladies' Club in the 1730s had been
regarded by many as a dramatist unusually sympathetic to women and
unusually appropriate to female readers and spectators. (Given that James
Harris's cousin was the 4th Earl of Shaftesbury, whose first wife,
Susannah, had been the most prominent member of the Shakespeare

Ladies' Club, this influence may have been fairly direct: Harris was an enthusiastic supporter and correspondent, moreover, of the leading female Shakespearean critic of the time, Elizabeth Montagu.)[54] Only a year after the Harris girls' performance of *The Sheep-Shearing*, for instance, Mrs Apphia Peach, in her anonymous novel *The Correspondents*, published a warm paean to Shakespeare which urged all British women to pay him homage as 'the only poet (that I know of) who has delineated to perfection the character of a *female friend*'.[55] Peach was referring in particular to Rosalind and Celia in *As You Like It*, but she might have cited Hermione and Paulina too, and although Morgan's version of *The Winter's Tale* excises both of them, his afterpiece, in the Harrises' hands, nonetheless became a celebration of female friendship and female solidarity. If Louisa identified Perdita with herself by equipping Shakespeare's royal shepherdess with her harp on stage, she identified herself with Perdita just as strikingly offstage, when, in a touching pair of poems composed after the last performance, she and Miss Henchman, who played Florizel, sought to preserve their characters' heterosexual love as their own female friendship:

> Miss Louisa H—s, to *Miss H—n, after their performing the characters of Florizel and Perdita.*
> No more shall we with trembling hear that bell,
> Which shews me, Perdita; thee, Florizell.
> Thy brilliant eyes no more with looks of love
> Shall in my bosom gentle pity move.
> The curtain drops, and here we both remain,
> You without love, I free from mimic pain.
> Grant me this favor, though our drama ends,
> Lett the feign'd lovers still be real friends.[56]

> *Miss H—n's Answer.*
> No longer now the lover, but the friend,
> To you these lines with temper'd warmth I send;
> The first kind offer of a heart was thine,
> Deign to accept the poor return of mine.
> Hence may our thoughts, our wishes all conspire,
> In harmony, like thy sweet voice and lyre;
> May concord's sweetest note swell on till death,
> And leave us only with our latest breath.[57]

There is much more going on here, in short, than is implied in the summing-up offered by this production's only previous historian, Arnold Hare, who in 1958 wrote dismissively of 'fashionable ladies who used drama to help to divert the tedious years between adolescence and

marriage'.[58] For one thing, this form of diversion was still highly controversial, as the responses to this double-bill written by those outside its cast
and sometimes outside its audience suggest. For a respectable woman
to impersonate a fictitious character, however meek and decorous, was
a potentially transgressive undertaking, even in the Cathedral Close.
Innocently maidenly as the Harrises' enterprise sounds, the single-sex
rehearsals properly quarantined against the unacceptable boy–girl embraces
so carefully banned from the Blenheim *All for Love* or the sort of cross-class
romance inadvertently fostered chez Fox, this private double-bill did not
escape criticism, directed in the first instance at its cross-dressing. The *Bath
Journal* published two disapproving poems on this subject, the first carefully
timed to appear on 17 November, the anniversary of Elizabeth I's accession,
which until recently had been celebrated as a national holiday, Queen
Bess's Day. The poem looks nostalgically back to a time when single-sexed
theatre was a male preserve:

> *On the Ladies of the Close of Salisbury now acting* Elvira
> In good Queen Elizabeth's reign,
> In a decent and virtuous age,
> That they ne'er might give modesty pain,
> No female appeared on the stage.
>
> But lo! what a change time affords!
> The ladies, 'mong many strange things,
> Call for helmets, for breeches, and swords,
> And act Senators, Heroes, and Kings.[59]

The following issue printed something even more hostile 'To the Ladies
of Salisbury acting Elvira', this time signed 'An Old Maid':

> Happy dames, ye have found a plan
> To learn what outwardly belongs to man.
> Follow the lucky thought, encore, encore,
> The Fates decree ye never shall know more.[60]

(This malicious prophecy may in one case have come true, in so far as Louisa
Harris, however advantageously displayed to the admiration of potential hus-
bands with her harp, chose never to marry.)[61] Loyal to its local gentry, however,
the *Salisbury Journal* took a more supportive line, assuring readers that

Great judgement and elegance of fancy appeared in the choice of [costumes];
particularly the dresses of those who personated men; their habits were well-
suited to their characters, and at the same time appeared so well-contrived, as to
leave no room for censure, had they been viewed by the most evil eye.[62]

As the titles of the two satirical poems suggest, the focus of the antagonism generated by the Harrises' private theatricals was on *Elvira* rather than on *The Sheep-Shearing*. In selecting Morgan's pastoral as their afterpiece, with its depiction of a courtship fully sanctioned by Perdita's foster-father – in which not only Florizel but also Perdita are only picturesquely dressed up as rustics, and underneath they are social equals – the girls had lighted on Shakespearean sentiments with which they might identify with impunity.[63] It was identification with the amorous sufferings of she-tragedy heroines that might break social taboos. The *Salisbury Journal*, unfortunately, underlined just this identification when early the following year it printed 'A RHAPSODY *by* W.B.E. *Esq.; addressed to Miss* W-D-M [Laetitia Wyndham, who played Elvira, as well as Dorcas in *The Sheep-Shearing*], *on seeing her in a late dramatic performance in the Close of* Salisbury' (a poem which ends with the words 'every smile proclaim'd thee Queen of Love').[64] More scandalously, the *Journal* printed an equally admiring poem on the subject by the Dean of the Cathedral himself, and not anonymously either: it appeared as ' *To Miss* W-D-M, *by the* D-N *of* SARUM, *on her acting the Part of* ELVIRA'. (Sadly a whole manuscript collection of further unpublished verses written on the occasion, called 'Heliconian Trifles, on the ladies who performed male and female parts in the Private Theatricals, held in the Close of Sarum',[65] last glimpsed in 1843, is now lost.)[66] The Harrises, along with others in the congregation, were not at all pleased that the Dean's specimen (together with Louisa's own poem to Miss Henchman and Miss Henchman's reply) had been made public. 'Louisa has been most violently offended with the printers of the *Salisbury Journal*,' wrote Mrs Harris, '... they have printed those [verses] the Dean made on Miss Wyndham. 'Tis not the thing for a Dean of a Cathedrale to be writing gallant verses to young ladies who act plays.'[67] It certainly is not, especially when the gallant verses in question, however different in intention to those of the *Bath Journal*'s old maids, suggest so clearly that these women were using Mallet's play, despite its script's advocacy of bashful modesty, as the vehicle for a spectacular piece of self-performance. The Dean's ill-advised poem registers this with both enthusiasm and anxiety, choosing to construe Miss Wyndham's performance as Elvira as a courtship display, a public exhibition of her marital eligibility. In fact he sounds a little concerned that this overpoweringly attractive tragedy queen in his canons' midst, with her 'beauteous form', had better be married off sooner rather than later:

'Tis not your mimic arts our praises gain,
You are the very thing you seem to feign;
No wonder that so well you act your part,

> Elvira only speaks Laetitia's heart,
> And shows your beauteous form contains a mind
> Fraught with each virtue of the fairest kind.
> To animate that form each virtue strove,
> Good sense, good nature, tenderness and love:
> Oh! may you soon perform, in real life,
> The tender mother, and the faithful wife.[68]

(This concluding wish might have been more respectable in 1774 if the rhyme had not obliged the Dean to put the projected motherhood before the imagined marriage.) The Dean may be trying to praise Miss Wyndham for being properly self-identical despite indulging in histrionics when he claims that Wyndham is the very thing she seems to feign and that Elvira only speaks Laetitia's heart. But in identifying her so thoroughly with this she-tragic paragon – a young woman to whom dissimulation is so foreign and love so paramount that she more or less dies of her secret marriage, not at all unlike Whitehead's Creusa, whom Wyndham had played four years earlier – his poem risks diagnosing her as feminine to a pathologically operatic degree. As with Mrs Harris' account of the costumes, which recognizably remain fancy dress ornamented with the family jewels, Wyndham's role in the play, as so often in private theatricals, is understood less as something into which she disappears than as a self-revelatory masquerade.[69] Not for nothing was she known, apparently, as one local historian tells us, as 'the admired Miss Wyndham, afterwards the wife of Sir William A'Court'.[70]

SHAKESPEARE AT KILKENNY

The nature of my third major example, the great Kilkenny theatricals of 1802–19, was in large part determined by the need to respond to a mounting level of hostile public comment about domestic theatrical performances. Mrs Harris, transcribing the rhyming attacks on her daughters' theatrical efforts, which she called 'vile verses from the Bath Journal', and sending them to her son, dismissed such criticism of private theatricals as motivated by envy: 'You may easily imagin these verses were sent by some vinegar merchant in Salisbury who [could] nott get admitted to the performance.'[71] This factor alone, however, cannot explain the widespread public concern over the vogue for domestic amateur drama revealed by journalists, clerics and even novelists and playwrights from the 1770s into the early decades of the nineteenth century. While the feigning of passion, seduction and betrayal might just be an acceptable pursuit when carried out by professional actors, safely quarantined from polite society on the stages of designated public playhouses, the knowledge that real people, and especially real young women, were now simulating such behaviour in the bosoms of real influential families was for some profoundly disturbing. According to Thomas Gisborne, for example, domestic theatrical activity was 'almost certain to prove, in its effects, injurious to the female performers',[72] and he would be famously seconded by Jane Austen's depiction of what happens to the Bertram daughters as a result of their participation in a domestic production of Kotzebue's *Lovers' Vows* (in *Mansfield Park*, 1814) – significantly, a production mounted behind their father's back and in defiance of his authority. For most published critics of the private stage, however, the paradigmatic dangerous and unsuitable script for home use was not a modern work of Continental liberalism but the most celebrated and well-loved depiction of secret love and forbidden marriage in the dramatic canon, the Shakespearean ancestor of she-tragedy, *Romeo and Juliet*.[73] However acceptable a single-sex rendition of the romance between Florizel and Perdita might be in a domestic setting, *Romeo and Juliet*, although at the time Shakespeare's most popular play on the professional stage, was almost entirely avoided by eighteenth-century amateurs. Here, conspicuously, the Shakespeare of the Theatres Royal and the Shakespeare of the drawing rooms diverged: depicting a doomed clandestine marriage undertaken in defiance of Montagues and Capulets alike was a much less attractive proposition to the parental sponsors of domestic theatricals than were the feudal heroics and unheroics of *Henry IV*. Even the Christmas seasons of plays mounted by Sir Watkin Williams Wynn and his son at Wynnstay House in Denbighshire (1770–87 and 1803–10), which included a *Twelfth Night* in which a Miss Wynne was allowed to wear Turkish pantaloons as Cesario, along with productions of *The Merchant of Venice*, *The Merry Wives of Windsor*, *Much Ado About Nothing*, *Othello*, *Cymbeline*, *Richard III*, *Macbeth*, *As You Like It*, *The Winter's Tale*, *The Tempest* and, outdoing Sir Edward Dering, both parts of *Henry IV* in full, did not include a single performance of *Romeo and Juliet*.[74] (Offering an attractive cameo to Lady Percy but including no actual courtship scenes, *Henry IV part 1* was certainly a safer bet in mixed company.)[75]

The very idea of the improprieties that might be involved should any respectable woman play Juliet in a domestic setting, despite the fact that it scarcely ever happened, haunted the imaginations of the opponents of private theatricals for generations. A fictitious production in which, most improbably, an amateur Juliet is paired with an apparently professional

Romeo dominates the plot of the one full-length play inspired by the amateur theatrical boom of the 1770s and 1780s, and it is a thoroughly disapproving piece of work. James Powell's *Private Theatricals* (1787), although it nominally celebrates the elopement of an heiress with an actor, is more concerned to decry amateur drama as a menace to the moral welfare of the young. In the main plot Alderman Grubb, father of the ingenue Lucy, has recently married a second and very stage-struck Lady Grubb, who has spoiled his country estate by putting a marble bust of Shakespeare in his favourite grotto and renaming his hermitage 'Prospero's Cave'. Furthermore, she has built a stage in his drawing room, and with the help of some London professionals she is busily rehearsing *Romeo and Juliet*, with Lucy as Juliet. It is at last revealed even to Alderman Grubb that the supposed actor who has been playing Romeo is really Juliet's forbidden but perfectly eligible suitor Villars, but in the inevitable reconciliation scene, Villars, forswearing his assumed profession with contempt, assures his future father-in-law that he is no William O'Brien:

Forgive, Mr Alderman, the stratagems of love, I am no player (tho' in its proper place, an enthusiast in the art). And I think the present rage for theatrical private performances, has grown to a ridiculous pitch, and is productive of much mischief to the morals of society, by admitting the loose and profligate (who are a scandal to the age) into the houses of virtue, whose reputation and honor they generally endanger.[76]

Powell, the writer of this pious speech, is careful to make a comparable social disclaimer for himself. Scorning to be identified either as a professional playwright or as a corrupted dilettante, he has this play 'Printed and sold by the Author', namely 'James Powell (of the Custom House)' – neither self-styled thespian nor theatrical hack, but a civil servant and a gentleman.[77]

   For their own slightly different reasons, those in the professional theatre could be just as critical about amateur Romeos and Juliets, though most preferred to be amusingly snide rather than determinedly moralistic, doubtless recognizing that some opponents of the private stage were enemies of theirs too. Powell's sense that those who impersonate Juliet on the recreational stage are liable to wind up as brides in earnest, for better or worse, is shared in a different register by Captain Topham's epilogue to Thomas Morton's comedy *The Way to Get Married* (1796), essentially a comic monologue written as a vehicle for the actress Isabella Mattocks. David Garrick had already ridiculed an unglamorously middle-aged upper-class couple for playing the love scenes from *Romeo and Juliet* together in private in his *A Peep Behind the Curtain* in 1767:

LADY FUZ. Pray don't you adore Shakespear, Sir Mac?
SIR MACARONI. Shakespear! *(yawning.)*
LADY FUZ. Sir Toby and I are absolute worshippers of him—we
    very often act some of his best tragedy scenes to divert ourselves.
SIR MACARONI. And it must be very diverting, I dare swear.
SIR TOBY. What, more family secrets! for shame, Lady Fuz—
LADY FUZ. You need not be ashamed of your talents, my dear—I
    will venture to say you are the best Romeo that ever appeared.
SIR TOBY. Pooh, pooh!
SIR MACARONI. I have not the least doubt of Sir Toby's genius—
    But don't your Ladyship think he rather carries too much
    flesh for the Lover—Does your Ladyship incline to tragedy too?
LADY FUZ. I have my feelings, Sir—and if Sir Toby will favour you
    with two or three speeches, I will stand up for Juliet.
SIR TOBY. I vow, Lady Fuz, you distress me beyond measure—
    I never have any voice till the evening.
MISS FUZ. Never mind being a little husky, Papa—do tear your
    wig, throw yourself upon the ground, and poison yourself.[78]

Though embarrassing, however, this peccadillo at least seems innocuous. Performing the same scenes while unmarried, however, according to Topham, might have serious consequences. During his epilogue's compendium of fashionable ways of securing marriage partners, Topham describes an overweight widow who nonetheless cherishes an incongruous enthusiasm for performing Shakespeare:

> Good sixteen stone to carry—but yet strong:
> She rolls a wool-pack Venus,—broad as long!
> Yet she's a tender passion for the stage!
> With her, dear *private acting* is the rage.
> Shakspeare in her finds beauties, not his choice,
> And Juliet grieves in – a fine manly voice ...[79]

This unlikely Juliet has found her counterpart in the person of a thin and pallid peer equally addicted to amateur theatricals, and despite their physical and vocal inappropriateness to the roles of young Veronese lovers they find themselves possessed by Shakespeare's amorous poetry:

> In tones like these their mutual passions run; –
> Says he, (*a lisping, effeminate voice*)
> 'It is the east, and Juliet is the sun! ...'
> Then she – (*very gruff, hoarse tone*)

'Good nurse! I am a child! Tut! do not speak,
Else would a maiden-blush bepaint my cheek ...'

Just as at Holland House or in Powell's satirical play, the amateur
performance of such inflammatory material leads inevitably to a misalli-
ance: 'Accents so sweet, what mortal can withstand? / The stage-struck
peer makes tender of his hand.' The concomitant of the pejorative,
professional view that amateurs are not very good at pretending to be
what they are not seems to be the view, shared with the anti-theatrical
moralists, that it is impossible for them not to adopt in their own persons
the sentiments they incompetently feign.

   Among the more established playwrights, Frederick Reynolds confined himself to flippancy about private theatricals, dismissing the
amateur competition as feeble-mindedly vague in a brief digression in
his play *The Dramatist* (1789),[80] and as merely inaudible in the wise-
crack he made after watching a later generation of Marlboroughs
performing at Blenheim in 1787: 'I was unable to hear one line out
of twenty which these *really private* actors uttered.'[81] His colleague
Richard Cumberland, however, took the subject as seriously as any
cleric, objecting to such performances on grounds more moral than
technical. The period's most detailed and informed critique of the
phenomenon of private theatricals, Cumberland's 'Remarks upon the
Present Taste for Acting Private Plays' (1788), is, perhaps surprisingly
for an essay by a practising playwright, even more disapproving of
productions in which well-bred young women displayed themselves
on the stage than were the *Bath Journal* or James Powell. Characteristically identifying the central motivating dynamic of home theatricals
as misguided vanity on behalf of exhibitionist daughters, Cumberland
structures his essay as a sermon addressed to doting fathers. 'Let the
foolish parent, whose itching ears tingled with the plaudits that
resounded through the theatre, where virgin modesty deposited its
blushes,' cautions its peroration, 'beware how his aching heart shall
throb with sorrow, when the daughter *quae pudica ad theatrum acces-
serat, inde revertur impudica* [who arrived at the theatre chaste, returns
from it unchaste]'.[82] What Cumberland's essay reveals with particular
clarity is that even a hardened career dramatist could be morally
shocked by the artifices of the theatre, once no longer insulated from
them by their being confined to a professional caste. Cumberland
affects to resent what he describes as new competition from a class
which ought to have other things to do: it used to be, he claims, that
people admired a great professional actor as a prodigy, but now 'the

nobility and gentry to their immortal honour have broken up the monopoly, and new-made players are now as plentiful as new-made peers'. The perceived rivalry between aristocratic amateur players and professionals is especially unfair when it comes to playing certain kinds of roles, which the nobs have been rehearsing all their lives:

In all scenes of high life they are at home; noble sentiments are natural to them; love-parts they can play by instinct; and as for all the casts of rakes, gamesters and fine gentlemen, they can fill them to the life. Think only of what a violence it must be to the nerve of a humble unpretending actor to be obliged to play the gallant gay seducer, and be the cuckold maker of the comedy, when he has no other object at heart but to go quietly home, when the play is over, to his wife and children, and participate with them in the honest earnings of his vocation: can such a man compete with the Lothario of high life?[83]

The full-time, paid actor, paradoxically, is 'unpretending' – but he may be trumped in his unpretending and even unwilling performance by a wicked aristocrat who really is what he pretends to be. (No wonder, then, that Lord John Delaval should have made such a suave and convincing Iago, 'his whole deportment so much the gentleman', when his rakish brother Sir Francis hired Drury Lane in order that his family and friends might show off in *Othello* in 1751.)[84] Once again, the implicit claim is that amateurs cannot really act but are theatrically interesting only by virtue of what happens in the process of casting: if they are innocent women, they will be corrupted by actually becoming what they are only supposed to impersonate, and if they are guilty men they will be unfairly convincing without the need for any thespian expertise at all.

The place to respond to such public assaults was in prologues and epilogues, some of which, fortunately, survive, even from very small theatres. William Fector, who bought the Assembly Room in Snargate, Dover in 1783 and offered short seasons of amateur drama there for the remainder of the decade (as well as founding a dining society in honour of Shakespeare, called the Shaksperian Institution, complete with its own livery),[85] riposted to the moralists simply by arguing that private theatricals were at least less harmful than other aristocratic diversions. A prologue by one Mr Gillum spoken at Fector's playhouse in the year of Cumberland's essay, 1788, defends the pastime on the grounds that it keeps 'acting Peers' from more deleterious pastimes:

> The Stage will never wound a parent's heart,
> 'Tis Dice and Faro point the cruel dart.
> By private Theatres no heir's undone –
> Estates by different Play are lost and won.[86]

This defence, sadly, was being undermined even as Gillum's lines were being spoken, by the prodigal and ill-fated Earl of Barrymore. A wild Prince Harry who did not live long enough to renounce the dissipations of his youth and give up his enthusiasm for mischievous plays extempore (he died in a firearms accident at twenty-three), in 1788 Barrymore spent (or promised to spend) £60,000 on his private theatre at Wargrave, near Reading. Its properties were confiscated and auctioned in 1792 to cover some of the unpaid bills incurred during its construction. Appropriately, the final extravagance Barrymore managed to commit was a major expenditure on Falstaff: the last production he staged before the bailiffs arrived was *The Merry Wives of Windsor.*[87] Regarding the private amusements of the governing classes as a matter of serious public concern, the judge in the legal proceedings involved, Lord Kenyon, took the opportunity to reflect on the Earl's favourite hobby in terms which might have been seconded by Powell or Cumberland. Once more, the paradigmatic play which sprang to mind was Romeo and Juliet. As the *Morning Chronicle* reported on 20 February 1792,

With respect to the tendency of private theatrical entertainments, his Lordship doubted very much whether they had ever inculcated one single virtuous sentiment. He had known instances where they had a contrary effect; and they usually vitiated and debauched the morals of both sexes; the performers seldom retired from the entertainment, but every Romeo knew the estimate of his Juliet's virtue.[88]

In this climate of opinion, it is not surprising that those few amateurs who insisted on staging *Romeo and Juliet* regardless generally hired in their leading ladies from the professional stage, as did Edward Hartopp-Wigley at Little Dalby Hall, near Melton Mowbray, in 1798 and 1802.[89] But the best hope of being allowed to play-act without incurring the disapproval meted out by Lord Kenyon was to perform not simply for the amusement of one's servants, friends and neighbours, but in an avowedly good civic cause: in fact, private theatricals might become less objectionable by becoming more public. The professional theatres had mounted charitable benefit performances in a bid to appease anti-theatrical opinion for years (such as the annual performances of George Lillo's *George Barnwell* given for apprentices in London), and in the later eighteenth century this strategy was adopted by some semi-professional and amateur theatres too, throughout the growing Anglophone world. An expatriate performance of Isaac Bickerstaff's *The Padlock* in February 1788, for example, in aid of 'an Asylum for Female Orphans', promoted Madras from being at the exotic fringe of a nascent empire to somewhere able to outdo the homeland itself: 'Tonight, superior ev'n to *Britain*'s boast, / Virtue's own Drama crowns this favoured coast.'⁹⁰ The most extensive and impressive example, however, was nearer home, in the form of the annual two- or three-week seasons of charitable performances mounted by a confederation of wealthy non-professional thespians at Kilkenny in Ireland from 1802 through 1819, which included productions of fifteen plays from the Shakespeare canon, with *Romeo and Juliet* prominent among them.⁹¹ Using a hired playhouse in a town rather than taking place on wholly domestic premises, this venture represented private theatricals at their nearest point of convergence with the public stage, but in the effects produced by its casting and its social dynamics it offered a very different Shakespeare to the playwright whose work was a staple of the mass-market repertory at Covent Garden and Drury Lane. Performing under the sign not of the Old Shepherd but of the élitist Hamlet, the genteel actors of Kilkenny sought to redeem Shakespeare from the vulgarity of the commercial stage, and to perform their own status as civic benefactors in the process.

The detailed records and published reviews of these performances lovingly assembled by their participants (who included the important Romantic poet and songwriter Thomas Moore, author of *Moore's Irish Melodies*), together with eyewitness accounts by spectators (who included the likes of Maria Edgeworth and Henry Grattan), certainly suggest that this was Shakespeare's finest hour on the Georgian private stage. The prime mover of the Kilkenny theatricals, Richard Power, had originally developed his interest in amateur drama in strictly domestic productions at his elder brother Sir John's nearby stately home, Kilfane House, but in 1801 he convened a group of prosperous local gentlemen who clubbed together, as the 'Kilkenny Theatrical Society', to lease the town's playhouse (as the 'Attic Theatre' or 'Athenaeum') for more ambitious performances.⁹² Although in adopting this cooperative approach Power was in part following the recent example of the Pic-Nic Club in London (of whom more in my next chapter), this was not an amateur dramatic society as we would now understand it, since there was no formal system of subscriptions or memberships, and nor was it a private theatre club, since, although a high proportion of its audience consisted of friends of the players, many tickets were freely sold to any members of the public who could afford them. What distinguished the Kilkenny Theatrical Society most clearly from the Pic-Nics, though, was its commitment to raising surplus funds which it could donate to local organizations for poor relief. 'No vagrant Actors asking alms you see, / But *joint Proprietors* of some

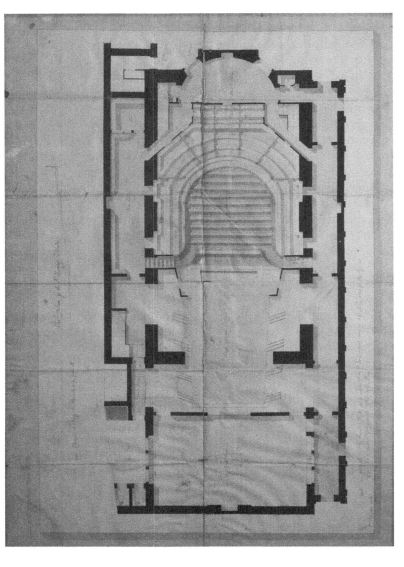

Figure 2. Plan of the Kilkenny playhouse, as altered by the architect William Robertson in 1818, further to the alterations he had already carried out in 1805. In order to increase the capacity of the house, the division of the pit area into boxes had now been abandoned, although places there still cost six shillings each. Note the luxurious size of the new green room added behind the newly enlarged stage.

degree, / A chartered company of *charity*,' as one epilogue put it.[93] Despite this noble claim on the money left over from ticket sales after the deduction of necessary expenses, and although the performers paid for their own costumes, considerable sums were reinvested from the takings in rendering the Kilkenny performances as tasteful and elegant as possible. The Society, for example, hired actresses and musicians from the Smock Alley theatre in Dublin to assist with what became, with balls, dinners, concerts and horse-racing in between nights at the theatre, an annual city festival. With professionals available to spare decent women from being compromised by playing its heroine, they were thus able to offer their public the period's favourite Shakespearean tragedy, *Romeo and Juliet*, in two different seasons.

The social and artistic assumptions of this project were built into the very shape of the Kilkenny theatre's expensively refitted and remodelled auditorium (Figure 2). Although its admission prices were the same as those of the major London theatres – one shilling for a place in the gallery, six shillings for a more comfortable place in a private box – this playhouse effectively excluded the lower orders altogether, since nearly all of the auditorium consisted of boxes, with only a tiny area at the rear of the gallery offering one-shilling places. In a pit-free theatre thus restricted to its casts' rich and polite social equals, the dramatic arts could be pursued for their own and the commonweal's sweet sake, without any need to stoop to the coarse tastes of the denizens of the gods. Regularly invoked as one figure-head of this enterprise, that disinterested and compassionate genius William Shakespeare, according to the Kilkenny theatricals, was himself an honorary gentleman amateur.

These performances thus provide a glimpse of an unfamiliar Romantic Shakespeare, declared for once not to be too transcendently good for the theatre, but just to be too transcendently good for the mercenary and socially heterogeneous Theatres Royal. Appropriately Richard Power had his portrait painted in the role of Prince Hamlet (by the young Joseph Patrick Haverty, Figure 3), which he played in 1803, 1809 and 1818. This was not only a presumptuously confident gesture – given that this was the role on which every great professional actor-manager since Betterton had staked his claim to be Shakespeare's truest current representative on earth – but one which aptly reidentified the play itself as a specimen and vindication of non-commercial theatre. Hamlet, regarded even in the professional theatre of the time as the gentleman *par excellence*, the glass of fashion and the mould of form,[94] is a connoisseur of just those pieces of drama that 'pleased not the million', and he himself privately enacts part

Figure 3. 'Mr Power ... is eminently gifted for the performance of the Danish Prince,
a character in whom are combined all the qualities of the soldier and the gentleman'
(*The Private Theatre of Kilkenny*, 105). Portrait by Joseph Patrick Haverty, *c.* 1818.
Power has expensively researched and commissioned a replica of the Order of the
Elephant, worn only by members of the Danish royal family.

of a play that in the public playhouses was 'caviare to the general'
(2.2.437–40). Power's own performance, too, this portrait implies, was
too good for groundlings capable of nothing but inexplicable dumb shows
and noise. Even the hiring of professional actresses in one instance
contributed to this sense of the private theatre's superiority to the public.

One of the professionals Power brought in from Dublin was no less a performer than Eliza O'Neill, who after playing comic roles in the 1812 Kilkenny season left Ireland to become the leading young tragedienne in London. (Here she earned such a reputation for moving audiences to tears that, before going to see her play the title role in Thomas Southerne's *Isabella, or, The Fatal Marriage* in 1814, Jane Austen picked up an extra handkerchief).[95] Having refused many lucrative offers to appear in private theatricals in England, she returned to Kilkenny to, play Juliet and Desdemona (and Belvedira in Otway's *Venice Preserved*) in October 1819 (Figure 4). O'Neill had amassed a sizeable fortune as a London star and was now as wealthy as her patrician fellow players: elevating herself to their status as disinterested social benefactors, she generously refused to accept any payment. One side-effect was that these appearances at Kilkenny were the very last performances she ever gave, since in December 1819 she married her amateur Friar Laurence and Iago, William Becher, MP for Mallow and a considerable landowner, and once married she retired from the stage altogether, never acting again for the remaining fifty-three years of her life.[96] For O'Neill, private theatricals offered an ideal transitional stage between the public theatres and the higher realm of genteel private life.

Despite the respectability of its participants, its commitment to charitable purposes and a conspicuous success in attracting impressive catalogues of Ascendancy socialites to the town every autumn, the Kilkenny Theatrical Society was still subjected to public criticism, and once more moral strictures focused particularly on women. The vicar of the town's principal church, St Mary's, the Reverend Peter Roe, was 'much grieved to witness the scenes of dissipation and folly which annually took place in Kilkenny during the theatrical season', and from the inauguration of the private theatricals in 1802 he and 'some other zealous clergymen and energetic preachers opposed these unhallowed amusements'.[97] 'The city is a scene of riot and revelling both day and night,' wrote Roe to his father at the opening of the 1805 season, lamenting the 'mania for stage-playing amongst the people in this quarter': 'Now, in my mind, attendance at the theatre affords as strong a proof of the existence of the carnal mind, as swearing or Sabbath-breaking.'[98] Although he apparently despaired of the souls of the Dublin women who performed in the playhouse, Roe was particularly anxious to keep his female Kilkenny parishioners from joining their audiences. In 1812, for instance, he wrote a long letter to two sisters he had heard were planning to attend a performance, sternly warning them to shun

Figure 4. Kilkenny's she-tragedy guest star Eliza O'Neill as Juliet, from a painting by
George Dawes, 1816.

that place of folly, where not only the dresses, decorations, company, conversation, music, attitudes of the performers, &c &c, are calculated to banish from the
mind every chaste, every correct, I will not say religious thought, but where the
glorious truth of God has been reviled ...[99]

The argument that the Kilkenny private theatricals were permissible and even laudable because motivated by benevolence clearly did not persuade everyone. 'It is stated that, in the space of six years, a sum exceeding one thousand six hundred and seventy-eight pounds was given to charities from the theatre,' snorted one of Roe's evangelical sympathizers, looking back on the whole project some years later, 'but how much more was given to folly and sin? How much was wasted on the inevitable expenses of a theatre? How much misery was engendered by the vices which accompany it?'[100]

Countering this familiar view, the amateur performers of Kilkenny sought to remind their audiences of their entertainments' claims to virtue on every occasion. Their philanthropic purpose was advertised by a surtitle visible throughout every performance: 'Over the proscenium of the stage is written the following elegant and expressive motto, from the pen of general Taylor,' reported the travel writer Sir John Carr, '"Whilst we smile, we soothe affliction."'[101] Beneath this slogan, the Kilkenny players offered a wholesome selection from the repertory of the Dublin theatres of the time,[102] carefully excluding any controversial or sensational recent material (such as what one prologue calls the 'monstrous' compositions of 'Monk' Lewis or Friedrich Schiller).[103] Each night there was an afterpiece as well as a mainpiece, as would have been the case at Drury Lane or Smock Alley (or, indeed, at Salisbury), and local poets contributed a number of special prologues and epilogues (which addressed cast and audiences alike as familiar friends). Unlike at the Theatres Royal, however, there were no additional dancers, singers or novelty acts to fill out the bill, other than an occasional 'Comic Ballet' or a more elevating item such as Miss Smith reciting Collins' *Ode on the Passions* ('With Appropriate Music', 12 October 1808), or Thomas Moore reciting his own *Melologue on National Music* (3 October 1810).[104] The company offered a clutch of standard respectable comedies such as Sheridan's *The School for Scandal* and Garrick and Coleman's *The Clandestine Marriage*, but, as O'Neill's valedictory star turn suggests, what the Kilkenny players really specialized in was the evocation of pity, whether in she-tragedy or in Shakespeare. Of the fifteen Shakespeare plays offered at Kilkenny (of which at least one was offered in each season), only four were comedies.

The connection between this repertory's investment in pathos and the players' devotion to charity was carefully made before the first performance of the first season, in February 1802, when the play was Thomas Otway's *The Orphan*, to be followed on the next night by his *Venice Preserved*. (Shakespeare joined the repertory only in a second season held that autumn, initially with *The Merchant of Venice*.) In Mr Langrishe's

Shakespeare in private

prologue, spoken by Mr Rothe (scion of the town's longest-established family of wealthy merchants), the charitable purpose of the entertainment is not only presented as redemptive: the actors claim that the audience for this production has its virtuous motives completely undiluted by any expectation of entertainment whatsoever. They are consequently able to disown most of the criticisms directed by the likes of the Reverend Roe at professional and amateur theatre alike:

> ... 'Tis not the curious that comes here today;
> 'Tis not the lounger, idling life away;
> 'Tis not the beauty, to display her charms,
> Nor vain coquet, nor fop with folded arms;
> Not to see *us*, you've heard so oft before,
> Nor hear old Otway, you've heard o'er and o'er;
> No – 'tis benign *Compassion* brings you here,
> Swells the fond sigh, and prompts the willing tear,
> And Pity, guardian of the helpless poor,
> Leading her *vot'ries* to our grateful door.

The extent to which this prologue nonetheless registers a lingering anxiety about the morality of deliberately stimulating unreal emotions is underlined by its conclusion, which does much to gloss the preference of this charitable theatrical enterprise for lachrymose tragedy:

> ... *Fictitious* tears bid *genuine* cease to flow,
> And our *feign'd* sorrows lighten *real* woe.
> Thus shall our Motives justify our Means,
> And Mercy consecrate these well-meant scenes.[105]

In paying to suffer emotionally with tragic characters, the audience are not only contributing to poor relief but demonstrating their compassionate ability to understand the sufferings of their less fortunate fellow citizens. This exclusive playhouse, then, could sell not just pathos but the added pleasures of self-congratulation. The point was duly taken by a correspondent from the *Dublin Evening Post* in 1809: 'While we are delighted with the Mimic scenes of woe so powerfully represented by Messrs. Rothe, Power, &c, it is no trivial increase of gratification, that such powers are exerted finally to relieve real scenes of distress.'[106]

Hand in hand with what amounted to a claim of moral superiority over the public theatres went a claim to artistic superiority, which was not only demonstrated by the heavy presence of Shakespearean tragedy in the Kilkenny repertoire but which, according to its enthusiasts, made his plays more at home there than on a commercial stage accused of having substantially abandoned them in favour of more populist fare. 'We congratulate ourselves on having Actors who can represent, and an audience who can relish, the long-neglected beauties of SHAKSPEARE and of OTWAY', observed the *Kilkenny Paper*.[107] As philanthropic amateurs, this company, in its own and its supporters' estimation at least, was worthier to perform high tragedy than mere professionals. In an age beginning to regard Shakespeare as a sublime artist raised above the degrading realm of show business, the Kilkenny theatre regularly proclaimed its elevation over the simultaneously vulgar and oversophisticated metropolitan houses, where the most crowded new plays were those designed to show off performing dogs ('*Carlo*'s the Roscius of our modern Plays'), and where unheeded Shakespeare was 'vanquish'd':

> For *you*, from London far, more wise, more plain,
> Who sense refine not, till no sense remain,
> Here, vent'rous, do we dare present to view,
> What *Nature* dictated, while *Shakspeare* drew.[108]

The phrase 'from London far' deliberately alludes to Samuel Johnson's satirical poem *London* (1738), which wistfully dreams of escaping 'From vice and London far', and claims that Ireland and Scotland are nowadays preferable to the corrupted metropolis: 'For who would leave, unbribed, Hibernia's land, / Or change the rocks of Scotland for the Strand?' To Sir John Carr, watching *Henry IV* in 1805, the Kilkenny players, restoring Shakespeare's awe-inspiring power to make audiences cry, might well succeed in luring the playwright's spirit to Kilkenny, not just from London but even from unspoiled rural Warwickshire:

> Blest be the reas'ning mind, the social zeal,
>   That *here* bids Folly from the stage retire;
> And while it teaches us to think, to feel,
>   Bids us in tears our godlike bard admire.
>
> Thus aided, see his rescued genius spring,
>   Again he pours the frenzy of his song,
> With every *feather in his eagle's wing*,
>   Once more in majesty he soars along.
>
> Oft deck'd with smiles, his spirit shall explore,
>   Erin! thy beauteous vales and classic ground,
> And every ripple of thy winding Nore
>   To him shall sweetly, as his Avon's, sound.[109]

This view that Shakespeare actively needed rescuing by amateurs from the debasing and indifferent commercial stage would become even more important a century later, as my next chapter will show. In the meantime, the Kilkenny theatricals of 1802–19 maintained three older traditions of private Shakespeare, dating back all the way to Edward Dering's domestic productions at Surrenden almost two hundred years earlier. One was an interest, despite their private nature and status, in matters of state, since one further justification which their proponents urged in the face of criticism from Roe and others was that the Kilkenny theatricals contributed not just to the welfare of the local afflicted but to the well-being of the nation. To some, these performances constituted virtuous incentives for remaining from vice and London far, by which Ascendancy landowners might be bribed not to leave Hibernia's land. However worryingly topical Shakespeare's depictions of rebellion and conspiracy might have looked in an Ireland still absorbing the aftershocks of 1798, the enjoyment and discussion of such plays was a means of both economic and social consolidation, since the Kilkenny theatre

collected together a great portion of the educated and the affluent, and induced them to spend their time and money at home; which, probably, but for its attractions, would have been spent abroad. Nor is this all – it often brought into the same social circle, many who at other seasons of the year were separated by differences of politics or religion, that too frequently, and too fatally, divide us.[110]

Drama as a disinterested art-form, according to this chronicler of the Kilkenny stage, was a force for social cohesion, and the lists of those public figures and politicians who came to the Kilkenny playhouse (printed, season by season, in a lavish privately published memorial tribute, *The Private Theatre of Kilkenny*, in 1825) bear comparison with the lists of fellow courtiers and local worthies associated with Dering's politically minded theatrical activities two centuries earlier. ('Kilkenny', remembered one spectator years later, 'was the Athens and the Bath of the Emerald Isle'.)[111] As a result of this perceived patriotism, the memory of the Kilkenny theatricals, despite the Ascendancy and Unionist cast of their participants (who regularly included 'Officers of the Garrison'),[112] could be invoked without embarrassment even by twentieth-century Irish nationalists. The centenary of Powers' first season was marked in 1902 by the inauguration of a new and decidedly Shakespeare-free 'Kilkenny Theatre', which was supported by the Gaelic League (which now met in Mr Rothe's old house in the centre of the town) and was specifically founded to promote 'Irish plays on Irish lines'.[113]

A second feature which the Kilkenny theatricals preserved from earlier private theatricals was a willingness to show off the precocious children of its sponsors, whether Masters Heilsham or Cooke as Fleance, Masters Gumbleton and Blakeney as the little princes in *Richard III*, Master Langrishe as Arthur in *King John* and a page in *Romeo and Juliet*, or Master Dalton as Young Marcius. This latter performer, according to the *Leinster Journal*, was the making of the climactic scene in *Coriolanus* in 1818:

The effect produced by the group was greatly heightened by the happy manner of the lovely child who personated the character of *Young Marcius*, Master GUSTAVUS DALTON. The attention paid by this fine boy to the business of the scene was scarcely to be expected in one of his tender years, and excited an uncommon degree of interest.[114]

The Kilkenny prologues may have occasionally ridiculed London theatre-goers for preferring Master Betty to Kemble and Siddons, but their audiences, no less than those at Surrenden or in Salisbury, would still pay an uncommon degree of interest to a cute real child. Like Laetitia Wyndham, seen not as a performer but as an exemplar of her onstage role, a non-professional infant might appear really to be that which he represented, and blamelessly at that.

One last feature which ties the Kilkenny theatricals, despite their anticipations of differently conceived amateur Shakespearean productions still to come, to the smaller-scale private theatricals of the preceding period is the interest taken by their participants and spectators in the reality and value of their props and costumes, just as everyone had taken due note of the jewels and swords shown off at Blenheim and in Salisbury. Sir John Carr's brief account of seeing *Henry IV* in 1805 is characteristic in this respect: 'I saw Henry the Fourth performed: the principal characters were admirably supported, and the dresses [i.e. costumes] were uncommonly superb. Lord Mountjoy appeared one night in a dress valued at eight thousand pounds.'[115] This, surely, is another example of amateur drama supplying a masquerade which displays rather than disguises the identity and status of the performer. Part of the appeal of Shakespearean tragedy and history to the likes of Power and Mountjoy seems to have been the opportunity it provided for them to dress up as the feudal lords and princes they really felt themselves to be, and Carr's insider knowledge of the price tag attached to Mountjoy's gleaming stage armour allows him to enjoy not only a visually magnificent production of *Henry IV* but a privileged sense of the different personal investments which it dramatizes for its performers.[116]

Despite its ostentatiously expensive mise-en-scène, one prop used in this particular play at Kilkenny ties this performance to the earlier, less

generously funded traditions of private Shakespeare with particular vivid-
ness. Preserved in the Bodleian Library is a part-book used by Richard
Power as Prince Hal, complete with notes as to the lengths in minutes of
the different acts, markings for cuts and notes of stage business.[117] In their
scenes at the Boar's Head, Hal and Falstaff do a great deal of laughing, as
do most of the other characters ('*They all laugh as loud as possible thro the
scene,*' says one interpolated stage direction in the margin, '*whenever
Falstaff laughs*'.)[118] While Falstaff mainly does his laughing while installed
in 'a large armchair', the Prince prefers an article of furniture much more
obviously associated with the luxurious domestic interiors familiar to this
production's cast. Listening to Poins' suggestion as to how he and the
Prince should rob Falstaff of his booty after the proposed highway
robbery, '*the Prince retires to sopha & lies all along it laughing immoder-
ately*'; soon Poins too '*retires and leans on sopha laughing with the Prince*'.[119]
If ever a real piece of borrowed contemporary furniture introduced a
suitably Regency note of upper-class raffishness to an amateur production
of Shakespeare, this unabashedly unmedieval sofa surely was it. Since the
time of Edward Dering some ambitious private Shakespearean performances might have migrated from domestic settings in country houses to
hired professional auditoriums, determined to assert their exponents'
superior judiciousness to whole public theatres of others, but this show
at least still bore vivid traces of the drawing room. Whether or not this
particular Hal and Falstaff were more dramatically compelling than their
predecessors at the Globe or Surrenden or their contemporary rivals at
Smock Alley or Drury Lane, at least they were probably more
comfortable.

CHAPTER 2

Shakespeare in public: the resisted rise of the amateur dramatic society

QUINCE Is all our company here?
BOTTOM You were best to call them generally, man by man, according to the scrip.

(*A Midsummer Night's Dream*, 1.2.1–3)

The Kilkenny Theatrical Society, convening to hire, decorate and in some accounts even buy their town's playhouse ('the small and elegant theatre,' according to Sir John Carr, 'is the private property of the gentlemen who perform'),[1] marks an important halfway stage between the private theatricals of the eighteenth century and the emergence of amateur dramatic organizations as Britain still knows them. It was an example, however, which it proved all-but impossible to follow in England for the best part of a century. At the start of the nineteenth century, the founding in 1802 of what has been termed the country's 'first amateur dramatic society',[2] the Pic-Nic Club, which unlike the Kilkenny theatricals was run on a formal, subscription basis, was greeted with moral panic. It was not until the start of the twentieth century, in 1901, that the establishment of the acknowledged pioneer of the Little Theatre movement, the Stockport Garrick Society, which definitely did buy a theatre of its own, could be celebrated as a breakthrough in the virtuous redemption of public life. By then the Pic-Nic Club had been forgotten, and enthusiasts instead hailed the Stockport Garrick and its emulators as marking a return to an imagined Elizabethan cooperative tradition of amateur theatricals supposedly depicted in the mechanicals' scenes of *A Midsummer Night's Dream*.

Between 1802 and 1809 a fierce debate about the social allegiances of the national drama affected the amateur and the professional stage alike. It would continue to rumble on even after the monopoly on legitimate professional drama in the metropolis long enjoyed by the two Theatres Royal was finally abolished in 1843. By now regarded as the embodiment of British public culture, Shakespeare was inevitably a major focus of this debate, and it would affect the amateur performance of his plays in the Anglophone world for the rest of the century and beyond. From the 1800s onwards, non-commercial Shakespeare split into two distinct and some-times colliding tendencies. One was the upper-class tradition of private theatricals, by now moving down-market into upper-middle-class villas and gentlemen's clubs. In the wake of the class wars for possession of the national poet that raged in London during the first decade of the nine-teenth century, such domestic performers often shied away from full-scale productions of Shakespeare in favour of drawing-room-scale abbrevi-ations of the comedies and burlesques of the tragedies. The other was a more artistically ambitious and altogether less bashful civic tradition of public readings and societies for cultural improvement. This came to ally itself with intermittent agitations for a subsidized national theatre, and it was especially vigorous in the industrial North. Only at the end of Victoria's reign would these two come together, and give rise to the 'Little Theatre' movement.

This chapter falls into two sections. The first explores the social competition for the right to perform Shakespeare which shaped both amateur and professional stagings of his plays in the nineteenth century. The second examines the kinds of Shakespeare favoured by amateur societies during their early twentieth-century heyday. If during the early nineteenth century Shakespeare was being performed by amateurs who might otherwise be happier staging *Bombastes Furioso*, in the early twenti-eth Shakespeare's plays instead found themselves more characteristically sharing the stages of amateur dramatic societies with the plays of Henrik Ibsen and George Bernard Shaw. After years of being accommodated to a genteel amateur repertory otherwise dominated by farce, burlesque and musical comedy, Shakespeare's plays were taken up in the twentieth century by volunteer thespians who, in default of the establishment of a national theatre, were now consciously occupying the artistic avant-garde of contemporary drama.

STATUES, SNOBS AND SPOUTERS

In 1864, during the celebrations of Shakespeare's tercentenary, two benefit performances were organized to raise money towards the erection of a statue of Shakespeare in London. There was nothing innately unusual in this — star actor-managers at the major London playhouses had staged fund-raising performances to pay for statues of Shakespeare before — but on this occasion the venue was not a famous West End theatre but the local playhouse in Cambridge, and the cast were not metropolitan celebrities but non-professionals, who sold their tickets through 'Mrs Martin's, Tobacconist, Sidney-street'.[3] In a tercentenary year otherwise alive with committees, processions and commemorative schemes to venerate the playwright, moreover, these performances of *The Merchant of Venice* and *As You Like It* constituted the city's only public homage to the national poet. 'Strange to relate,' a contemporary pamphlet on the subject remarks,

> yet no more strange than true, the only way in which the Tercentenary of SHAKSPERE, – the great poet of humanity, – was recognized in Cambridge, was by the Amateurs of the town giving two performances at the Theatre. No other gathering of any kind took place, – no meetings were held in honour of the poet, – either among the members of the University or the Inhabitants of the Town.[4]

The two performances at the Theatre made a profit of £23 5s 6d, which was sent to the London Shakspere Committee 'in aid of the London Shakspere Memorial'. This was to be a statue of the poet, framed by an imposing structure worthy of comparison with the monument to Sir Walter Scott in Edinburgh, to be erected either at the summit of Primrose Hill (at the focal point of a Champs-Elysées-like avenue leading all the way to it from Portland Place), or in Green Park, or at a prominent point on the Thames embankment.[5]

This statue, had it ever been erected, would have joined a tradition of commemorative images of Shakespeare which had begun with the monument installed by his family in Holy Trinity Church in Stratford, but which in the eighteenth century had been successfully co-opted by the professional London theatres. The question of a London monument to Shakespeare was first considered in the First Folio (1623): nineteen lines into his dedicatory poem, Ben Jonson is already considering whether Shakespeare ought to be commemorated in what would become Poets' Corner in Westminster Abbey, alongside Chaucer, Spenser and Beaumont. Jonson professed to think otherwise (though he arranged to be buried there himself when the time came), but his decision was reversed a little over a century later, when the Earl of Burlington convened a committee in order to raise money towards the installation of a monument to Shakespeare in the Abbey, eventually unveiling Peter Scheemakers' statue (made to a design by William Kent) in 1741.[6]

Both this monument and the poems composed during Burlington's fund-raising campaign declare it to have been paid for by the population at large rather than by the patronage of particular patrons or institutions:

'To future times recorded let it stand, / This head was lawrel'd by the public hand,' declared Benjamin Martyn's prologue to the benefit performance of *Julius Caesar* mounted on 28 April 1737;[7] 'Amor Publicus Posuit' reads an inscription on the monument itself. Having helped to pay for the monument, however, London's two Theatres Royal (which had enjoyed a monopoly on performing 'straight', non-operatic drama such as Shakespeare since 1660) made sure that they got as much of their money's worth from this and similar likenesses of Shakespeare for the remainder of their existence. Both playhouses displayed copies of the Scheemakers monument during the public excitement over its installation in 1740–1 and thereafter; Covent Garden, for instance, staged a special epilogue to a revival of *King John* in April 1741 'on occasion of the Monument erected by the Publick to his Memory … With an exact Representation of the said Monument'.[8] David Garrick commissioned another replica of the same object for Drury Lane, where it regularly appeared in his pantomime *Harlequin's Invasion* (1759) and more grandly during the climax of his most successful afterpiece, *The Jubilee* (1769): here the assembled company sang songs in praise of Shakespeare and representatives of Tragedy and Comedy crowned his votive image with flowers.[9] The statue was much paraded, too, when the rebuilt and enlarged Drury Lane reopened with John Philip Kemble's production of *Macbeth* in April 1794. Echoing Garrick's *Ode upon dedicating a building, and erecting a statue, to Shakespeare, at Stratford-upon-Avon*, the epilogue declared the new playhouse to have been built 'In tribute to the genius of our Isle', concluding with the lines, 'And now the image of our Shakespeare view / And give the Drama's God the honor due!', at which 'the statue of Shakespeare was displayed, and was crowned with bays by Miss *Farren*'.[10] When the building was remodelled in 1820, this sacred icon was displayed on top of the portico, where the young Charles Dickens would remember seeing 'rain-drops coursing one another down its innocent nose in piteous chase'.[11] Throughout their different incarnations, as each periodically burned down and was rebuilt, both Drury Lane and Covent Garden displayed at very least a bust of Shakespeare in their foyers. (Drury Lane still exhibits Garrick's copy of the Scheemakers sculpture, now brought inside from the portico.) When John Philip Kemble commissioned Robert Smirke to design a new Theatre Royal, Covent Garden, which opened in 1809, the building boasted not only a whole new post-Scheemakers statue of Shakespeare (by Rossi) in its anteroom (standing, as Leigh Hunt described it, 'in an easy assured attitude, making a sling of its cloak with its left arm, and holding a scroll in the other'), but a spectacular new safety curtain, depicting a temple dedicated to Shakspeare, who stands in the vista in his usual attitude, while your eye approaches him through two rows of statues, consisting of the various founders of the drama in various nations, Aeschylus, Menander, Plautus, Lope de Vega, Ben Jonson, Molière, &c.[12]

All these likenesses of Shakespeare effectively served as a trademark ('You cannot miss the sign, 'tis *Shakespeare*'s Head,' as Garrick's prologue to *Florizel and Perdita* had put it in 1756). The statues reiterated the message of those numerous prologues and epilogues in which Theatre Royal employees claimed to be Shakespeare's true present-day representatives: 'Sacred to Shakespeare was this spot design'd, / To pierce the heart and humanize the mind ...', as Garrick declared at the opening of the 1750–1 season. The way in which all this Shakespearean iconography was supposed to work was helpfully spelled out by Lewis Theobald in the prologue for the *Hamlet* staged at Covent Garden to raise money towards the Abbey monument in April 1739:

> For the dead Bard, receive our thanks and praise,
> And make us Sharers in the Tomb you raise ...
> Then think, this Pile his honour'd Bones contains,
> And frequent Visit – here – the lov'd Remains.[13]

In other words, in the eighteenth century the Theatres Royal were marked as sacred to Shakespeare by becoming his honorary grave, the place where his corpus could most suitably be visited – hence by 1817 Covent Garden was even displaying a cast of Shakespeare's Stratford monument.[14] Dickens too would recognize this funerary dimension to the Theatres Royal, though to rather different effect, in a speech rebuking Drury Lane for substantially dropping high-quality Shakespeare from its repertory in favour of musical spectaculars after the abolition of the patent-holders' monopoly in the 1840s: 'the statue of Shakespeare is well placed over its portal,' he lamented, 'since it serves as emphatically to point out his grave as does his bust at Stratford-upon-Avon.'[15] The legitimacy of the two legitimate playhouses had been staked on their status as at once Shakespeare's tombs and the homes of his only authorized executors, and Shakespeare had become shorthand for a properly public and inclusive national culture.

This identification of Shakespeare as the property of the legitimate public Theatres Royal had important consequences for those outside the profession who nonetheless wished to stage his plays. Most of the examples of large-scale amateur Shakespeare mentioned in my last chapter took place well away from London, and often well away from any professional playhouse, even after licensed provincial theatres began to proliferate in the 1780s: one reason the Wynnstay House theatricals stayed vigorous for so long, for instance, and could be safely encouraged even by Garrick, was that there were very few alternative sources of cultured amusement for the gentry within miles of the place.[16] Similarly, it is not just a mark of the social confidence and artistic ambition of the Kilkenny theatricals that their proponents were willing to stage as much Shakespeare as they did: it was also a function of distance. From vice and London far, claiming that their refined and artistic performances had lured Shakespeare's spirit from the banks of the Avon to those of the Nore, on occasion they were even prepared to borrow (albeit in a cut-price, two-dimensional manner) the patent houses' favourite Garrick-sanctified iconography. At the close of the final performance of the 1810 season, for instance, believed at the time to be their last,

> a scenic Painting representing the statue of SHAKESPEARE on an elevated Pedestal, appeared in the centre of the Stage, round which were grouped the whole of the theatrical Company, and, as they moved forward, a plaintive song was sung by them, taking leave of the Audience ... 'Here at the SHRINE we've lov'd so long, / Tonight we breathe our parting Song ...'[17]

In London, however, for amateurs to perform Shakespeare outside the Theatres Royal, let alone while making this sort of claim to be his true disciples, risked looking like an illicit private appropriation of the national drama. According to the patent houses, the grandeur which their mono-poly allowed them to maintain made them the only fit venues for Shakespeare. Thomas Morton of Drury Lane, for instance, questioned by the Parliamentary Select Committee on Dramatic Literature in 1832, quoted lines from the prologue to *Henry V* as evidence for the sort of theatre in which Shakespeare himself wished his plays to be enacted ('A kingdom for a stage, princes to act, / And monarchs to behold the swelling scene', 3–4), and he insisted that it was 'a command upon [Shakespeare's] countrymen that his pieces should be produced only in the noblest Temples of the Muses'.[18] This view had consequences for amateurs as well as for commercial would-be competitors: although Garrick had been happy to allow Sir Francis Delaval and his friends hire Drury Lane for their production of *Othello* in 1751,[19] it would be quite another thing when titled thespians presumed to perform at more private venues just around the corner.

Although much opposition to private theatricals had been voiced in the 1780s, a full-scale ferment over the aristocracy's place in relation to the stage, private and public alike, came to a head in the first decade of the

nineteenth century over the activities of a metropolitan group known as
the Pic-Nic Club. In 1802, the year of the peace of Amiens, when
hostilities with Napoleon briefly ceased, Lady Albina (or Albinia)
Buckinghamshire, formerly Mrs Hobart, initiated a series of Francophile
parties at the house of Anthony le Texier at Lisle Street near Leicester
Square, at which amateurs recited from the plays of Molière and Racine.
These amusements emulated the Anglo-French theatricals which the
Margravine of Anspach (née Lady Elizabeth Berkeley, and subsequently
Lady Craven from 1767 to 1791) had been mounting at Brandenburgh
House, Hammersmith, since her marriage to the Margrave in 1792.[20]
The Margravine, excluded from being received at Court due to having
co-habited with the Margrave while her previous husband, Lord Craven,
was still alive, decided to make herself the centre of an alternative social
circle much enlarged by émigrés fleeing the French revolution, and as a
cultural draw she commissioned a theatre in the grounds of her home
beside the Thames at Hammersmith. Some of the plays staged here were
new, including French scripts prepared by Le Texier, who had in the past
engaged in private theatricals with Voltaire at Ferney, but who now lived
in London working as a sort of theatrical fixer, helping to stage social
events and supplying the likes of Elizabeth Inchbald with current French
plays to translate.[21] Many, however, were older, native works, but the
Margravine of Anspach seems to have been highly self-conscious about
her amateur dramatics' off-centred relation to the mainstream of English
drama. Her theatrical repertory at Hammersmith was both substantially
modern and scrupulously not-quite Shakespearean. It is true that in 1796
she planned to produce *Twelfth Night* (in a classic piece of private
theatrical casting, she proposed to play Viola to her son's Sebastian,
presumably in order to prompt charming remarks about the family
resemblance and her youthful good looks), but in the event she staged a
latterday derivative instead, her own Mediterranean comedy of mistaken
identity *The Smyrna Twins*. On other occasions too she signalled her
theatre's supplementary status in relation to the legitimate Theatres
Royal by staging only appendices to the Shakespeare canon. Instead of
mounting either *The Taming of the Shrew* or *Henry IV part 1*, in the
summer of 1795 she staged John Fletcher's sequel to *The Taming of the
Shrew*, *The Tamer Tamed* (with herself as the heroine, Petruchio's second
wife, Maria), and in 1797 she produced William Kenrick's 1760 sequel
to the Henry IV plays, *Falstaff's Wedding* (with herself as Falstaff's bride,
Ursula).[22] Alongside their instigator and hostess, these performances
starred a number of titled personages, including the Comte d'Alet

('the best comic actor, I think, I ever saw,' remembered the Margravine)[23] and the Vicomte de Brécy, who has left an enthusiastic account of the Brandenburgh House production of Molière's *Les précieuses ridicules*, and an even more enthusiastic one of the supper which followed it. De Brécy's memoirs convey a vivid impression of a flourishing non-professional theatrical scene around London in the 1790s, during which he found himself appearing in both English and French plays.[24] His only appearance in Shakespeare, however, came in a French verse translation of (Cibber's) *Richard III*, prepared by a Genevan employee of the Aliens Office, Charles Michel Lullin, at his house in Pimlico. In this production the Vicomte – in a perfect royalist fantasy of martyrdom, exile and restoration – doubled the roles of Henry VI, murdered at the beginning of the play, and Richmond, who returns home to avenge and replace him at the end.[25]

Lady Albina was among the native participants in the Margravine's productions, attracting more notice than the Vicomte ever did as the rustic ingenue Cowslip in John O'Keeffe's *The Agreeable Surprise* in 1795. This performance was sufficiently memorable to become the subject of a caricature by Gillray and, less forgivably, a poem by the Margravine herself:

> Tho' her Ladyship's figure,
> Was some little bigger,
> Than Cowslip's; yet all must allow
> That her fat Ladyship,
> Might have cut off the slip
> And famously acted the cow.[26]

This extremely personal review must have been a sharp and lasting spur to social competition. Lady Albina, however, lacked the financial resources to build her own theatre to vie with the impressive Gothic structure which the Margravine had erected at Brandenburgh. ('One should rather suppose it to be a Bastille,' commented *The Times* during its construction in 1792, in a deliberately tactless allusion to its émigré habitués, 'than a temple dedicated to the Muses.')[27] Instead Lady Albina's rival soirées chez Le Texier off Leicester Square evolved into a whole season of exclusive social gatherings for a 'Dilettannti, or Pic-Nic Society', with one Colonel Henry Greville as master of ceremonies and chief administrator. Constituting her circle as a club, Lady Albina pioneered a new, cooperative model of amateur theatrical funding. The society's varied social and cultural events generally concluded with a supper for which the participants themselves supplied the refreshments (this being the derivation of the modern sense of the word 'picnic').²⁸ The members of this society clubbed together for their dramatic entertainment too, paying subscriptions to cover the hire of the New Theatre on Tottenham Street in Fitzrovia and the payment of professional assistants.²⁹ Motivated initially by dissatisfaction with the spectacular, crowd-pleasing repertory then available at the oversized Theatres Royal,³⁰ the Pic-Nics organized their own productions of new works by both English and French authors. As a result their repertory resembled that of Brandenburgh House, only without any plays or performances by the Margravine of Anspach.³¹

This new way of organizing recreational theatre – as a club rather than as the private amusement of a particular host – immediately attracted both legal opposition and public hysteria, which the society's cosmopolitan orientation only fanned. The proprietors of both Theatres Royal threatened to sue on the grounds that these private performances of 'straight' drama within a few streets of their playhouses constituted unfair competition which violated their duopoly (according to one amused member of the Pic-Nic Society, the managers seemed improbably afraid that 'the rage for these pic-nic dramas might leave the legitimate dramatic corps to play to empty boxes').³² The press, meanwhile, decided that these aristocratic goings-on behind closed doors could only be motivated by a desire to evade the moral and political censorship to which the public stage was subject. For over a year, after a judgement was passed against the patent houses and in favour of the Pic-Nics' right to their private amusements, the London newspapers and magazines were agog with titillated speculation, elaborate facetiousness and serious outrage. 'The *éclat* of the Pic-Nic Society', remembered one of its aggrieved actors nearly thirty years later in an appropriately Frenchified vocabulary,

afforded subject for lampoon in every other society. Hence the writers for the daily press, pamphleteers, and other waspish scribblers, dipped their picked-pointed pens in gall, and attacked the Pic-Nics *péle méle*.

It was as if amateur theatricals constituted high treason:

Every day, during the season of their mighty doings, as many literary crackers and squibs were played off against these harmless *players*, as would have furnished ammunition for a fifth of November, to blow up that old offender, the tatterde-malion Guy Fawkes.³³

As a voluntary society of thespian enthusiasts, the Pic-Nics could be criticized much more openly than any single aristocrat. The fact that it hired professional actresses to take female roles, so that its members could claim that no respectable women actually appeared on a public stage under its auspices, did nothing to calm the press's tireless innuendo. The playwright and former professional actress Elizabeth Inchbald, always scrupulously careful of her reputation, declined an invitation to perform with the Pic-Nics on the plea of the fatigue it would induce ('The acting would tire me to death, and the hour of returning home totally disqualify me for the next day'),[34] and she was probably prudent to do so. Rumours that the Pic-Nics' late-night amateur theatricals were simply a cover for sexual and political misbehaviour continued to spread, and they were fanned by another malicious verse from the pen of the Margravine of Anspach, which sarcastically described Lady Albina's associates as a group of 'True genuine Illuminés' who

> Agreed ten times a year to meet
> To Act, to Dance, to Chat, to Eat;
> Whatever else they were to do
> That I must leave to them and you.[35]

Other commentators had clearly long regarded private theatricals as innately immoral anyway, the expression of a Satanic discontent with one's own lot and identity: 'The Pic Nic actors may be pleased with their *managers*,' sneered *The Chronicle* on 5 January 1803, 'but they seem much discontented with the *parts* assigned them by *Providence*.' Many voiced a more immediate and local fear that a libertine faction of the British aristocracy (exercising what one sarcastic journalist called a 'liberal licence . . . freed from vulgar prejudices')[36] was conspiring to secede from public culture and subvert public morality. As well as generally ridiculing the appearance of these titled dilettantes, in *The Pic-Nic Orchestra* (25 April 1802), James Gillray published two cartoons to this effect. One depicts the Lady Albina and other members *en déshabillé* backstage while the Prince of Wales and two of his mistresses disport themselves in the background (*Dilettanti Theatricals; – or – a Peep at the Green Room. Vide Pic-Nic Orgies*, 18 February 1803). The other ridicules both the Pic-Nics and one of their most vocal opponents, Richard Brinsley Sheridan, proprietor of Drury Lane, who in a series of articles in newspapers castigating the Society had sought to present himself as a disinterested champion of public taste. In *Blowing up the PIC-NIC's; – or – Harlequin Quixotte attacking the Puppets. Vide Tottenham Street Pantomime*, 2 April 1802 (Figure 5), a rotund Sheridan, in a harlequin costume, lashes the Pic-Nic Society (including a topless Lady Albina) with his diatribes from *The Morning Post, The Morning Chronicle, The Courier* and *The Morning Herald* as the amateurs guzzle their supper

Figure 5. The legitimate Shakespearean theatre versus amateur dramatics: James Gillray, *Blowing up the PIC NIC's; – or – Harlequin Quixotte attacking the Puppets. Vide Tottenham Street Pantomime*, 2 April 1802.

after staging Henry Fielding's burlesque *Tom Thumb*. He is backed up by
Kemble (in his Hamlet costume), Sarah Siddons (clutching a dagger as per
her Lady Macbeth), and the entire legitimate dramatic corps, a crowd of
actors and actresses who carry a large tattered banner labelled 'Shakespeare'
amongst smaller, equally faded ones labelled 'Otway', 'Rowe' and 'Jonson,
Congreve, Addison'. Betraying the commercial theatre's real allegiances to
whatever sensational, democratic, modern continental drama would sell
tickets, however, they also carry less tarnished and more dangerous-looking
banners labelled 'Schiller' and 'Kotzbue'. The ghost of Garrick rises through
the floorboards to look on in mingled shock and amusement.

This hysterical invocation of a legitimate if shopworn Theatre Royal
Shakespeare as a charm against the Pic-Nics was not confined to Gillray's
cartoon. It seems the more disproportionate, given that the Pic-Nics, for
all the abuse directed at them as wicked splitters and privatizers of the
national drama, never performed Shakespeare at all save in one fleeting,
diffident self-identification with the mechanicals from *A Midsummer
Night's Dream*. At their Christmas ball at Crewe House in 1802, a
performance of Kane O'Hara's burletta *Midas* was introduced by a
version of the proto-burlesque prologue to 'Pyramus and Thisbe', 'altered
and made applicable to the occasion'.[37] But despite this careful avoidance
of the national poet, an annual round-up of selections from the London
papers, *The Spirit of the Public Journals for 1802*, devotes more than twenty
pages to letters, articles and satirical poems attacking the Pic-Nics,[38] and
many of these are quick to appeal to Shakespeare as the wholesome time-
honoured antithesis to this sinister fashionable novelty. *The Oracle*, for
instance, published a 'Shakespearian Parody on the Pic-Nic', attributed
to 'The Tottenham Rosalind', which adopts both the verse form and
the tone of Touchstone's send-up of Orlando's love poetry (*As You Like It*,
3.2.99–110):

> HITHER, ye Muses! hither quick,
> And sing the praises of *Pic-Nic*.
> Who but would go through thin and thick,
> To taste the joys of dear *Pic-Nic!*
> 'T would raise the dead and heal the sick,
> To pass an evening at *Pic-Nic*.
> The Duke, the Lord, the 'Squire, and Dick,
> All seem impatient for *Pic-Nic*.
> What Phyllis does behind the rick,
> We'll slily practice at *Pic-Nic*.
> E'en anchorites their lips might lick
> At recollection of *Pic-Nic* . . .

All morals out of doors we'll kick,
And sacrifice them to *Pic-Nic*.
There every cock shall have his *chick*,
Cluck, crow, and cackle at *Pic-Nic* . . .[39]

More apocalyptically, *The Morning Herald* invoked not *As You Like It* but *King Lear*, in the course of a series called 'Dramatic Predictions, or, Theatrical Intelligence for 1812'. These spoof theatre reviews from the future imagined what sorts of show might be received with approbation on the West End stage after a decade of corrupting Pic-Nic activity, accusing this aristocratic club of being in the vanguard of an impending proliferation of illegitimate theatres and pornographic entertainments. The hits anticipated in horror by this column include a revival of John Dryden's notoriously lewd Restoration comedy *Mr Limberham, or, The Kind Keeper*, complete with a new 'Sapphic Epilogue' ('the public spirit that first established the rights of *Dilettanti* Theatres' having at last banished all 'contemptible squeamishness'). From the now well-established 'Cognoscenti Theatre, Tottenham Street' the reviewer reports on an evening of 'Bacchanalian Glees', and at the 'Subscription Theatre, Queen Anne Street' he describes a lavishly applauded erotic 'Pas de Trois' performed by ballerinas clad only in flimsy transparent gauze. A 'Dramatic Saloon of Comus' and a 'Cyprian Circus' (since Cyprus was the legendary birthplace of Venus, 'Cyprian' was at the time a slang term for a prostitute) are cited among seventeen other 'Subscription Theatres' 'established since the odious Monopoly was assailed'. Thanks to the Pic-Nics, too, more familiar venues have changed almost beyond recognition. The Haymarket has been converted into a store-room for animal fodder, 'The Royal Hay-Loft, late King's Theatre', while the 'Ci-devant Theatre Royal, Covent Garden' is now exhibiting zoo animals, a use of which the fictitious reviewer mainly approves, though he admits that 'the stench . . . is intolerable, and the more so, since it cannot fail to remind the fashionable visitants of the effluvia of the *Canaille* in the Pit, which so sorely annoyed the Quality in the Side Boxes, while this place was a Theatre'. Only the Theatre Royal, Drury Lane has to date held out, but not for long:

This Theatre closed last night (and we trust for ever) with Shakespeare's Tragedy of *King Lear*. Though much insidious exertion had been made to interest the public feelings, there could not have been a receipt sufficient to pay for the candles. Mr. Kemble, however, exerted himself so as to extort considerable applause from the few auditors present; and we are informed, that there was something affecting in his manner, when announcing the final close of the scene

where Shakespeare and Garrick had so often triumphed. But the obstinate
manner in which this Theatre has so long withstood the will and mandates of
Fashion, renders its fall deservedly unpitied ... [W]e are assured that a celebrated
Architect has undertaken to turn the stage part of the Theatre into a Tennis
Court; and for the audience part, it is known that advantageous terms have
already been offered to convert it into a receptacle for Wedgwood's ware,
a lucrative branch of British commerce, which is well entitled to every advantage
of exhibition.[40]

Within two years the Pic-Nic Club had disbanded in the face of this level
of opprobrium. In March 1804 the officers of the Life Guards supplanted
the Club from their former venue, hiring the Tottenham Street theatre for
an all-male performance of Edward Young's *The Revenge*, before an
audience that included the Margravine of Anspach,[41] and a decade later
its next amateur theatrical booking was made by her cousin, Colonel
William Berkeley (later Earl Fitzhardinge). A veteran of the Brandenburgh House theatricals, Berkeley took this opportunity to show off in the
metropolis the productions which he had earlier mounted back home at
Berkeley Castle. While the Pic-Nic Club had been founded in consequence of a rivalry between fashionable cosmopolitan women (and hence
in part the agitation it provoked in masculinist commentators),[42] the
shows for which Berkeley hired Tottenham Street were far more insular
and patriarchal affairs. Berkeley's officer-led theatricals offered older and
broader fare than had either the Margravine or the Pic-Nics, including
Henry IV part 1, *King John*, *Othello* (in which Berkeley, like Lord John
Delaval before him, made a disturbingly convincing Iago), *Cymbeline*,
Julius Caesar (in which Berkeley played Brutus, a performance he commemorated by commissioning an immense portrait of himself in costume), and Garrick's abbreviation of *The Taming of the Shrew, Catherine
and Petruchio*, along with other stock dramas such as Sheridan's *Pizarro*,
Samuel Foote's *The Mayor of Garratt* and Susannah Centlivre's *A Bold
Stroke for a Wife*.[43] In his non-military capacity as a Member of Parliament, Berkeley appeased the Theatres Royal (of which he was a conspicuous patron, notoriously taking the actress Maria Foote as one of his
mistresses) by speaking vigorously in defence of the professional status
quo, opposing the multiplication of inferior playhouses which he feared
might follow from any abolition of the patent-holders' monopoly.[44]
During his regular visits to Cheltenham to attend the races he also
pioneered an alternative form of compromise between the amateur
stage and the commercial by paying theatre managers to include him
in otherwise professional casts.[45] When he did speak up for the moral

acceptability of dramatic activity Berkeley referred only to revivals of Shakespeare. To the sporting Colonel, theatre, so long as Shakespeare was involved, should be an art lawful as horse-racing: 'I hope from the bottom of my heart,' he declared in a much-quoted speech,

that I shall never see the time when an Englishman shall be reduced to such a state of mental degradation as to believe that he cannot see a race run, or a play of Shakespeare acted, without having reason to dread the vengeance of offended Heaven.[46]

The disappearance of the Pic-Nic Club in favour of Berkeley's more robustly British troupe of upper-class amateurs, however, did not settle the simmering contention for the soul of the national drama between the quality in the side boxes and the *canaille* in the pit. Although the actor-manager John Philip Kemble had featured in the *Morning Herald* and in Gillray's *Blowing up the Pic Nic's* as a personification of legitimate, uncorrupted popular Shakespeare to set against the Pic-Nics' supposed aristocratic vice, he appeared on precisely the opposite side of the contention for the stage between the élite and the general public during the much more serious struggle over the class allegiances of the London theatre which took place in 1809. Even if Smirke's rebuilt Covent Garden prominently displayed the proper Shakespearean statues as ever, the design of the new auditorium itself suggested that Kemble had sold out completely to the aristocrats whose alleged antics in the privacy of the Pic-Nic Club had inspired such reprobation a few seasons earlier. Kemble made annual summer visits to perform in Dublin, and he was in close contact with many of those involved in different capacities in the Kilkenny theatricals: now, whether consciously or not, he seemed to have deliberately adjusted Covent Garden towards the model offered by Kilkenny's utopian, patricians-only playhouse. Far more of the available space in its auditorium was now given over to private boxes (twenty-six more than before the fire), so that the space for the general public in the pit and galleries was much reduced. The occupants of the remaining public areas, moreover, had to pay increased admission charges to help pay for the proportion of the building costs that had not been covered by Kemble's high-born friends the Prince of Wales and the Duke of Northumberland. Suddenly one of the only two professional theatres in London permitted to perform Shakespeare appeared to have been transformed into an aristocratic plaything, in which the Covent Garden company would in effect be performing private theatricals at the behest of titled libertines in the private boxes, while a limited proportion of commoners eavesdropped from the cheaper seats. To add insult to injury, the privileged could now reach their boxes via a separate staircase, so that, just as the *Morning Herald*'s imaginary Pic-Nic snob might have wished, they could entirely avoid mingling with the *canaille*.

The disorder which this state of affairs provoked, soon dubbed 'The Old Price Riots',[47] disrupted not only Kemble's performance as Macbeth on the first night of the 1809–10 season, 18 September, but every successive performance for sixty-seven consecutive nights. In part organized by veterans of the pro-Jacobin 'Corresponding Societies' of the 1790s, this sustained fracas was as close as London ever got to having a revolution along Parisian lines. The nightly demonstrations in the Covent Garden pit and galleries, significantly, were explicitly made on behalf of a people's Shakespeare against an encroaching élite (regularly pillorying Kemble, for instance, as two of the Shakespearean usurpers he habitually impersonated, King John and Macbeth). They attacked aristocratic immorality in just the same terms as had earlier diatribes against the Pic-Nics: one banner unfurled at frequent intervals, employing a tabloid term for adultery borrowed from journalistic reports on upper-class divorces, demanded that there should be 'No Crim. Con. Boxes!' A Hamlet taken unexpectedly to task by the groundlings, Kemble was ultimately forced to capitulate, removing the offending new boxes and restoring the old prices. A sense that the Theatres Royal could no longer be trusted with the soul of the national drama, however, fuelled repeated bids to repeal their monopoly on the performance of straight plays over the following decades, which at last succeeded in 1843. •

Despite the eventual abolition of the monopoly, many English theatrical dilettantes remained diffident about performing Shakespeare's plays in full-length, unadapted form. As we've seen, in the 1770s the Harris girls and their friends were more than happy to tackle ambitious five-act high tragedies, such as David Mallet's *Elvira*, but their only Shakespearean performance was a heavily abbreviated version of *The Winter's Tale*, Macnamara Morgan's *The Sheep-Shearing*. Surviving marked-up copies of Garrick's similar *Florizel and Perdita* suggest that this shortened version of the play too was also widely used by amateurs,[48] and Garrick's other Shakespearean afterpiece, *Catherine and Petruchio*, also became a perennial favourite with non-professionals. An elaborate ticket for a production at the 'Amateur Theatre of Gibraltar' in 1820 provides a vivid glimpse of the nineteenth-century repertory into which Shakespearean afterpieces like these were assimilated: here *Catherine and Petruchio* forms part of a variety bill alongside Stephen Storace's operetta *No Song No Supper* and

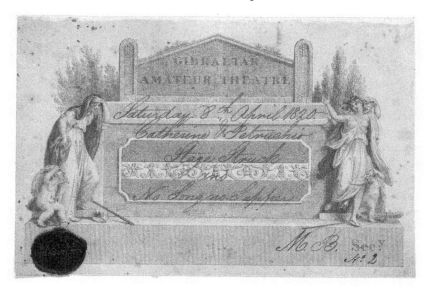

Figure 6. Shakespeare abbreviated for a variety bill: ticket for a performance of David Garrick's adaptation of *The Taming of the Shrew, Catherine and Petruchio,* Amateur Theatre of Gibraltar, 1820.

William Dimond's one-act farce *Stage Struck* (Figure 6).[49] Later in the century, the well-bred performers who appeared in the 'Oak Room Theatre' at Hampton Court Palace in such shows as Henry Danvers' *A Conjugal Lesson,* John Buckstone's *Popping the Question* or Haynes Bayly's *A Legal Fact, or, You Can't Marry Your Grandmother* offered only one piece of Shakespeare in almost forty years of dramatic activity, and it was a programme of 'Scenes from *The Tempest*'.[50] In 1861 the first-ever programme mounted by Richard Barham's Ingoldsby Club, similarly, featured numbers of songs, the whole of a comedy (*The Farce of A Fast Train! High Pressure!! Express!!!*), and just the trial scene from *The Merchant of Venice,* with Portia and Nerissa played by men.[51]

Many went further, insisting that genteel amateurs should avoid playing Shakespeare even in cut form but should offer his work, if at all, in even more self-deprecatingly light and comic modes. Garrick himself had reserved Shakespearean tragedy proper for the boards of Drury Lane by playing *Julius Caesar* among amateurs only in the form of his outrageous burlesque of the quarrel scene, *Ragandjaw* (1746). This cheerfully obscene playlet was performed, with scenery by

William Hogarth (who also played Caesar's ghost, here represented by the Devil's cook Grilliardo), at the home of their friend the Reverend Hoadly in Alresford, during an intimate house-party well away from Garrick's place of work and the Reverend Hoadly's parishioners.[52] (A version of 4.1 of *Julius Caesar* transposed to the low-life milieu of Henry Fielding's *Covent Garden Tragedy*, *Ragandjaw* depicts a foul-mouthed row between two watchmen, Brutearse and Cassiarse.)[53] The later emergence of Shakespearean burlesque as a trademark of the illegitimate theatres in the early nineteenth century was similarly associated with amateur stages from the first.[54] The comic actor Charles Mathews, for instance, author of *Othello, the Moor of Fleet Street* (1833), was already performing Shakespearean parodies and travesties in private at the home of John Rolls in Camberwell in 1809,[55] and the 1811 stage debut of John Poole's lastingly influential *Hamlet Travestie* (first printed in 1810) took place at the New Theatre on Tottenham Street,[56] a venue by then, thanks to the Pic-Nics and Colonel Berkeley, notoriously associated with non-professional actors.

The most important purpose served by Shakespearean burlesque before 1843 was to allow the minor commercial theatres condemned to playing musical comedy and melodrama by the duopoly on 'straight' drama exerted by the Theatres Royal to produce shows based on Shakespeare nonetheless, often drawing attention to the absurdity of the prohibition in the process. After 1843, though, burlesque might still usefully distinguish a frivolous and self-mocking strain of Victorian amateur Shakespeare from any embarrassingly serious attempt at emulating the professionals. As the once aristocratic pastime of private theatricals continued to move down-market into the upper-middle-class drawing room and the gentlemen's club, the first wave of amateur-dramatic how-to books began to advise amateurs to avoid Shakespeare in favour of afterpieces and burlesques. Charles William Smith, 'Professor of Elocution', for instance, opposed the amateur staging even of excerpts from Shakespeare's plays in his *Family Theatricals Selected From Standard Authors* (1860), preferring that non-professionals should confine themselves to pronouncing the great speeches which he had anthologized for the purpose in one of his other publications: 'Scenes from Shakespeare,' he advises, 'are far too complex for Amateurs; who, however, may vary their Entertainments by the recitation of passages from the Great Dramatist, which will be found in the "Book of Recitations".'[57] He is prepared to countenance, however, the performance of *Catherine and Petruchio* (which requires, he advises, 'ten males and three females; Venetian costume', 31), and he has no objection to reducing famous scenes from Shakespeare to tableaux for the purposes of elaborate games of dramatic charades. To act out the word 'lawsuit', for example, he recommends a full-dress mime of the climax of the trial scene from *The Merchant of Venice* for 'law' and then another of the wooing scene from *The Taming of the Shrew* for 'suit' (followed by one of the trial scene from Dickens' *The Pickwick Papers* to represent the whole word, 58–9).[58] Smith notes in passing that military men on leave are especially useful at theatrical house-parties (78), and in this and on other points he is seconded by William J. Sorrell, author of *The Amateur's Hand-book* (1866), which includes a section called 'How to "get up" theatricals in a country house, by Captain Sock Buskin'.[59] Sorrell is insistent throughout on steering amateurs away from the preserves of Drury Lane: 'if they *will* plunge into the fathomless depths of "the legitimate drama",' he advises, '. . . they will most surely fail' (6). Disclaiming the artistic ambitions of the previous century's country-house theatres, Sorrell dismisses serious five-act plays out of hand as inappropriately demanding, both technically and emotionally, for recreational performance: 'In short, if you wish to weary your friends and utterly disgust them with Private Theatricals, collect your troupe, and select *Othello*' (24–5). In Sorrell's military alias, however, he does not object to the presentation of short extracts from tragedies, just so long as they aren't Shakespeare's: 'If scenes only are played, Mr Tragedian will have many opportunities. The choice should be from Bulwer's or Sheridan Knowles' plays, rather than from hackneyed Shakespeare' (51). He much prefers, however, that amateurs should perform well-chosen short comedies followed by cut versions of burlesques (25), with only experienced players in the leading roles, but unfortunately the social situation of a house-party may leave one at the mercy of an overweening host: 'This however cannot always be managed in a private house, where the ambitious tyro can revel in Shakespeare's most difficult parts if he desire it' (64).

Sorrell's advice is largely addressed to men: briefly and unconsciously concurring with Sir Edward Dering, for example, he insists that 'All the men should wear wigs, taking care to try them on previously. There will be no difficulty in obtaining them from London by railway, &c' (65). When it comes to women, he is firm: 'Do not have too many ladies performing . . . two or three gentlemen to one lady is a good division of the sexes on stage' (50). Although the bulk of Sorrell's book seems to assume that these ladies will be members of the house-party, its more practical supplementary section, contributed by the theatrical publisher Thomas Hailes Lacy, supplies not only a three-page list of plays 'for male characters only' (79–82, including a sole Shakespearean item, once again the burlesque-avant-la-lettre 'Pyramus and Thisbe'), but the names and addresses of eight actresses, 'Ladies Who Assist In Amateur Performances', available for hire should mixed performance be required (119). But this expedient could not be adopted everywhere, once again mandating a resort to burlesque:

At Oxford, Cambridge, and other leading Colleges and Institutions, female assistance must be dispensed with. Almost all the modern Burlesques are well suited for performance under this restriction, and few need to be told that such representations have generally been attended with most satisfactory results. (81)

Even when subscription-based amateur dramatic societies had begun to reappear outside Oxford and Cambridge during the Victorian period, they had mainly been heavily male-dominated affairs. In January 1839, for instance, George Hodder, a future *Punch* journalist, appeared in a *Hamlet* mounted by just such an all-male theatrical club, which used to meet at a tavern in Covent Garden. As Lacy would have recommended, they hired competent professional women to play Ophelia, Gertrude and the Player Queen, but while their Hamlet was good enough to have later repeated the role with a professional company before embarking on a proper career in the Indian Civil Service, the rest of the cast were not, and an invited audience of their friends, clearly expecting that any amateur performance of a high tragedy could only be intended as a spoof, found the whole performance hilarious. Thirty years later, Hodder candidly admitted that the overlarge hired tights he wore as Horatio might have suited a lighter genre than tragedy: 'had I been equipped for a burlesque the result could not have been more effective'. The audience, clearly connoisseurs of just that genre, found this *Hamlet* 'droll enough to gratify the most inordinate lover of burlesque'. Fortunately only the lessee of the venue, a Mrs Pym, seems to have been much offended by this transformation of Shakespearean tragedy into light comedy, rising at one point to harangue the assembled hysterical company with a cry of 'Do you call yourselves gentlemen?'[60]

Most of those involved in amateur dramatic societies around the West End over the next three decades and more, apparently, did. Lacy prints a list of the names, addresses and office-holders of thirteen 'Metropolitan Amateur Clubs', including the Byron Excelsior, of Bloomsbury, the Siddonian Dramatic Club, of Soho, and the Strand Amateur Dramatic and Musical Club, all of whose officers are men. He helpfully prints the rules of the latter, established in 1864, as a model, the first of which specifies that 'This Club shall consist of Twenty Acting Members (inclusive of the Managers and Secretary, and exclusive of Ladies)' (74). It is indicative of this particular amateur theatrical milieu that the one English club already in existence in Sorrell's time that still survives – the Canterbury Old Stagers (established by the Hon. Frederick Ponsonby, later the Earl of Bessborough, in 1842, and given its current name in 1851) – began as the side-effect of an annual cricket tournament, originating in comedy performances mounted by the sporting gentlemen in the evenings after their matches.[61]

The relation between respectable amateur performers and intense tragic emotions, especially those involving sexual desire, remained especially problematic for those Victorian amateurs who persisted in mounting mixed-sex productions, but here again a recourse to burlesque might provide a partial answer. Neville Lynn's *The Thespian Papers, being a series of humorous essays on subjects of professional and amateur dramatic interest*, for example, is particularly illuminating about the inhibiting social difficulties experienced by nineteenth-century amateur players of love scenes:

Who ... ever saw an amateur rush from the wings and clasp his fair one to his manly breast? No one, I venture to say. The Romeo either rushes on and falls over some properties (which he stoops to pick up), or else goes on gingerly, fully conscious that Capulet is watching his antics through a formidable pair of opera-glasses, and that all Juliet's relations are critically sitting, in joyful anticipation of his making a complete hash of it ...

Juliet, also, has too many conflicting emotions to help the unhappy Romeo in any way. She is wondering what 'mamma' is staring at her for, and devoutly wishes that she were in the auditorium to slap her little brother for making frightful faces at her at this trying moment ...[62]

The solution, for Lynn as for Sorrell, is that amateurs should embrace burlesque instead, a genre dedicated to reframing the transgressive social situations depicted in tragedy within limits appropriate to domestic performance:

[C]all the performance a farcical version and add a few little intellectual bits of business, such as in the Balcony Scene ... contrive that a flower pot with loose mould, shall descend on Romeo's head in the middle of an impassioned utterance, and introduce a botanical sentence or two on the Primrose League, and some meteorological observations on our English weather. To supplement this sort of thing, there might be a topical song, and a ballet with Juliet as *première danseuse*. I know I shall be thought brutal for saying so, but I should infinitely prefer a comic Shakespeare to a performance badly acted.[63]

Neville would have approved, then, of the Bourne family's choice of play for a performance at Cowarne Court in Herefordshire, the anonymous *Romeo and Juliet, or, The Shaming of the True, An Atrocious Outrage in*

Five Acts (1868).[64] Just as he might have advised, this version of the play reduces Shakespeare's traumatic Renaissance feud to a disagreement over Victorian politics, laced with topical gags: Capulets and Montagues become Whigs and Tories, with Capulet 'President of the Verona Reform League' and Romeo 'a Conservative and a Gentleman'. This performance gave entire satisfaction, and, bathetically degrading its heroine from appealing she-tragic role-model to pert minx, it even had the additional benefit of tending to render its star less vain rather than more so. 'The servants on the stairs were very appreciative and clapped everything,' Ruth Bourne recorded in her diary. 'Faith did Juliet very well. She talked in a short sharp impertinent way. Her hair was frizzed in a vulgar fashion.'[65]

The same solution to this play's potential embarrassments had occurred to George M. Baker in Boston in 1869, whose *The Mimic Stage*, 'a series of Dramas, Comedies, Burlesques, and Farces, for Public Exhibitions and Private Theatricals', manages to render even *Romeo and Juliet* 'particularly appropriate ... for temperance gatherings'. The trick as ever is to transpose the play into a painlessly modern frame of reference, in the process making the lovers merely a little forward rather than embodiments of irresistible sexual passion. Baker converts *Romeo and Juliet* into *Capuletta*, a pun-infested semi-musical abbreviation not only freed from troublesome intimacies and supplied with a happy ending (Romeo, instead of drinking poison in the tomb scene, merely takes some Winslow's Soothing Cough Syrup) but naturalized (like the version of *Macbeth* which Jo March hopes to stage with her sisters in Louisa M. Alcott's *Little Women*, 1868) into the drawing rooms of New England.[66] To Baker, apparently, rhyming burlesque and emigration provide perfect antidotes to Old World tragedy:

> CAP[ULET]. Vile Montague, begone, or you shall sweat!
> I'm on my native heath, my name is Capulet.
> JUL. Give me my Romeo, or I shall die:
>   I'll cut him up in little stars –
> ROM.   Oh, my!
> CAP. No, no, my child, you'll cut up no such capers:
>   Do you want to figure in the Boston papers?
>   Go home and sew, and so your morals mend:
>   This fool I'll straight about his business send.
>   If you two marry – why, then, I'm a noodle,
>   Who dare dispute me –
> *Song. Tomb opens and MERCUTIO appears as Yankee Doodle.*
> *(Allegorical dress of America.)*
> MER.   Only Yankee Doodle! ...

ROM. What say you, Juliet? shall we westward go?
    Speak up, my darling, do not color so.
JUL. I like those colors well, I do confess:
    Those stripes are just the style of my new dress.
ROM. To seek that blissful land, I think we'd orter.
JUL. But I'm so horrid sick upon the water!
MER. Come, Capulet, your blessing I command;
    Then pack up trunks, and off for Yankee land.
CAP. What! end a tragedy without a death?
    It's horrible! you take away my breath!
MER. Then we shall have one, sure, let's move along:
    We'll end our tragedy with a yachting song.
    Finale, 'A Yankee Ship and a Yankee Crew.' . . .[67]

Even in the less democratic surroundings of the British Raj, this same aesthetic was recommended to stage-struck military officers in the 'Letters on Amateur Acting' published in the *Bombay Miscellany* for 1862, again under the pseudonym of 'Captain Sock Buskin', who sends minute and voluminous advice to his nephew, the theatrical novice 'Ensign O'Trigger'. 'Gentlemen amateurs should never attempt tragedy – their tears will be laughed at,' advises Buskin, '. . . severe pieces must not be attempted by amateurs.' Quite apart from the potential for embarrassment, there are practical problems: 'Shakspeare (and the authors of tragedy generally) is particularly difficult to understand.'[68] Instead, O'Trigger is advised to stick to well-tried short farces (such as J. M. Morton's *Box and Cox*), melodrama, and, for variety, burlesque, since in the latter 'there is plenty to see. Processions, tableaux, etc, please the eye, and prevent the ear noticing bad acting – and acting is bad, very bad, sometimes.'[69] Buskin particularly commends William Barnes Rhodes' popular 1810 burlesque *Bombastes Furioso* ('There is none like it. It is a dressy piece. It is short. The action is capital. It has good songs and fights. It contains only one woman'), but under the right circumstances he likes more recent, Shakespearean specimens of the genre too: 'More difficult burlesques, such as "Shylock Travestie", "Macbeth [Travestie]", &c, are well worth playing, as first pieces, if the company be good enough.'[70] This latter specimen, *Macbeth, Somewhat Removed from the Text of Shakespeare*, had been written for all-male amateur performance in the first place. Francis Talfourd's play was originally performed by Oxford undergraduates (including Talfourd himself, who played Lady Macbeth) at Henley Regatta in 1847, and it was later staged at his house.[71] A succeeding troupe of 'Oxford Dramatic Amateurs' performed their own *Hamlet Travestie* in 1849,[72] and a number of other Shakespearean burlesques, like Baker's

Capuletta, were similarly purpose-made for non-professional performance, among them the cherished *Hamlet! The Ravin' Prince of Denmark!!
Or, The Baltic Swell!!! And the Diving Belle!!!* (1866).[73]

In this context, the fact that the amateurs who celebrated the 1864
tercentenary in Cambridge chose to perform full-length, unadapted,
unburlesqued Shakespeare – giving *As You Like It* and *The Merchant of
Venice* as mainpieces – marks them as belonging to a different social
milieu, with a very different agenda. Although the artistic seriousness that
had once characterized the aristocratic performers of Wynnstay and
Kilkenny may have been disavowed by burlesque-loving Victorian undergraduates, it survived among townspeople, since in the meantime the
radicalism of the Old Price rioters had fed a new strain in amateur
Shakespeare. Artisan engagement with Shakespeare had been on the rise
since the early 1800s, producing both organized societies for the reading
and discussion of his works and ad hoc groups committed to performing
them, in extracts at least. Lower-class amateur actors, reciters and debaters
had been mocked as 'spouters' since the mid eighteenth century: see, for
example, William Woty's *The spouting-club: a mock heroic, comico, farcico,
tragico, burlesque poem* (1758), or the encounters with eighteenth-century
amateur performers in the West Country chronicled in John Bernard's
Retrospections of the Stage (1832).[74] A 'spouting club' was defined in Francis
Grose's *Dictionary of the Vulgar Tongue* (1811) as 'a meeting of apprentices
and mechanics to rehearse different characters in plays: thus forming
recruits for the strolling companies',[75] but just as important as the
imputed theatrical aspirations of spouters was their engagement with
controversial public issues.[76] The years following the Old Price Riots
saw a new spate of cheap publications designed to cater to those literate
workers who were committed to finding themselves a voice through the
public rehearsal, often in hired rooms at public houses, of the perceived
masterpieces of English rhetoric, dramatic and political alike. (See, for
example, *The Spouter's Companion*, c. 1821, and *The Spouter's Album*,
1825.)[77] Leman Thomas Reade's *The Modern Speaker; containing selections
from the works of our most approved authors, in prose and verse; with extracts
from the Parliamentary speeches of some of the leading men of the past and
present day* (1826) provides a good snapshot of the milieu and mind-set
into which, in the years preceding the first Reform Act, Shakespeare was
now being adopted. Orlando's account of rescuing Oliver from the lioness
appears, in a section headed 'Narrative Pieces', under the heading 'Frater-
nal Affection', but there is much more Shakespeare among 'Orations,
harangues, etc', where Margaret of Anjou, Richmond and Henry V rub

shoulders with Pitt the younger and William Wilberforce (opposing slavery) and Napoleon Bonaparte (rallying his army on behalf of the liberties of France).[78] This newly visible workers' Shakespeare has been documented by Andrew Murphy in *Shakespeare for the People: Working-class Readers, 1800–1900*, which points out how thoroughly Chartist agitators pressing for the extension of the franchise in the 1840s incorporated phrases and rhythms taken from Shakespeare's rhetorical set-pieces into their own speeches.[79] Although his study, as its subtitle suggests, does not deal directly with the performance of Shakespeare, Murphy does describe one key incident in the career of the Chartist arch-spouter Thomas Cooper, who in 1847 mounted an entire production of *Hamlet* in Leicester, with himself as the Prince, in order to raise money to meet the legal expenses of his trial for sedition.[80]

Less openly polemical urban self-improvers also began to move from the reading and recitation of Shakespeare into the full-scale performance hitherto associated only with the aristocrats of the preceding century. The Sheffield Shakespeare Club, founded in 1817, it is true, simply paid a subscription towards commissioning a designated annual Shakespearean performance from professionals at the local playhouse, and held a large annual dinner after it, featuring grandiloquent Bardolatrous speeches, songs and toasts.[81] A 'Manchester Shaksperian Society' was operating on similar lines by the 1850s, when it would organize an annual charity benefit at the Manchester Theatre Royal:[82] by then, however, the Manchester Athenaeum Dramatic Society, established in 1847 (as the 'Athenaeum Literary & Dramatic Reading Society') to read 'the works of Shakespeare and other authors' so as 'to cultivate a taste for standard dramatic literature and poetry and to be a source of mutual improvement and amusement to its members', had graduated to giving its own public readings. By 1861 this society was mounting its own amateur performances, with scenery, and with hired professional actresses taking the female roles:[83] their first productions were benefits in aid of St. Mathias's Working Men's Club, Salford, and the Working Men's Institute, Hulme.[84] In 1864 the Athenaeum decided to celebrate the Shakespeare tercentenary by raising money towards a scholarship at the non-denominational Owens College (which later evolved into Britain's first civic institution of higher education, Manchester University). They did so, like their Cambridge colleagues, by mounting a full-length production of *The Merchant of Venice*.

The members of the Cambridge Amateur Theatrical Society who, 'ever alive to promote a knowledge of the great master of the dramatic art, to

pay homage to his wonderful genius, and to cultivate the dramatic taste
of their fellow townsmen', staged the same play 'in aid of the London
Shakspere Memorial' were in one respect more permissive than their
Mancunian colleagues, in that although they hired the professionals
Helen Paget and Kate Rivers to play Portia and Nerissa, they did allow
their own Miss Matthews to play Jessica. (In *As You Like It* the professionals similarly took Rosalind and Celia, but Miss Matthews played
Phoebe, and Mrs W. Ball played Audrey).[85] Their performances, however,
were clearly felt to belong to the same noble tradition of representing
Shakespeare as the poet of all Britons: 'To all classes his works appeal,'
declared *A Memorial of the Tercentenary of Shakspere, at Cambridge*, '– all
classes can gather wisdom and knowledge from his pages; for all classes are
by him truthfully pourtrayed.'[86] This, at last, was a non-professional
Shakespeare offered to a socially heterogeneous audience, aimed not at a
network of like-minded social equals but at an entire local community. In
practice, however, not only did the supposedly educated classes fail to stir
themselves on this great occasion, but some of their younger representatives in the audience gave every impression that Shakespeare was not
for them at all:

The slight honour that was rendered in Cambridge to the name of
SHAKSPERE, had its origins among the people. Those who got up and gave
the performances, belonged chiefly to the class that is governed, and not to that
of the governors ... Excepting some interruptions from a few noisy members of
the University, – roistering blades, more familiar with the patter of the turf, with
short pipes, heavy wet [hard liquor], grooms, jockeys and ballet dancers, than
with the sweet lines of Father WILL, – the performances passed off with great
spirit and to the satisfaction of the audiences.[87]

This satisfactory popular event (which even came complete with 'A
Comic Song by Mr Wilkins' and afterpieces, namely 'the farce The
Railroad Station' after *The Merchant of Venice* and 'the farce The Artful
Dodger' after *As You Like It*) was in marked contrast to the celebrations
mounted in Stratford, which enraged popular opinion by being mainly
confined to the rich.[88] Live amateur Shakespeare had by now definitively
passed from the hands of the aristocratic dilettantes and into those of
the artisan class, largely by-passing a bourgeoisie left to amuse itself
with burlesques and farces. Furthermore, the right to certify oneself as
Shakespeare's true heir by erecting his latest tombstone had now passed
from the monopolizing Hamlets of the Theatres Royal and into the hands
of such everyday groups as the Amateurs of Cambridge. Once such
popular organizations had erected a fitting monument to the people's

poet in London, the scandalous absence of a national holiday to mark Shakespeare's birthday would be their next target. 'The day is coming,' promises *A Memorial of the Tercentenary of Shakspere, at Cambridge,* 'when the people themselves will wipe out this national ingratitude. What the powerful and the wealthy have left undone, the masses of the community will ultimately carry into effect.'[89] In the event, sadly, as Richard Foulkes explains, the national organization of the 1864 tercentenary was so riven with faction and incompetence that not only was no holiday instigated but no monument was erected either, despite the £23 5s 6d sent from Cambridge.[90] Instead Samuel Phelps, the actor-manager whose low-cost productions at Sadler's Wells had largely taken the baton of popular Shakespeare from the old patent houses, simply planted a patriotic oak in the poet's name at the proposed site of the memorial, on Primrose Hill. This came at the climax of a march from Russell Square, organized by just that division of the tercentenary's ad hoc bureaucracy with which Cambridge's polite mechanicals apparently sympathized, the Working Men's Shakespeare Committee. The fact that this march doubled as a demonstration protesting that the liberator Garibaldi had just had his visit to Britain cut short by the covert intervention of Her Majesty's Government only underlined its significance as a milestone in the extension of the Shakespearean franchise.[91]

There is an ironic postscript to the 1864 campaign to install a statue of Shakespeare that would not belong solely to the privileged or the professional. A public successor to Shakespeare's Abbey monument and the imitations flaunted by the Theatres Royal *was* installed in central London after all, but a decade later. In 1874 the dubious financier Albert Grant, *né* Abraham Gottheimer, bought Leicester Square, in the heart of London's theatre district, and in a gesture that might have been imitated from Julius Caesar's will he threw it open 'to be preserved for ever for the free use and enjoyment of the public'.[92] He consecrated this new public space by erecting, at its corners, statues of four general benefactors who had lived locally: Isaac Newton, William Hogarth, Joshua Reynolds and the pioneering surgeon John Hunter. At its centre, however, he placed a replica of Scheemakers' statue of Shakespeare, in his usual attitude, but this time labelled not 'Amor Publicus Posuit' but 'There is no darkness but ignorance'.[93] Words with which Feste taunts the imprisoned Malvolio in *Twelfth Night* are here ingeniously redeployed to adopt Shakespeare as another hero of the Enlightenment public sphere. Sacred to the people's poet despite everything, albeit through the patronage of a single millionaire, the original home of the Pic-Nic Club thus became another of Shakespeare's honorary tombs.

The tercentenary campaign to erect a new monument to Shakespeare was ultimately subsumed, as Richard Foulkes points out, within a much longer struggle to establish 'a National Theatre in London to be regarded as a Shakespeare Memorial'.[94] This was conceived as a publicly funded institution which would constitute just the sort of deserving 'Temple of the Muses' which the Theatres Royal had not been since the time of Garrick.[95] The amateur productions of Shakespeare offered in Cambridge in 1864 might well be seen as prescient forerunners of this movement, since in the years preceding the establishment of subsidized theatres, when Shakespeare proverbially spelled ruin on the commercial stage, it was volunteer casts who filled the gap between the lost glories of the monopoly-funded Augustan stage and the imagined future of a state-supported Shakespeare-for-Shakespeare's-sake. The fate of the first National Shakespeare Theatre site in London offers a piquant emblem of this. Just when the committee to establish the theatre had finally acquired somewhere to build it, on Keppel Street in Bloomsbury (close to the Royal Academy of Dramatic Art), the First World War broke out, and the project had to be shelved. In 1916 the plot was loaned to the YMCA, and instead of housing a Temple of the Muses it was soon occupied by a structure known as the 'Shakespeare Hut', which mainly provided entertainment and warm meals for servicemen on leave. But to mark the tercentenary year of Shakespeare's death, the Hut also hosted performances of extracts from the plays – which were given by amateurs.[96]

The task of supplying an amateur stop-gap in lieu of a national theatre had first been explicitly recognized and embraced at the turn of the twentieth century, when various kinds of society devoted to saving the national drama, generally by supporting the performance of new plays unsuited to the existing commercial stage or the existing system of censorship, sprang up all over the country.[97] For those societies whose members did the performing themselves, the presence of Shakespeare in their repertories might function just as had the presence of statues of Shakespeare in the lobbies of the old Theatres Royal: as the declaration of a claim to the centre ground of the national theatrical tradition. One such democratic successor to the Pic-Nics came into being on 24 October 1901, in the Church Coffee Tavern on St Petersgate in Stockport, Lancashire, at a meeting held to discuss 'A Proposed New Stockport Dramatic and Literary Society'. By the time the local newspapers were reporting this event, the Society's newly elected president was already expressing visionary hopes for the future:

Amateurs may set an example to the professional theatrical world if they will. Theatrical managers are unfortunately bound down [sic] by commercialism and tradition … Is not the time approaching when even in conservative England it will be considered as necessary to have municipal theatres – conducted on artistic as distinct from profit-making lines – as to establish libraries, art galleries, &c? At any rate, until this happy consummation [sic] is attained, let amateurs work their hardest to raise the standard of the art. – Yours &c.

EDWIN T. HEYS

31, Tatton-road North, Heaton Moor, October 30th 1901[98]

At the same time that the society embraced this view of the future, it chose a name identifying it with the greatest achievements of the Shakespearean theatre's past. As the printed constitution issued the following month declares, 'The Society shall be called THE STOCKPORT GARRICK SOCIETY.'[99]

The Stockport Garrick is usually cited as the most important of the early twentieth-century amateur dramatic societies, for three reasons. It was the first amateur club to acquire its own playhouse (in 1905: their current building, converted from a warehouse on Exchange Street and as intimate as the Pic-Nics could have wished, dates from 1920); it helped to stimulate a revival of artistically inclined theatre in the North-west more generally, including the important work of Annie Horniman's Manchester repertory company at the Gaiety;[100] and it was the first amateur group to play Ibsen and Shaw, praised for so doing by the likes of Harley Granville-Barker.[101] Its dealings with Shakespeare are especially instructive, since (like the Society's forward-looking aims and backward-looking name) they reveal the amateur Shakespearean performers of the modern period to have been conflicted about their artistic niche from the outset. As both the Garrick's early programmes of social and intellectual activities and their productions of Shakespearean drama show, the invocation of Shakespeare served to sanctify much of what such amateur dramatic societies did, but their originality and imagination were rarely directed towards rethinking how his plays might be performed. When early twentieth-century amateurs did pioneer new methods of staging Shakespeare, their speciality turned out to be turning backwards to the Elizabethans rather than looking forwards into modernism.

If ever Bardolatry trespassed on established religion, it did so in the case of the Stockport Garrick, which only came into being after the dramatic society at the local Unitarian church was 'broken up', as Heys put it, 'under circumstances which need not here be discussed'.[102] Those circumstances included the row which had broken out when Heys, as part of his preparations for the Society's most ambitious production to date, of *The Merchant of Venice*, turned out to have started digging an unauthorized tunnel underneath the Unitarian Hall so as to enable actors to cross unseen from one set of wings to the other. Noticing that in any case many of the Society's members had no interest in Unitarianism but had only joined for the sake of the drama, and hoping that even more would come if the society were re-established on secular lines, Heys set up the Stockport Garrick, charging a subscription sufficient to enable them to do without the Unitarian Hall and hire the local Mechanics' Institute instead. The subscription also covered the production of official stationery, which marked the Society as sacred to Shakespeare by incorporating an engraving of Anne Hathaway's Cottage. This was at once a cheaper alternative to commissioning their own statue of the playwright and a gesture identifying this society's Shakespeare not with the corrupted and ambitious metropolis but with provincial innocence and humble, rustic courtship.[103]

From the first, the Society, pledged 'to foster and further the higher forms and aims of dramatic art and literature',[104] ran a social programme almost as full as that offered by the church from which it had seceded. While membership of the Kilkenny Theatrical Society had been limited to a handful of very wealthy men who gathered to mount plays for only three weeks in the year, the Stockport Garrick could provide a year-round way of life for anyone who could afford its five shilling annual subscription. Its primary purpose was to stage at least three plays every season 'by masterminds like Shakespeare, Ibsen, G. B. Shaw etc., the production of whose works would in most towns involve a monetary loss', and to this end the Society hired 'Mr Ryder Boys, an elocutionist of the highest standard' to undertake 'the onerous task of training and stage management'.[105] But the Garrick, open to both men and women and thus attractive to young people of courting age, also held monthly social evenings involving recitations and music by members; it hosted festive occasions, such as 'Ye Merrie Spinsters' Partie' (April 1903), which featured a throwback to the genteel drawing-room amusements of earlier times in the form of *tableaux vivants* billed as 'The Garrick Waxwork Show', and 'Benedict's Party' (January 1904), which featured progressive whist; it ran its own orchestra; it organized cycling excursions; it held an annual dance; it threw garden parties; it held an annual picnic (initially at Redesmere, whose woods provided, as a local paper coyly remarked, 'ideal spots for budding Romeos and Juliets');[106] and it ran a junior section for children, the logical concomitant of the Society's view that 'drama is a

great educational and moral force'. (Another concomitant was an energetic campaign of letter-writing to advertise special rates for school parties
at the society's Shakespearean revivals.) It also ran well-advertised and
well-attended fortnightly literary discussions and lectures. In its inaugural
season lectures were given on 'David Garrick', '*The Merchant of Venice*',
'Shakespeare's London', 'Wagner: The Reformer of Opera', 'The Flowers
of Shakespeare' and 'A Pilgrimage to the Shrine of Shakespeare'.[107] This,
clearly, was a society which saw drama as an instrument for the renewal of
public life, rather than a club like the Pic-Nics or the Old Stagers founded
for its own private amusement, and as such its activities and ambitions far
exceeded those of the subsidized national theatres which would eventually
join it as purveyors of serious live drama fifty years later. It is indicative of
how rapidly the Garrick was embraced as a benign civic force that the very
first of these lectures was introduced by the Mayor, who implicitly
declared Stockport to be a worthy successor to classical Athens: 'In a brief
introductory address, the Mayor referred to the elevating influence of the
drama, and eulogized the dramatic fervour of the Greek poets.' However,
the Mayor's enthusiasm for the work of the Society was conditional on
their productions aiming for a moral and aesthetic tone well above that of
most contemporary theatre, since in recent years the playgoing public

had allowed examples to be put on the stage which had made it degrading and
debasing, and which met with the disapprobation of every right thinking man
and right thinking woman. If the drama was to be of service to humanity and of
service to the heart of mankind it must be kept grand, beautiful and pure . . . This
society was doing an ambitious thing . . . If they had human passion shown, if
they had all that was heroic and beautiful in the human character displayed, the
joy and benefits would all be high and pure. Then under those circumstances the
drama was educational, it was religious, and it was in every sense a sermon such as
no cardinal would be able to preach, and in all, pure and good.

Those sharing this perspective would not always be happy with the
Society's productions of controversial modern plays such as Ibsen's *Pillars
of Society*, staged in 1904.[108] But the Mayor certainly had no qualms about
going to see revivals of plays by

the great master of the art, the truest of all poets, and the poet of all times,
Shakespeare. He had heard it said that a true student of Shakespeare should never
enter a theatre, and that he who desired to know what the drama really was never
went to see it acted. He would not subscribe to such a proposition.[109]

The Society's first production, *The Merchant of Venice*, which had four
performances at the Mechanics' Institute in February and March 1902

(and was subsequently played at the Theatre Royal, Stockport, in December 1903, along with a new production of *Twelfth Night*), clearly satisfied the Mayor, who could not resist the opportunity to go up onto the stage during the curtain call at the end of the Friday performance to speak 'a few words of encouragement and praise'.[110] Supportive reviews in the area's vigorous local press (the Society's archives preserve five, each from a different publication) reveal, however, that, although this was an impressive and large-scale production (involving most of the Society's 130 members in one capacity or another), it was not in any respect a ground-breaking one. As surviving photographs show (Figures 7 and 8), the costumes were such as might have been used in almost any professional Shakespearean production of the preceding seventy years, and in fact advance notices had promised as a selling-point that they would indeed be exactly the same set of costumes which had already been seen on the commercial stage 'in Mr. R. Flanagan's Revival, at the Queen's Theatre' (for which they had been supplied 'by Mr F. A. Smith of 10, Peter Street, Manchester'). The 'Synopsis of Scenes' supplied in the programme, together with the listing of some thirty cast members as 'Magnificoes of Venice, Heralds, Standard Bearers, Gaoler, Halberdiers, Attendants to Portia, Attendants to Morocco, Attendants to Bassanio, Flower-sellers, Gentlemen of Venice, Children, Pages, &c &c', suggests vividly what a pictorial piece of proscenium arch staging Ryder Boys had produced. The show used six major sets ('Venice – A Street'; 'Belmont – A Room in Portia's House'; 'Another Street in Venice'; 'Belmont – Portia's Chamber'; 'Court of Justice' and 'Portia's Garden'), the changing of which required three scheduled twelve-minute intervals (during which the Garrick's thirty-two-piece orchestra played the music Yorke Sheffield had composed for the Queen's Theatre production, and 'Chocolate &c' was 'offered for sale by the Lady Attendants'). There were also seven shorter pauses for scene-changing within the four acts into which these intervals divided the play. Like the costumes, the scenery was acquired from a professional supplier, 'Messrs F. Le Maistre & Co, Manchester'. The novelty of the occasion, as one journalist makes clear, resided not in the style in which these amateurs performed Shakespeare, but in the fact that they had the nerve to attempt Shakespeare at all:

Last evening the members essayed a public performance, and the presentation was none other than Shakespearian. Theatrical managers have with few exceptions avoided Shakespeare as they would the bankruptcy court. In fact the two have not infrequently been associated. Rarely, indeed, has Shakespeare been exploited with financial success, and the difficulties which the production of Shakespeare's plays have involved have daunted even the most experienced of managers. But our local Garrick Society may succeed where others have failed,

Figure 7. *The Merchant of Venice*, Stockport Garrick Society; the 1903 revival at the Stockport Theatre Royal of the Society's initial production at the Stockport Mechanics' Institute the previous year. Shylock (Robert J. Smith) and Portia (Josephine Gaul).

and after last night's performance of 'The Merchant of Venice', we can only congratulate the members of this body upon their courage and their splendid success.'[111]

As the *Manchester Evening Mail* remarked, 'The play was presented in a very thorough manner, and the staging and dressing were all that could be

Figure 8. *The Merchant of Venice*, Stockport Garrick Society, 1903. Bassanio
(Burley Copley).

desired.'[112] The point of the exercise, clearly, wasn't to do Shakespeare
innovatively; it was to do it properly, as any theatregoer of the time would
have understood it, emulating the production values attained by professional companies.

This remained the Garrick's house style for playing Shakespeare for decades, despite one potentially transformative encounter in 1904. In April of that year the Society teamed up with another organization dedicated to bringing culture to the masses, the Ancoats Brotherhood, to arrange a week-long excursion to Stratford-upon-Avon. At the time of this pilgrimage to the shrine of Shakespeare, the Memorial Theatre was still out of season, but in the evenings after their sightseeing the Stockport visitors arranged recitations and rehearsed readings at their hotel, the Swan's Nest, given by a few veterans of Frank Benson's company. These included Janet Achurch, her husband Charles Charrington, and their daughter Nora, who had been named after Achurch's most famous role, in the first English production of *A Doll's House* in 1889. The members of the Garrick were particularly pleased to have an opportunity to compare notes about Henrik Ibsen:

We must not forget to mention among the many items of this evening a short recital from 'Peer Gynt', and it was greatly interesting to hear Mr Charrington's opinion that Ibsen was to be ranked second only to Shakespeare, a further justification of the Garrick's temerity in producing 'Pillars of Society'.[113]

But the bulk of these evenings were given over to Shakespeare, including readings of some passages which the visitors knew extremely well. One night Achurch, Charrington and others gave 'a highly interesting recital of the principal scenes from *The Merchant of Venice*. In this intimate setting 'it was truly a revelation to witness the remarkable effect that could be given to a Shakespearean play beautifully interpreted, but without stage effects or costumes'.[114]

Revelation or not, this was not a direction which the Garrick's own productions of Shakespeare would follow for more than fifty years. Their *Macbeth* in 1903 had boasted more scenery by Le Maistre and Co. (and five five-minute intervals to go with it), more costumes reused from the Queen's Theatre, and more orchestral music by Yorke Sheffield similarly reused from the Queen's Theatre, with Hecate and the 'Three Singing Witches' of theatrical tradition backed up by a thirty-two-piece 'Chorus of Witches and Bards'. Their *Merry Wives of Windsor* in 1906 had 'New and elaborate Scenery', and its climax (always in any event liable to resemble a Shakespearean premonition of amateur revivals of *A Midsummer Night's Dream* to come) featured a 'Special Fairy Dance by Miss Dora Whalley and 20 Children'. Their *Winter's Tale*, produced, along with *King Lear*, in the same year, was equally Victorian in its largely classical mise-en-scène, and in one detail of its casting it unconsciously echoed an

Figure 9. *The Winter's Tale*, Stockport Garrick Society, Stockport Theatre Royal, 1906.
Gladys Crawford and Maggie Howard as Florizel and Perdita.

even earlier production, since 'Miss Gladys Crawford made a handsome
Prince Florizel, and played her lover's part with delightful freedom, while
Miss Maggie Howard was a delightful and winning Perdita'[115] (Figure 9).
Although the Garrick considered its 'great Shakespearean revivals' to be
'the most important part of its work',[116] most of the intellectual energies
of the Society went into its lectures on modern German drama, its
correspondence with Shaw, its triple bills of modern one-act plays (by
W. B. Yeats and others), and its fostering of new scripts by members.
'Had this society done no more than continue with programmes of
Shakespeare it would probably have foundered,' comments Adrian
Rendle, 'or settled down to become a large, colourfully costumed, mutual
admiration society … The society's really important contribution came
with the presentation of Ibsen's *The Pillars of Society* in 1904.'[117] A century
earlier it had still been possible for amateurs to perform *Catherine and
Petruchio* or a modern farce in much the same manner, and at Kilkenny
Shakespeare's tragedies had fitted seamlessly into a repertory and set of
performance practices equally comfortable with more recent specimens

of the genre by Otway or Rowe or Mallet. For the new amateur societies
of the early twentieth century, however, Shakespeare belonged in a special
category of his own: rather than being the first of the moderns, he was
now the sole survivor of the ancients, and his plays demanded an entirely
different manner of presentation to anything else in their repertoire.
However daring they might be in staging new realistic social dramas on
their realist proscenium stages, when it came to producing plays written
some three hundred years before most of their other material they adopted
the standard methods and aesthetics of the late nineteenth-century commercial theatre, leavened only with lingering traces of the genteel drawing
room. The Garrick's opening *Merchant of Venice*, for instance, charmingly
showed off Miss Jennie Harrison, who in the best tradition of Salisbury
Cathedral Close accompanied 'Tell me, where is fancy bred?' on her
harp (Figure 10).

The fact that Shakespeare's plays now seemed more archaic than they
had when amateur theatres were aristocratic playthings, however, was also
part of the point of reviving them, and indeed of reviving them in modes
which made them look as boldly old-fashioned as possible. As pillars of
an alternative theatre repertory otherwise dominated by Ibsen and Shaw,
Shakespeare's defiantly outmoded plays were identified not just as
uncommercial but potentially as anti-commercial into the bargain. In
Britain there has always been a nostalgia of the left as well as one of
the right, and it is clear from the archives of the Garrick and other
societies like it that the underlying ideal of twentieth-century amateur
Shakespeare, derived ultimately from John Ruskin and William Morris,
was the restoration of the organic society, the return to an imagined
collective artisan life of unalienated labour. Shakespeare's hand-made
drama, in this reading, belonged less to commercial modernity than
to the spacious, ceremonious harmony of an idealized Middle Ages. This
view was shared by some idealistic professionals too. Another stage-struck
Edwardian visitor to Stratford, for example, the young H. V. Morton,
would as a sadder and wiser post-war adult remember meeting Frank
Benson himself:

I remember him telling me, as I sat worshipping him, that only through
Stratford, the common meeting place of the English-speaking world, could we
heal the pains of Industrialism and make England happy again. We were to make
the whole world happy, apparently, by teaching it to morris-dance and to sing
folk songs and to go to the Memorial Theatre. With the splendid faith of Youth
we pilgrims believed that England could be made 'merrie' again by hand-looms
and young women in Liberty gowns who played the harpsichord.[118]

Figure 10. *The Merchant of Venice*, Stockport Garrick Society, Stockport Theatre Royal, 1903. Miss Jennie Harrison, who accompanied 'Tell me, where is fancy bred?'

Or the harp, presumably. It was not for nothing that in 1907 another ardent young disciple of Benson, Barry Jackson, called his own amateur company the Pilgrim Players, a venture which evolved into the Birmingham Repertory Theatre (1913–), destined in 1935 to become just the sort of pioneering municipal theatre Heys had dreamed of.[119]

For the Stockport Garrick and many of the civic amateur dramatic societies which followed it, this widespread sense of Shakespearean drama as a short-cut back to Merry England – as implicitly promised by the

picture of Anne Hathaway's Cottage on the Garrick's stationery –
mandated a loyalty to the Victorian theatrical tradition of historical fancy
dress. As a result, theatrical costumiers catering to the amateur market
addressed themselves to producers apparently terrified above all else of
committing historical mistakes. Under the heading of 'Costumes of
HISTORICAL ACCURACY', for example, an advertisement for one
long-established West End firm ('One minute from Piccadilly Circus')
promises reassuringly that 'No anachronisms will mar your production if
it is dressed by Rayne's. Every one of their thousands of dresses is not
only beautiful but authentic in every detail ... Complete wardrobes are
always in readiness for all the plays of Shakespeare ...'[120] For a few non-
professionals, however, historical authenticity in costumes alone was not
enough, and they embraced styles of production and even architecture
dating back to well before J. R. Planché and Sir Walter Scott had initiated
the archaeologically correct style of nineteenth-century stage dress. Late
Victorian and Edwardian attempts to rediscover Elizabethan playing styles
on conjectural reconstructions of Elizabethan stages invariably depended
on amateur casts, from William Poel's experimental production of the
first, 'bad' quarto of *Hamlet* at St George's Hall in London in 1881
onwards. Although Poel's background was in the professional theatre,
the performers in his now celebrated Elizabethan Stage Society (1894–
1905) were all volunteers.[121] As the cartoon published in *Punch* on the
occasion of the Society's 1896 production of *The Two Gentlemen of Verona*
suggests (Figure 11), the idea of performing Shakespeare without scenery
and with only a small cast struck most contemporary theatregoers as
absurd (albeit economical), and it would be many years before such
experiments with what in more recent years have been optimistically
dubbed 'original practices' would be a paying proposition for any commercial playhouse. The fact that the Elizabethan Stage Society's productions seemed retrospectively to imply that the Shakespearean theatre had
in itself been amateurish, however, as this cartoon suggests, would not
have entirely displeased Poel and his supporters, who generally preferred
to think of the Lord Chamberlain's Men as a happy band of disinterested
artistic pioneers than as the employees of a flourishing capitalist business.

The most influential of those supporters, the director Nugent Monck,
cooperated with Poel in 1910 when his production of *The Two Gentlemen
of Verona* was revived by invitation of Sir Herbert Beerbohm Tree at Her
Majesty's Theatre (its mock-Tudor thrust stage jutting incongruously out
over the gilded orchestra pit), and in the following year he too set out to
pursue a vision of Elizabethan revival far from the modern theatrical

Figure 11. William Poel's amateur group, the Elizabethan Stage Society, retrospectively
making Shakespeare look amateurish: *Punch*, 21 November 1896.

marketplace. In 1911 Monck co-founded the deliberately medieval-
sounding 'Guild of the Norwich Players', later to become the Norwich
Players, who in 1921 would move into the first-ever permanent conjectural
replica of an Elizabethan playhouse, the 250-seat Maddermarket Theatre
(Figure 12).[122] For Monck, the great advantage of using amateur actors,
explained his admirer Charles Rigby, was that they were 'preoccupied
with the stage, not as a means of livelihood, but as an art-medium'.[123]
(They were also sufficiently ensemble-minded to agree not to have their
names listed in any of the programmes.) In 1933 Monck became the first
director ever to have staged every single one of Shakespeare's plays.
Watched by the likes of Harley Granville-Barker, Robert Atkins, Barry

Figure 12. Nugent Monck's antiquarian plaything: *The Taming of the Shrew*,
Maddermarket Theatre, Norwich, 1927.

Jackson and Tyrone Guthrie, Monck's fast-moving and uncluttered productions at the Maddermarket, now well documented and much studied,
may have been the most influential performances of Shakespeare ever
given by amateur players.[124]

By then philanthropically inclined public amateur dramatic societies
were far from being the novelties they had seemed in the early days of the
Stockport Garrick. In the years immediately following the First World
War, the art-form which had already been charged in Edwardian days
with healing the pain of industrialism was seized upon even more avidly as
'a great spiritual force'.[125] 'The moral exhaustion that was the aftermath of
the War has left mankind at the mercy of the mechanical-economic
elements in modern civilization,' explained Geoffrey Whitworth. This
tendency, 'if pushed to its logical conclusion, would deny to us all that
sense of personal vitality which is a prime condition of happiness. Here
Drama comes to the rescue.'[126] Drama needed especially to rescue the
post-war public from a new form of entertainment that was now supplanting even the vitiated commercial theatre of pre-war days, the cinema.
The film business, according to Patrick Carleton, was 'in the hands of

capitalists less hampered by a sense of social or artistic obligation than any other body of men on earth':

> But there must be an alternative. The poor and under-educated must not be left to suppose that there is no Drama except the pseudo-drama of Hollywood, or our cultural outlook will be black indeed ... [T]he professional theatre is not now ... in a position to supply this alternative. There remains only one source from which it is available: the Amateur Drama.[127]

The benefits arising from this healthy antidote to moral exhaustion and the flicks, moreover, were personal as well as social. 'Apart from its value to the community as a whole,' observed Barry Jackson, introducing the monumental 1,267-page manifesto and how-to book *The Theatre and Stage* (1934), 'the Amateur Dramatic Movement, by the outlet that it offers to creative work, can enrich the lives of countless individuals.'[128] In this belief, not only did more towns, suburbs and cities acquire major amateur societies – such as the Questors Theatre in Ealing (1929), the Middlesbrough Little Theatre (1930) and the Bolton Little Theatre (1931) – but some enlightened employers set up their own works amateur dramatic societies to improve employee morale. The London Transport Players, for instance, performed at the Scala Theatre, built in 1904 on the site of the Pic-Nics' old haunt in Tottenham Street, but others had less lavish facilities. In 1919, for example, a former amateur actress from Darlington was hired as a 'welfare officer' by the personnel department at a Shredded Wheat factory in Welwyn Garden City, where for three years her duties included running a drama society in a converted dining hall – though she subsequently abandoned this promising career in the breakfast cereal industry to return to the professional stage, under her own name, Flora Robson.[129] New societies flourished in rural areas too. At Great Hucklow in the Peak District, for instance, L. Du Garde Peach instigated the Village Players in 1927, with a production of *The Merchant of Venice* mounted in Peach's version of the Maddermarket manner: 'Without hesitation I decided to use an Elizabethan stage, with a forestage and an inner stage, separated by a simple traverse curtain.'[130] By then there was already a flourishing national Village Drama Society, founded by Mary Kelly in 1919, though Kelly disapproved of revivals of Shakespeare, who to her represented a centralized court culture inimical to local folk tradition.[131]

Despite this reservation, Kelly's organization would later merge with the British Drama League, which had no such misgivings about Shakespeare. The League worked simultaneously for the establishment of a National Theatre legally obligated 'to keep the plays of Shakespeare in its repertory' (fittingly, they held their inaugural conference in Stratford, in 1919), and for the coordination and encouragement of amateur theatrical activity. As their president, Geoffrey Whitworth, put it, 'a National Theatre, for all its costly elaboration, for all its perfection of professional technique, [is] nothing more and nothing less than a Community Theatre writ large'.[132] No fewer than 2,500 societies would be affiliated to the League by 1934, and, according to Norman Marshall, by then, 'at an extremely conservative estimate', over 5 million people each year (out of a total population of about 44 million) were paying to see amateur performances.[133] By the end of the 1930s, a higher proportion of the British population had practical experience of putting on plays than at any time before or since, a factor which, as we will see, was to have intriguing cultural consequences during the next world war.

'Hence comes the enormous growth of the Amateur Dramatic Movement,' summed up Barry Jackson in 1934,

which does far more than merely keep pace with the decline of the professional stage. Consequently there is no doubt whatever that the Drama will not only live, but will increase in stature through the coming years, and – observing what they have already done – I look to the amateur societies to win for it nothing less than a complete renascence.[134]

In keeping with the longer-term aims of the British Drama League, Shakespeare remained a major feature of many of these amateur societies' programmes, mandating the publication, for instance, of Frank Humpherson's how-to book *Shakespeare for Amateurs: A Handbook for the Amateur Actor and Producer* (1935, reprinted 1936). Humpherson's background was in teaching at boys' schools, but this only partly explains his Victorian-sounding enthusiasm for the gender division of roles in the Shakespeare canon:

But there is one feature of Shakespeare's plays which is particularly valuable from the point of view of casting, and that is the small number of female characters required. Usually, three good women will be sufficient for the main parts in most of the plays, and the remainder can be fitted in as ladies-in-waiting.[135]

Humpherson clearly expects that in the dramatic societies of the 1930s the principal demographic problem will be a shortage of competent and experienced women, rather than of competent and experienced men, and it is a sign of how non-professional theatre has lost kudos since the war that amateur dramatics are nowadays notoriously short of males instead. Many civic groups of the 1930s, however, could field at least three good women, and Shakespeare was a regular and often lucrative fixture of their repertories. The Middlesbrough Little Theatre, for instance, staged their first Shakespearean production, a popular *Merchant of Venice*, in 1935 (a 'safe' play, according to Humpherson, which 'never fails to appeal', 136–7);[136] the Questors, mounted *Twelfth Night* in 1936,[137] and the Bolton Little Theatre produced *Much Ado About Nothing* in 1937,[138] and each continued to perform Shakespeare thereafter, generally showing the same preference, noticeable since the time of the Amateurs of Cambridge, for the comedies of courtship over the tragedies and histories of masculine honour favoured by the private theatricals of the preceding era.

Given the presence of Shakespeare as a mainstay of the amateur repertory, then, it was not surprising that this inter-war dramatic 'renascence' was understood by some of its proponents in terms of the preceding dramatic Renaissance, and vice versa. To the founder of the British Drama League, it appears, the world of the Globe and the world of the Stockport Garrick Society seemed very much alike. 'It would be no exaggeration to assert,' wrote Whitworth,

that Shakespearean Drama as we know it – not excluding the work of the master himself – would never have come into existence but for the facilities for dramatic experiment that had been provided by the amateur stage of the period ... And the amateur movement of the day – in one of its less exalted manifestations – comes in for some pointed yet not unsympathetic satire in the clown scenes of *A Midsummer Night's Dream*. Bottom and his troupe of 'rude mechanicals' suggest that amateur acting was not even then confined to the social strata exemplified by royal courts and seats of learning, but that it had spread, as in our own day, to the ranks of the 'workers'.[139]

From being an honorary gentleman dilettante at the start of the nineteenth century, Shakespeare had in the early twentieth become a beneficiary, well-wisher and keen observer of artisan amateur theatricals. Even if there was still no massive new public monument to him in London, and no National Theatre as a memorial to him there either, it appeared that by the 1930s Shakespeare's name, too, along with those of Thomas Cooper, Edwin Heys and L. Du Garde Peach, could at last be added to Quince's scrip.

CHAPTER 3

Shakespeare in exile: expatriate performance

MOWBRAY ... The language I have learnt these forty years,
My native English, now I must forgo,
And now my tongue's use is to me no more
Than an unstrungèd viol or a harp,
Or like a cunning instrument cased up,
Or, being open, put into his hands
That knows no touch to tune the harmony.

(*Richard II*, 1.3.153–9)

The movement from private theatricals to civic amateur dramatic societies
charted across the two previous chapters – whereby non-professional
productions of Shakespeare ceased to address themselves solely to lateral,
aristocratic networks of connoisseurs and applied themselves instead to
serving entire local communities, across class lines – had effects which
were felt not just within Britain but wherever English-speaking people
found themselves with time on their hands and an audience within hailing
distance. In 1607, when whichever member of the *Red Dragon*'s crew cast
as Mowbray in *Richard II* lamented the linguistic impotence enforced by
banishment from England, he could not have foreseen the extent to which
Britain's growing mercantile, diplomatic and military commitments
around the globe would come to make such sentiments seem largely
obsolete.[1] Shakespeare travelled with the national language, whether its
speakers were in foreign parts voluntarily or under duress. The most
spectacular instances of British expatriate Shakespeare, though they are
now largely and perhaps deliberately forgotten, undoubtedly occurred
during the Second World War, when a combination of the pre-war Little
Theatre movement, mass conscription and the scale of early Allied defeats
produced a captive army on Axis soil which was better qualified to keep its
spirits up with amateur dramatics than any military force before or since.
This, it proved, was a body of men more than capable of doing justice to a
playwright by then regarded both as England's national poet and the third

German classic. Before exploring these controversial prisoner-of-war productions of Shakespeare, however, I shall trace their precursors among
both diplomatic and military performances, and in particular look at what
distinguishes expatriate amateur performances mounted for audiences of
Anglophones alone from those addressed to members of other linguistic
and national groups.

Shakespeare's plays occupied a special place in the repertories of each of
these kinds of expatriate theatre, for a number of reasons. The most
important was their status as the supreme and representative achievements
of the national culture: by the time the British Empire was being consoli-
dated as such in the latter half of the eighteenth century, the Bard had for
many come to exemplify the freedom-loving, all-inclusive, anti-French
spirit of the imperial project itself, so that to perform Shakespeare in a
distant land became the theatrical and social equivalent of planting a
Union Jack there. This identification of Shakespeare with Britannia's
ambitions to rule the waves and ultimately the world is conveniently
summed up by an anonymous 'Ode to Shakespeare' from the 1760s:

> While Britons bow at Shakespeare's shrine
> Britannia's sons are sons of mine.
> Like him shou'd Britons scorn the Art
> That binds in chains the human heart
> Like him shou'd still be unconfin'd
> And rule the World as he the mind.[2]

Prominent overseas representatives of Britain from the Enlightenment
onwards, then, might well choose to stage a Shakespeare play as the
perfect social event by which to perform their own national identity,
much as Captain Keeling had produced his shipboard *Hamlet* and *Richard II* in 1607. Keeling, however, had only chosen to equip his galleon
with copies of *Hamlet* and *Richard II* because their quartos were currently
available printed samples of the domestic theatrical repertory; by the time
his successors were exporting Shakespeare on the global scale envisaged by
this 'Ode', Shakespeare's place within that repertory had changed. It was
not only that his works had acquired the status of national secular
scripture; it was that they were now, with the exception of two or three
comedies by Ben Jonson and Philip Massinger, the last plays still in use
that had been written for the long-lost all-male stage of the English
Renaissance. As we have already seen in the instance of the Gibraltar
performance of *Catherine and Petruchio* in 1820 (Figure 6), around the
edges of Britain's overseas dominions, and in the midst of its various war

efforts, Shakespeare now competed for space in repertories otherwise dominated by plays written with female performers in mind. These included, in particular, the latest farces, musicals and burlesques, which often used cross-dressing for exclusively comic effects unavailable in the days when male performers were the sole candidates for female roles in tragedy and comedy alike. In both the army and the navy, however, as in other all-male institutions such as boys' schools, serious in-house communal theatre remained socially important well into the twentieth century. It also often remained single-sexed, just as on board the *Red Dragon* in 1607, so that the armed forces provided one haven in which some of the conventions of the Renaissance stage had never quite died out. As in the case of the Harris sisters' all-girl abbreviated *Winter's Tale*, the gender composition of the available cast has often determined the nature and meaning of Shakespeare's plays in amateur performance. The special and sometimes extreme circumstances of diplomatic and military life overseas have typically posed the question of who gets to play Shakespeare's heroines, and in the eyes of which audiences, with particular force.

DIPLOMATS

When it comes to representing Shakespeare to overseas audiences, Captain Keeling's shipboard performances of *Hamlet* and *Richard II* again provide a founding precedent, in that, while *Richard II* was performed only for the actors' fellow English sailors, *Hamlet* was offered as a performance of the crew's native culture to an audience which included an embassy from the local African king. The divergence between amateur expatriate productions intended solely for the cast's compatriots and those offered with foreign spectators in mind is usefully exemplified by the changing fortunes of Shakespeare in Geneva, a notably international city with its own important traditions of salon drama and theatrical controversy. Here, as contrasting productions staged in 1739 and 1830 respectively show, Shakespeare's growing status as a definitively British playwright perplexed the movement from aristocratic private theatre to civic-minded club.

Live English-speaking Shakespeare first reached the shores of Lac Léman in the 1730s, in a context not of insular homesickness or self-assertion but of aristocratic cosmopolitanism. As an important stopping-off point for those taking the Grand Tour southwards into Italy, excitingly Francophone but reassuringly Protestant Geneva was a place where cultured young Englishmen abroad might safely meet people of their own rank, and preferably not just from their own country. Richard Aldworth Neville, for example, stayed in the city from 1738 to 1742, socializing with compatriots such as Lord Brook, William Windham (the future dedicatee of Garrick's *Ragandjaw*), Benjamin Stillingfleet (later an acquaintance of Hermes Harris, and another friend of Elizabeth Montagu), and Charles Churchill (future author of *The Rosciad*). He also associated with other visiting Europeans such as the Comtes de la Lippe, and with the Genevois themselves. In between pioneering tourism to the Alps,[3] this group, known as 'the Common Room', engaged extensively in private theatricals. In 1738 they staged John Hughes' congenially anti-Catholic tragedy *The Siege of Damascus*, and then on 15 January 1739, before an invited audience including most of the governing Conseil, Syndic François Calandrini among them, they performed an all-male *Macbeth*. Neville played the title role; the de la Lippes between them acted Ross, Donalbain, Angus and the Bleeding Sergeant (symptomatically promoted to 'Captain' in the cast-list); and George Hervey, son of the bisexual Lord Hervey pilloried by Alexander Pope as 'Sporus' in his 'Epistle to Arbuthnot', played Lady Macbeth. To accommodate the non-Anglophones in their audiences, Neville and his friends gave out printed texts of key extracts from the scripts, and on each of these ambitious bills literary tragedy was counterbalanced by a wordless comic pantomime offered as an afterpiece.[4]

Neville remembered this group's success in *Macbeth* as 'beyond imagination', convening an eager audience of supportive fellow expatriates from all over Switzerland and eastern France: 'our countrymen flocked from all parts to see us, and flattered us by declaring that we excelled the London actors'.[5] Decades later, he continued to believe this praise, insisting that despite its old-fashioned or schoolboyish single-sex casting the Common Room's style of performance had been years ahead of its time:

Indeed, at that time Garrick was not known; and we had the good fortune to strike out something in the same manner, which he carried afterwards to a much higher perfection. I mean by following Nature, and exploding the measured step and unmeaning rant, in which the periwig-pated heroes of the Stage at that time made all great acting to consist.[6]

In fact, in the manner in which these well-bred young men had made a virtue of the absence of women from their stage, this production, he claimed, had been ahead even of Garrick, in practice at least:

In this Play, we made several alterations; some from necessity, others from judgement. The omission of Lady Macduff was from the first consideration. The changing of the Witches and their brooms into Magicians with long beards and black gowns, was from the second. This alteration, instead of ridicule, produced additional awe and horror. Garrick has since approved the idea; but owned he durst not carry it into execution himself, for fear of offending the Gallery.[7]

This, clearly, was a classic instance of private theatricals. Like the gentlemen of Kilkenny, Neville claims that this group's Shakespeare was in better artistic taste than that on offer back in the Theatres Royal because it was not subject to the vulgar market pressures of 'the Gallery', the common herd in the cheap seats. Well-to-do English travellers and the Genevan élite constituted a much more discriminating audience, and in this context social rank was far more important than national origin. Like Neville's compatriots, Syndic François Calandrini was impressed by the whole enterprise – 'les seigneurs étrangers,' he wrote in his diary, 'ont joué leurs comédies avec beaucoup de succès' – and that was clearly much of the point; Neville subsequently married Calandrini's daughter Madelaine.[8] Just as he would function for Parson Yorick in Laurence Sterne's *A Sentimental Journey* (1768), this was Shakespeare as the passport to the right European connections.

After Waterloo, however, when British military power and diplomatic leverage had helped to install reactionary governments right across Europe, and long after the growing currents of romantic cultural nationalism visible at the 1769 Stratford Jubilee had declared Shakespeare to be an exclusively British national treasure, aristocratic amateur Shakespeare on the Grand Tour became rather more insular in tone. From 1820 onwards, one palazzo in Florence declared itself to be *de facto* British soil by mounting a series of untranslated productions of Shakespeare, including that established amateurs' favourite *Henry IV part 1*. The presiding actor-manager in this instance was not just an aristocratic traveller but a promising diplomat and politician, Constantine Phipps, 1st Marquess of Normanby, future Home Secretary and future British Ambassador to France. Normanby was best known in the 1820s for having resigned as MP for Scarborough after controversially supporting Catholic emancipation, after which he moved to sunnier climes, where he wrote a pioneering collection of short stories about expatriate life, *The English in Italy* (3 vols., London, 1825). This liberally inclined work is suffused with enthusiasm for one of Phipps' peers, Lord Byron, who himself put an abortive rival amateur production of *Othello* into rehearsal at the Casa Lanfranchi in Pisa in February 1822, with himself as Iago.[9] Normanby had been stage-struck for years: while still a Cambridge undergraduate and legally underage he had sent a proposal of marriage to the actress Eliza O'Neill, future star of the Kilkenny theatricals. (With a sharp eye for maintaining the respectability that would in time make her a fit match for William Becher, O'Neill sent it unanswered to Normanby's parents, who threatened to disinherit him.) Soon afterwards Normanby instead married the daughter of Baron Ravensworth, Maria Liddell (in 1818, the year he turned twenty-one, graduated from Cambridge and was first elected as an MP).[10] Maria shared his enthusiasm for the stage, so that unlike the bachelors of the Common Room Normanby could deploy both men and women in his expatriate productions, casting himself and his wife as the highest-ranking married couple in *Henry IV*, Hotspur and Lady Percy. They also played Benedick and Beatrice, and their other, predominantly Shakespearean mainpieces included *Richard III*, *Macbeth* and George Colman's *The Iron Chest*.

The cast of *Henry IV* featured both amateurs and one future professional, in the person of the quixotic architect Charles James Mathews, son of the actor Charles Mathews and destined in time to manage Covent Garden; Mathews was given the role of Falstaff in part as recompense for redesigning Normanby's theatre. Mathews took the opportunity to make experiments with the role which he felt would not have been permitted by the tradition-bound popular audiences of the Theatres Royal, dressing Falstaff in the early scenes as 'a superannuated beau' rather than a *miles gloriosus* so as to make his assumption of military dress for the battle scenes at once more incongruous and more dramatic.[11] Thanks to Normanby's rank, however, these Tuscan performances attracted comments that were more sycophantic than analytical, significantly not just in the local English newsletter but back in London:

English theatricals in Florence. Extract from a letter dated Florence, December 8, 1829 ... Last evening Lord Normanby opened the tasteful little Theatre he has had constructed in the Palazzo San Clementi [*sic*] which was filled by 400 persons of rank and fashion. Shakespeare's Historical Play of *King Henry the Fourth* (the first part), and the Farce of *Simpson and Co*, constituted the evening's entertainment ...'[12]

The cast's social status, furthermore, guaranteed that their performances would be unctuously well received by those keenest to boast that they had been present:

Where each filled his part so well it would be invidious to particularize. Lady Normanby acted delightfully ... Lord Normanby, Mr Craven [Prince Hal], and Mr Mathews evinced the greatest talent ... the whole performance went off with the greatest *éclat*.

A play that culminates in a ferocious medieval battle fought with broad-swords may seem like a tricky proposition to bring off with *éclat* in a private theatre, even in the lavishly converted hall of a palazzo, but this drama about male honour and homosocial rivalries had been a favourite with well-bred non-professionals since the time of Sir Edward Dering, and doubtless San Clemente had just as good a sofa as the one used in Kilkenny. Normanby, indeed, seems to have been in conscious competition with the last theatre in which his former beloved had appeared: on one occasion he even cast Maria in Eliza O'Neill's signature role of Juliet, with himself as Romeo, deploying a drafted-in selection of the daughters of other English expatriates in lavish masquerade costumes to offer an unprecedentedly sumptuous version of the Capulets' ball.[13] As architect and designer, Mathews too was acutely conscious of the comparison: 'no private theatre ever before attempted the thing in such perfection as it is here done,' he wrote to his mother,

and (perhaps excepting the 'Kilkenny', which I cannot speak of) certainly, out of London, no theatre is conducted with such care and attention … new scenery always painted for the occasion from good drawings, and all the costumes made from sketches by an English painter here from pictures in the gallery according to the correct examples of the time … Even if private theatres – the 'Kilkenny' for instance – have in all these matters equalled, they could not surpass, the present one.[14]

Mathews, significantly, sees this project solely in relation to the professional theatres of London and to private theatres elsewhere within Britain, without any reference to an Italian audience at all. Like private theatricals back home, these performances were very much occasions for insiders, only here conspicuously more so in that they were not even performed in the local language. They predictably infuriated the most articulate non-British member of Normanby's audience, the American novelist James Fenimore Cooper. Cooper had already been disappointed, on arriving in Florence with his wife in the spring of 1829, to discover how conspicuous English socialites now were in the cultural life of the city of Dante and the Medici. Throughout his European travels he had been astonished by the rudeness of the English aristocracy and the servile deference of their followers, and although he came to regard Normanby as one of the only four tolerable English lords he had ever met he was inclined to dismiss his amateur dramatics as part of a pointless social rivalry with the English ambassador to Tuscany, Lord Burghersh, who preferred to mount musical and operatic soirées.[15] As for the artistic value of these Shakespearean productions, the author of *The Last of the Mohicans* was considerably less

116   *Shakespeare in exile*

impressed than was the fawning correspondent who thought that all of
Normanby's cast could have held their own on the professional stages of
the West End. To Cooper, the performances amounted merely to medi-
ocre and inappropriate transplants from the stately homes of England,
produced with an insolent and ignorant disregard for their Italian surroundings. 'We have seen Shakespeare in the hands of these noble actors
once or twice,' he wrote in *Gleanings in Europe: Italy*,

and found the representation neither quite good enough to please, nor yet bad
enough to laugh at. Occasionally, a character was pretty well represented; but the
natural facility of the other sex in acting was sufficiently apparent, the women
making out much better than the men. It was like all private theatricals, good
enough for a country house, but hardly in its place in the capital of Tuscany.[16]

Despite this discouraging review, however, in 1830 another such group
performed *Henry IV part 1* in English, this time back on the far side of the
Alps, in Geneva.

The instigator and moving spirit of the 1830 *Henry IV* was not English
but a native Genevois, Charles Michel Lullin. The production, as a result,
offers a particularly intriguing and conflicted specimen of expatriate
amateur Shakespeare, divided between seeing Shakespeare as innately
British and as eminently transplantable. Lullin was a veteran, as we have
seen, of the Anglo-French amateur dramatic scene in London at the time
of the Margravine of Anspach's theatrical enterprise at Brandenburgh
House. After his patrician family were ruined by the French revolution,
Lullin, able to pass as either English or French, had been recruited by the
spymaster William Wickham in 1793 to infiltrate and monitor possible
political conspiracies among French émigrés in London.[17] (His responsi-
bilities at the Aliens Office included the granting and refusal of passports
to foreigners, and he may have changed the course of literary history when
his dealings with Alexandre d'Arblay in 1802 stranded both him and his
wife, Frances née Burney, in France at the end of the peace of Amiens,
forcing her to return to the novel instead of pursuing a career as a West
End playwright.)[18] Away from his desk, Lullin became a passionate
theatregoer, and a friend of the thoroughly counter-revolutionary Shakespearean actor-manager John Philip Kemble.[19] Combining work and
play, Lullin kept an eye on London's French community by engaging
key members in amateur dramatics, including a production of his own
French verse translation of *Richard III* at his house in Stafford Place,
Pimlico.[20] Lullin and his English wife staged other plays too: they were
condescendingly described as 'Swiss refugees and semi-gentlefolks' by the

future Countess Canning when they later performed Racine's *Mithridate* before the exiled dukes of Berry and Angoulême at 3 St James' Square,[21] but they were more warmly received when they and another cast of expatriates performed Racine's *Bérénice* at the home of an exiled Swiss doctor in Bloomsbury. (This was 23, Russell Square, subsequently the offices of Faber and Faber, just opposite what is now Birkbeck College.) Joanna Baillie's friend Mary Berry, for instance, among an appreciative and fashionable audience, was delighted to have this rare opportunity to 'admire the beauty of Racine's most French tragedy'.[22]

A combination of Nick Bottom and the Scarlet Pimpernel, Lullin clearly knew all about the potential cultural cachet to be gained from being the right kind of foreigner in the right wrong place at the right time: as the old maxim has it, 'when in Rome, do as the Greeks do'. Having performed Shakespeare and Racine in French in London, when Lullin returned home to Geneva on a British government pension after the defeat of Napoleon he took to performing in English instead. Dedicating himself to providing hospitality to British visitors (among them Kemble, who retired to Lausanne), founding an Anglican church and arranging performances of English plays at a purpose-built music room and expatri- ates' club known as 'the Cassino', Lullin became known in his homeland as 'Lullin l'Anglais'.[23] Augustin Pyramus de Candolle, for instance, writing to Madame de Circourt on 13 July 1831, reported that Geneva was having a particularly brilliant summer of culture: 'd'un côté Mlle Duchesnois joue au théâtre, et Mr. Lullin donne au Casino ses represen- tations anglaises'.[24]

In 1830 Lullin's offerings with this Anglophone amateur-dramatic- society-in-exile were much as might have been found on the playbills of Kilkenny two decades earlier, namely Thomas Otway's *Venice Preserved*, an unnamed farce, and *Henry IV part 1*.[25] He was fortunate in that Colonel Thomas Braddyll was at the time living in Geneva while his country house in the Lake District was being expensively remodelled: when still a captain in the Guards nearly thirty years earlier, Braddyll had played King John in an officer production at the Theatre Royal in Rochester, and he had subsequently become famous for his performances as Falstaff at Wellington's headquarters during the Peninsular War, a role which he was now happy to repeat in Geneva.[26] Along with his English wife, Nancy, Lullin's fellow actors may have included his sister Anna and her politician husband Jean Gabriel Eynard, both of whom had performed in scenes from Shakespeare in Madame de Staël's salons, and who built private theatres of their own in their apartment on the

Cour St Pierre, at their country house at Beaulieu outside Lausanne, and later in their commanding Genevan town-house, the Palais Eynard.[27] Lullin, like Normanby, probably took Kemble's old role of Hotspur. He added further Anglophile credentials to this season by commissioning prologues from Geneva's resident English poet. Sadly, he had missed Byron and Shelley by more than a decade, and he now had to resort to the notorious old bibliophile and snob Sir Samuel Egerton Brydges. Brydges had been acquainted with Byron, and was still in correspondence with major poets such as Robert Southey, William Wordsworth and Sir Walter Scott. He would have to do.

A decade of exile had at least compelled Brydges to give the question of national identity and culture some serious thought. Having bankrupted himself making unsuccessful and probably fraudulent claims to be the rightful Baron Chandos, Brydges had settled in Geneva in 1821, where he continued to dilate on his life and opinions, especially in a magazine which he grandly called *The Anglo-Genevan Critical Journal* but which nowadays looks more like a personal blog *avant la lettre*. Considering the Genevans a 'mixed race of French, Germans, Italians, &c.' (who have 'less imagination or sentiment' than either the French or the Italians, but compensate with Germanic *sang froid*, accuracy and 'laboriousness'), his *Autobiography* notes that 'notwithstanding the settlement of the English refugees, when they fled from the restoration of popery by Queen Mary' his countrymen have made little visible contribution to Geneva's ethnic melting pot, and he now cannot find any local families 'confessedly descended from male English stock'. Brydges put this down to the regrettable insularity of his fellow expatriates. 'It is the fault of the English ... when they come abroad,' he wrote,

still to live too much with one another. As islanders, it is long before we entirely abandon our strong peculiarities, and our conceit of the exclusive superiority of all our own modes and customs and ideas. The English are [not] only esteemed proud by other nations, but really are so. The consequence is, that though they are feared, they are little loved by them.[28]

Brydges was suitably gratified, then, to be made much of by Lullin, whom he praises in his poem 'The Lake of Geneva' both as one 'renown'd upon the private stage, – / The oracle, thro whose lips miraculous Shakespeare / Speaks' and as the 'warmest in friendship and in hospitality' of all the many local patricians he catalogues.[29] A report on his work in progress for Lullin is full of self-congratulation: 'I have written 4 Prologues for some intended Private Theatricals here,' he wrote to a friend in London, '– Two

for Venice Preserved – One for Henry IV. One occasional ...' Ever keen
to name-drop, Brydges went on to remember the previous occasion on
which he had been similarly employed:

You will observe that I never wrote but one Prologue before, and that was 44 years
ago for a private Theatre in Hampshire at Mr Austen's, the father of Jane Austen,
author of *Pride and Prejudice – Northanger Abbey*, etc. See *Quarterly Review*.[30]

Brydges was sufficiently pleased with these latest efforts to publish them
repeatedly, at first printing only his *Prologue for Shakespeare's Henry IV,
Written for the Private Theatre at Geneva*, then publishing all *Four Prologues for a Private English Theatre at Geneva*, 1830, which then reappeared
in *The Anglo-Genevan Critical Journal for 1831*.

These eloquent and largely incoherent pieces of verse demonstrate if
nothing else how badly suited the British nativist tradition of Bardolatry
was to the task of presenting Shakespeare to non-British audiences. In his
'Prologue. For Shakespeare's Henry IV. Written 13 Jan. 1830', for instance,
Brydges instinctively adopts the rhetorical mode of David Garrick's
Jubilee ode (1769), which commits him to an opening gambit of celebrating Shakespeare as utterly indigenous. *Henry IV* is initially offered as the
expression of a British national character acquired primarily through
genetics:

> IN every Land the sages say we trace
> Th'hereditary feature mark the face.
> But not alone distinct their outward forms;
> Their nobler part distinctive genius warms.
> With scornful pride each Nation boasts its Muse,
> Whose rays are tinted with unrival'd hues!
> Let but a Briton step upon the stage,
> Whence will he draw the glass for every age?
> To one lov'd fount of magic he will go;
> With one lov'd name his head and heart will glow;
> One only volume will his hand unroll;
> SHAKESPEARE, the mighty master of the soul!
> Him, with one voice whom varying critics praise;
> Him, the great theme of every poet's lays![31]

That's all very well for the British, clearly, but what about the locals?
According to this line of rhetoric, the kind of private theatricals which a
century earlier had enabled aristocrats of different nationalities to perform
Macbeth together were apparently no longer quite possible: as national
poet, Shakespeare had become a writer for all 'Britons' rather than for an
international educated élite. Despite his misgivings about the collective

stand-offishness of the British abroad, Brydges here slips easily into a
mode of boosting national prestige via praising Shakespeare which would
become familiar in later years around more formal diplomatic institutions
such as the British Council. It is telling that Lullin had to ask Brydges to
rewrite his prologue to *Venice Preserved* to include some remarks
addressed specifically to a Genevan audience, and it looks as though the
Henry IV prologue may have undergone the same process. Turning as if in
embarrassment to apostrophize Falstaff at first instead of the Genevois,
Brydges rather awkwardly and alienatingly classifies the fat knight's local
spectators as 'foreign':

> O soul of wit and humour, that attest
> The genuine sunshine of the social breast;
> Unseen before, unimitated since;
> Yet where each word, each look of life convince;
> Rare FALSTAFF, in the drama of life's stage
> Unique; to youth surprising; – new to age;
> Let foreign eyes thy form of fun behold;
> And foreign ears attend thy vein of gold![32]

When it comes to actually speaking to these foreign ears, Brydges finds
himself having to find ingenious ways in which the Genevans might
miraculously qualify to comprehend Shakespeare despite their foreignness.
Perversely, he has to argue that it is because the Alpine landscape is so
unlike that of Shakespeare's England that its inhabitants should appreciate
his work. Since the Genevans inhabit a romantic landscape, he claims, they
should be ideally susceptible to the romantic magic of Shakespearean
nostalgia. As befits an antiquarian and genealogist with a fatal partiality
for hereditary rank, Brydges hymns Prince Harry, Hotspur, the Douglas
and the play's overall presentation of the 'days of chivalry', urging this
republican and rational audience to succumb to the national necromancy
by which Shakespeare's art can reanimate the lost glories of feudalism:

> How at the picture, which the open'd tomb
> Gives back again to earth's recover'd bloom,
> The bosom swells, and the decaying fire
> Of an exhausted age begins respire!
> Ye, whom the blue Lake, clos'd by mountains hoar,
> Whispers to love all grand and genuine lore,
> Gaze on the glories of a British spell;
> Let your hearts on his vanish'd heroes dwell,
> And see how History can tell her tale,
> Clad in a poet's most transparent veil!

At this point Brydges remembers, fortunately, that Shakespeare is not only the poet of Britain but the poet of Nature:

> No feeble action; no bedazzling hues;
> No art that with its scentless flowers bestrews;
> 'Tis Nature's self that here we see in strife;
> Not life's reflection, but the very life!

In his thoroughly convoluted peroration, Brydges takes the connections between Shakespeare's art-transcending, natural genius and the natural landscape further, suggesting that since the liberty-loving Swiss take their character from a sublime Alpine landscape, they may be able to appreciate Shakespeare's sublime genius:

> Mid rocks and mountains and the torrent's roar,
> And cataracts that down precipices pour,
> If aught sublimer from the outward forms
> The spirit, that presides within us, warms,
> Here mayst thou have the seat of thy sublime!
> Here mayst thou listen to the noblest rhyme!
> Children of Freedom, born amid the show
> Of Nature's grandest works, may learn to glow
> With strains, from Nature's loftiest Bard that flow!

The problem of offering what he still regards as innately British national culture to a European audience, clearly, deeply puzzles Brydges – hence the big 'if' in that last passage. In the last of these prologues, indeed, contradicting his introduction to *Henry IV*, Brydges is forced to admit that national difference did nothing to prevent Lord Byron and Jean-Jacques Rousseau being spiritually akin. In his 'Occasional Prologue, being an apology for the necessity of substituting a farce instead of a tragedy. Written 17 Jan 1830',[33] he ends up suggesting that the Swiss may enjoy Shakespeare and his literary compatriots not because of their excitingly foreign landscape, but despite it. In Brydges' clinching couplet, instead of the playwright being marked as the object of a potentially narrow British enthusiasm, it is Britain which is marked as belonging to him. Just audible through Brydges' anxiously twisted syntax, a Romantic cosmopolitanism is here beginning to appear alongside the cultural jingoism which was otherwise supplanting the internationalist outlook of the preceding century's well-travelled aristocracy. Shakespeare, rather than speaking solely of the English to the English (as he did at Normanby's palazzo), is in this prologue part of the medium by which Britain can enter into communication with the world; the whole nation and its

canon – 'the land of Avon's matchless Bard' with its 'golden tales' – are
now available to Rousseau's compatriots for overdue appreciation:

> What then is MIND? does climate, image, lot,
> Or form of government, or choice of spot,
> Wealth, poverty, or joy, or grief, bestow
> The breath that bids the flame of genius glow?
> Ah, not confin'd to climate, country, state, –
> MIND is above all fortune, and all fate!
> Rousseau and Byron, sons alike of fire,
> In their own flames were fated to expire!
>
> Here then congenial is the generous breast;
> Tho' mountains, with eternal snows opprest,
> Hang on thy walls, and suns of rosy ray
> Unfelt upon thy cloud-capt mountains play, . . .
> Here may the land of Avon's matchless Bard
> Claim for its golden tales the fair reward![34]

It is hard to imagine these prologues producing much effect on any
non-Anglophones in the Cassino's audiences. Sadly, the sole extant
contemporary comment on the performances introduced by these prologues, – in the *Dublin Literary Gazette* – records only that the decor of
these productions was more impressive than their acting.[35] Certainly
Brydges' rhetorical efforts to present Falstaff to the Genevois as the
perfect ambassador for British culture appear to have produced no
long-term effects whatsoever; when it came to drama, the city still
belonged to Voltaire rather than to Shakespeare. In the long term,
Brydges and Lullin were at the wrong end of the country, and their
efforts to promote an English-speaking Shakespeare through polite
amateur productions would be outstripped by those of the Zurich-
based native translators and critics eager to adopt his work into their
own culture without the mediation of well-meaning English or Anglophile gentlemen.[36] The really significant event of the 1830s for the
subsequent development of Continental Shakespeare, both professional
and amateur, would not be these Genevan performances of *Henry IV* in
English but the completion of the Schlegel-Tieck translation of the
Complete Works into German. When it came to live Shakespeare,
much of Switzerland would in practice remain a province of Greater
Germany, presenting the plays not in English or French or *Schweizer-
deutsch* but in *Schriftdeutsch*. As in other parts of Europe, in Switzerland
Shakespeare would appear on stage not as Britain's national poet but as
the third German classic. As we will see, this would have remarkable

consequences when the circumstances of world war brought Colonel Braddyll's successors as military performers of Shakespeare onto German territory in the twentieth century.

If diplomats, whether official or self-appointed, found themselves inescapably drawn to the works of their national poet when staging theatricals abroad, so too did the military. However, if transplanting the eighteenth-century tradition of private theatricals to Geneva began in the hands of Lullin and Brydges to produce a form of voluntary-sector expatriate Shakespeare which anticipated the agenda of the British Council, that tradition mutated in very different directions when allied not with diplomacy but with military force. In all forms of amateur drama, the social situation is always paramount, and very different kinds of sociability are constituted on board warships and in military barracks and camps compared to those which prevail in the drawing rooms and clubhouses of artistic cognoscenti. While in 1829 *Henry IV part 1* offered a charming opportunity for Lord and Lady Normanby to demonstrate their hospitality, their cultivation and their prestige even while impersonating the impolite Hotspur and the downtrodden Lady Percy, other works of the national poet have looked very different when performed in social settings defined not by the cultural and social agenda of the Grand Tour but by the imperatives of colonialism and warfare.

Military theatricals have been ably analysed by Gillian Russell in her *Theatres of War*, who comments on their importance as a means of displaying and reinforcing rank and status.[37] One way in which young officers could at once display their courage, their education and their *esprit de corps*, it transpires, was by performing female roles. Often taking place in an environment enforcedly as single-sexed as that of the Lord Chamberlain's Men and just as obsessed with rank as the Elizabethan sumptuary laws, expatriate performances by servicemen raise with particular clarity the question of what constitutes a woman in the live performance of Shakespearean drama, and indeed what the category of 'woman' means among all-male communities far from home. Away from the professional stage, and away from Britain, who gets to be a Shakespearean heroine, and for whom?

This question gets raised and answered in different ways according to context. In some situations, the military assumed control of what had originally been civilian playhouses, and tried to maintain some façade of business as usual in as many aspects of their activities as possible, including the gender of their leading ladies. This was the case, for example, during the American war of independence, when Shakespeare's newly established status as national poet gave his work particular resonance in the theatrical repertory of an embattled garrison. Convinced of the importance of the drama for the maintenance of civilian and military morale alike, the British military authorities took over the Southwark theatre in Philadelphia for the winter season of 1777–8 and then, after that city fell, commandeered the John Street theatre in New York for each winter from 1778 until the end of hostilities in 1783.[38] Here they continued to mount stock plays from the London repertory of the time, using established local professional actresses in female roles where possible but sometimes resorting to cross-dressed junior officers as necessary. The repertory included a generous selection of works by the empire's playwright laureate, defiantly described to sceptical rebels by one 1778 Loyalist broadside (itself cast as the epilogue to the rebellious colonists' farce of 'Independence') as 'Old Shakespeare, a poet who should not be spit on, / Although he was born in an island called Britain'.[39] These familiar favourites with amateurs and professionals alike included *Henry IV part 1* (all about honour and defeating rebels), *Richard III* and *Macbeth* (all about the ultimate defeat of wicked usurpers), together with *Othello* (all about intrigue among garrison officers) and *Catherine and Petruchio*. The John Street theatrical seasons were so vigorously supported by the governor of New York, Sir Henry Clinton – who clearly recognized their importance in sustaining public attachment to the status quo – that the officers involved became known in some quarters as 'Clinton's Thespians'. In a prologue spoken in 1777, indeed, the entire British army is jokingly described as a touring theatrical company led by commanding actor-manager General Howe, its summer military campaigns against the American rebels out in the countryside conceived as continuous with its winter activities on the boards of the city playhouse:

> Once more ambitious of theatric glory,
> Howe's strolling company appears before ye.
> O'er hills and bogs, through wind and weather,
> And many a hair-breadth 'scape, we've scrambled hither;
> For we, true vagrants of the Thespian race,
> While summer lasts ne'er know a settled place ...[40]

Whatever their hardships when in combat rather than onstage, the financial records of this troupe, now preserved in the library of the New York

Historical Society, record a level of expenditure on costumes of which any country-house impresario back home would surely have approved, including 40 shillings for 'Sundry Millinery for Captain Watson', and 46 shillings and 6d for 'trimming a hat for Roderigo in Othello and Ld Trimmer in The Jealous Wife'.[41] They also document substantial profits, which were in part, in a gesture familiar from other contemporary theatrical enterprises eager for respectability, distributed to the widows and orphans of soldiers killed in the conflict and to other local charities.[42] This philanthropic dimension was advertised in the prologue quoted above via a phrase from Shakespeare's *Othello*:

> But soft! a word or two before I go.
> Benevolence first urged us to engage,
> And boldly venture on a public stage;
> To guard the helpless orphan's tender years,
> To wipe away th'afflicted parent's tears ...[43]

Despite this public commitment to charitable giving, it appears that soldiers could still supplement their ordinary pay by participating in performances: on 23 March 1779, for instance, £3.4s was paid out 'for the Guard of light Infantry, attending the Rehearsal and play of Rich: the 3^{d}',[44] and the terms of other such payments suggest that ordinary infantrymen, alternately doubling as extra security and as extras *tout court*, served both as bouncers in the auditorium and as supernumeraries on the stage. Under something like siege conditions, the cultural reassurance provided by these hybrid productions at what was still very insistently a Theatre Royal – even when half-amateur and half-professional, half-military and half-civilian – was clearly felt to be worth paying for.[45]

A different halfway stage between the traditions of aristocratic-cum-diplomatic amateur dramatics and those of military camp entertainment is provided by the case of less professionalized theatre in garrison towns abroad, where officers might support the civility represented by amateur English drama both as a police presence and as guest performers, joining civilian society at the same time as showing themselves prominently to it. A striking case-study is provided by the rendition of *The Merry Wives of Windsor* given, under the patronage of the Governor, in the unlikely setting of St Vincent in the Windward Islands in 1842. Here again the willingness of junior officers to play Shakespearean heroines was vital, though on this occasion they were supplementing not professional actresses but the bashful wives and daughters of colonists. We owe the surviving inside information about this Caribbean production to one

Captain George Valentine Mundy, whose letters home to his mother, along with other documents relating to his military career, are now preserved in the National Army Museum in Chelsea. Mundy was posted to Kingstown, the capital of St Vincent, in 1842, where British officers (part of a military presence maintained since the Carib wars, which had culminated in the forcible removal of a whole sector of the island's indigenous population in 1797) had long engaged in amateur drama supported by prosperous planter families in the town. The prominence of this activity is suggested by the venue they used; the 'Theatre Royal, Kingstown', was the upper storey of the brick-built court house erected in 1798 which also served as the meeting place of the island's governing assembly.[46] For the ruling élite of the island, these performances both exhibited and modelled the social order, while for the officers they served much the same function as other theatricals back to the *Red Dragon* and beyond, namely the preservation of morale and common purpose in circumstances which might otherwise have tended towards anomie and disaffection. Although in 1842 some feared that the expiration of the 'apprenticeships' conferred on the slaves officially freed in 1834 might yet lead to violent social breakdown, the great enemy in St Vincent was not rebellion but fever, which Mundy himself contracted (the dramatic changes in his handwriting as he narrates his illness and recovery are extremely poignant). Strikingly, he only fell ill after he had given up his participation in amateur theatricals. As in garrison life more generally, so in one of his first letters home after reaching the Windward Islands the theatre serves as a healthy and useful distraction from thoughts of disease and death. The first paragraph of this letter, dated 'St Vincents, October 23rd 1842 – Sunday', consists largely of a list of those in his company who have already succumbed to disease, but then Mundy abruptly realizes that this is not the sort of thing best calculated to entertain his anxious mother. Instead he humorously affects the tone of a dilettante as he describes the recent doings of '*we* amateurs':

– but I will change this *nasty subject* – Last Wednesday *we* amateurs acted the 'Merry Wives of Windsor' to a crowded house – all went off capitally – Falstaff, Sir Hugh, Mrs Quickly & Slender were perfectly acted, & your humble servant made his debut as Mr Page and was enthusiastically received – I was at first in a great fright but soon got pluck & they say I looked very well and also acted my part well, but it is rather a stupid one.[47]

Falstaff again serves here as a talisman to convene social gatherings of homesick Englishmen abroad, but by contrast with what Brydges sought to make of his appearance in Geneva he is not in this instance being consciously offered as an insight into British culture for the benefit of a non-British audience. Even more than Normanby's *Henry IV* in Florence, this production of *The Merry Wives of Windsor* seems to have been produced in deliberate and purposeful defiance of its location. In St Vincent the play could serve as part of a charade by which soldiers and colonists alike pretended to be in Merry England, or at worst in the West End, while actually in the midst of tropical fever and incipient discontent. Within the British empire of the eighteenth and nineteenth centuries, garrison theatre performed some of the same functions as do the multiple flavours of ice-cream served on US bases in the American empire of the twentieth and twenty-first, helping to maintain its consumers' sense that the norms of the national culture still apply and prevail even thousands of miles from home. Certainly at a practical level this St Vincent performance was in deep denial about the nature of the West Indian climate. It was mounted in a lavish, eclectic early Victorian fancy-dress version of Old English costume, which dominates Mundy's recollections of the production, or at least those which he thinks will best amuse his parents. The more one imagines the sheer bulk of the heavy fabrics and even additional hair which Mundy describes, the less surprised one is about the complete physical exhaustion that followed his performance:

My dress was very handsome, & I had let my hair grow for *six wks* – I wore a dark coloured doublet slashed with light blue satin, light brown trunk hose & blue long stockings, & your blue slippers with rosettes, my hose, hanging shoes & collar, trimmed with old point lace, and a purple velvet cap, with blue velvet bag hanging out of the top, a very becoming dress, with Mustachoes, just so so, and I don't think you wd have known your son George ... After our play *we* actors gave a very nice ball at a Sr Melville's house, where we danced till 4, when I was what with excitement & dancing thoroughly knocked up ...[48]

As the detail of Mundy's carefully cultivated long hair suggests, this performance had kept the officers in its cast usefully busy for a good while, and indeed it is nominally the burden of rehearsal which persuades Mundy, despite his exhilarating success as Page and the pleasing novelty of being able to speak of '*we* actors', to abandon this hobby thereafter:

I was very glad when it was all over, & I do not think I shall take the trouble to act again, as it is too much trouble having to learn a long part & rehearse so often as we are obliged to do – The next play to be acted is 'Virginius' [by Sheridan Knowles, 1820] in my opinion a most stupid one, and I think it will fail ...[49]

It is a pity that Mundy does not expand further upon his reasons for not thinking it worth his while to appear in the stupid *Virginius* (assuming that this dismissal is not merely cover for having failed to secure the offer of a role), which may conceivably have been related to the gender distribution of its roles. Whereas *The Merry Wives of Windsor* potentially offers opportunities for its male cast members to interact with three nubile women (those cast as Anne Page, Mistress Page and Mistress Ford), *Virginius* only provides one leading female role, that of Virginia, who is killed by her own father at the end of act 4. Otherwise a matter of togas, honour and tyranny, *Virginius* would certainly look less promising to any young captain as the prelude to a ball. In the vicinity of young women, comedies of courtship were much more to the point, and it may be that one perceived advantage of *The Merry Wives* as a piece for expatriate actors such as 'The Amateurs of the Garrison and Island' was not only its patriotic status as a work of true old English genius but the fact that two of its female roles could with reasonable suitability be played by the womenfolk of colonists or officers. *Virginius* was in fact much more like the sort of play that tended to be chosen when senior officers mounted full-length dramas to keep themselves and their immediate subordinates busy in the all-male environment of a camp (or a galleon, in the case of Keeling's *Hamlet* and *Richard II*), namely a high tragedy with fewer prominent roles for women. Away from married quarters and attractive civilians, military Shakespeare tended to be altogether less connubial than *The Merry Wives of Windsor*.

Even this production, however, was at best a halfway house in this respect. Caught up in the remembered social whirl of the play and the ball, Mundy does not comment on the gender balance of the casting, but he does make it visible to his parents by including an annotated copy of the playbill with his letter, amused at the instance of social pretension in a remote and exotic backwater which it represents: 'I enclose a bill of our last play – see how *strong we come it* at St Vincents!!'[50] (Figure 13). As the cast list shows, in practice only one of the play's female roles – Mistress Ford – was on this occasion played by a woman, one Mrs Hutchings, who was chaperoned throughout the production by her husband (who played Shallow) and her young son Charles (who played Robin the page, and who is described by Mundy's possibly sarcastic annotation as an 'Infant Phenomenon!!!!'). Mistress Page and her daughter, rather than being impersonated by potential dancing partners at the post-show ball, were instead played by male members of the prominent local Melville family, descendants of the island's first British governor and heirs to the titled host of the post-performance party. As we have seen, by the 1840s burlesque and travesty were beginning to displace Shakespeare from the

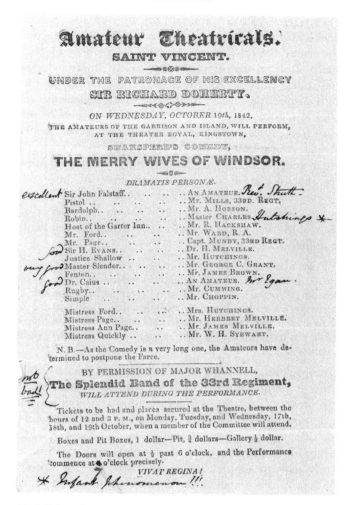

Figure 13. Playbill for *The Merry Wives of Windsor*, St Vincent's, Windward Islands, 1842, with annotations by Captain Valentine Mundy.

genteel theatrical repertory, and in the 1860s Captain Sock Buskin was recommending farce and burlesque to military personnel as preferable to straight drama.[51] This half-cross-dressed *Merry Wives* seems to have fallen usefully between the two. Long enough, as the playbill points out, to have displaced the usual farcical afterpiece entirely, it had in effect subsumed it already. Canonical but racy, this comedy forgives drag but at the same time supports reproductive respectability. Playing the role of Falstaff, however, who himself cross-dresses as Mother Pratt, remained unrespectable, to the extent that the performer on this occasion – a local clergyman, the Reverend Shuth, ruthlessly outed by Mundy's marginal annotation – had himself billed only as 'An Amateur'. The production was clearly a success, and despite the climate by the end of the nineteenth century the West Indies in general could be described by one expert in the colonial traditions of non-professional drama as 'a stronghold for amateurs'.[52]

In some parts of the empire, however, not only would respectable vicars not admit to playing debauched knights but respectable women would not accept any roles at all, no matter how many of the males in their families were prepared to appear with them. Lord William Lennox, beginning an entire chapter of his memoirs on the subject of military theatricals, would particularly remember this problem of early nineteenth-century colonial drama in 1878:

IN the early part of the present century, amateur theatricals were got up in almost every garrison town, in our colonies, to enliven the monotony of winter quarters; and good as the performances generally were, as far as the actors were concerned, there was always a dreadful dearth of female talent. Ladies could scarcely be persuaded to take a part in a drawing-room entertainment; to appear on the public boards was never dreamt of. The result was, that beardless ensigns had to appear in female attire.[53]

Drawing-room entertainments, in front of invited guests only, were one thing, and only perilously respectable for women at that; but when such amateur theatricals were offered in a real commandeered playhouse to an audience dominated by soldiers, it was quite another. Hence while sufficient male officers were perfectly willing to don the greasepaint in the cause of duty (in fact some who made their debuts in garrison theatricals subsequently took to supplementing their half-pay by turning pseudonymously semi-professional, such as Captain Prescott of the Royal Artillery, who, according to Lennox, 'under the *nom du theatre* of Warde, represented some of Shakespeare's characters in tragedy very well'),[54] female civilians were harder to co-opt. Under these conditions, becoming ladies for the occasion was a job particularly suited to those who bore an exalted social rank but so far a junior position within the officer corps. Lennox particularly recalls the titled cadets who distinguished themselves in this way at Wellington's headquarters in 1816 – Lord Arthur Hill and Lord Howden, who played Bridget Pumpkin and Kitty Sprightly respectively in Isaac Jackman's farce *All the World's a Stage*, and Sir Henry Barnard, who played Emily in Joseph Frederick's musical comedy

The Beehive. But he also remembers one way of avoiding even this nicely calculated expedient, the same tactic employed by Clinton's Thespians a century earlier:

Occasionally, abroad, professional actresses could be engaged, and when the late Field-Marshal Sir John Fitzgerald, at that time commanding a battalion of the 60th rifles, and myself, were joint managers of the Quebec garrison theatricals, we were fortunate enough to secure the aid of three professional ladies.[55]

Lennox's comments reveal how completely the casting of female roles in such amateur theatricals is a matter of rank. When it comes to playing heroines, there are ladies, professional ladies and lieutenants, and it isn't entirely clear from the anecdotes he goes on to recount whether the hired actress is definitely preferable to the well-connected beardless ensign.

Out on battlefronts during the campaigning season, however, away both from potentially paying civilian audiences and from potential female performers, military Shakespeare was not like this at all, represented in the independent United States, for example, by a substantially different set of favourite plays. *Othello*, with a doge in command rather than a king and a mere general as its protagonist, continued to recommend itself to the free citizens of the new republic, however controversial it might look in the antebellum South. Just three years after Captain Mundy made his theatrical debut in St Vincent in the role of Master Page, another officer in a different army made his own first appearance on any stage, at a temporary encampment in Texas, in the role of Desdemona. This was the young Ulysses S. Grant, then a (beardless) lieutenant, who while awaiting action against the Mexicans in 1845 was persuaded by a fellow officer called Longstreet to take part in an ambitious, if slightly abbreviated, *Othello*. (Apparently Grant 'looked very like a girl, dressed up', but the soldier playing Othello complained that he 'did not have much sentiment'.)[56] Shakespeare had been part of the entertainment repertory of the US army from the beginning – while Clinton's Thespians were diverting New York in 1778, for instance, the rebel soldiers encamped at Portsmouth, New Hampshire, saw *Coriolanus*, complete with a topical epilogue comparing the sufferings of Caius Martius at the hands of ungrateful civilians to those complained of by the American troops.[57] (When hostilities broke out between the two countries again in the shape of the War of 1812, a group of African-American sailors imprisoned in Dartmoor similarly passed the time by performing Shakespearean tragedy.)[58] Widely appropriated as a freedom-loving poet whose tragedies often recognized the necessity of tyrannicide,[59] Shakespeare had entered the consciousness of the American officer class as a powerful source of oratory, and in 1845 part of the appeal of *Othello* – quite apart from its depiction of intrigue among rival officers within a garrison, and the practicably small number of principal roles which had recommended it to the Delavals almost a century earlier – must have lain in its great rhetorical set pieces.

Certainly when the 7th New York Regiment found themselves quartered at Fort Federal Hill in Baltimore while waiting to be sent into battle in the Civil War in August 1862, the all-male Shakespearean performances which topped the weekly variety bills assembled by the '7th Regiment Amusement Association' were dominated by high-minded speechifying. As recommended in the how-to books of the time, these were only extracts from the plays, and they shared the billing once more with farce and burlesque. On 2 August, it was 'the Instigation Scene from *Othello*' (followed, 'by request of the Commandant', with the first act of Boucicault's *London Assurance*); on the 8th, 'the celebrated Trial Scene from *The Merchant of Venice*' (with John H. Bird as Portia, a performance he immediately followed by playing the title role in William Barnes Rhodes' ever-popular *Bombastes Furioso*); on the 15th, the (all-male) scenes from the first act of *Hamlet* in which the prince meets his father's ghost (followed by John Morton's farce *Box and Cox*); and, on the 22nd, the tent scene from *Julius Caesar* (followed not only by Gilbert Abbott à Beckett's farce *The Siamese Twins* but, 'by request', with a repetition of *Bombastes Furioso*).[60] Strikingly absent from these American bills, however, are any plays set in Britain; victorious kings such as Richmond, Malcolm and Henry IV were not felt to be appropriate material for the amusement of the US army. This is a Shakespeare whose status as English national poet has been carefully rescinded, allowed to remain in the emancipated former colonies strictly as a writer for aspiring utopian republicans rather than for homesick and nostalgic subjects of the time-worn English crown. Whoever else Uncle Sam may have wanted, he did not want Falstaff.

These Civil War performances appear to mark the high-water mark of American amateur military Shakespeare: as we will see, by the time of the Second World War American servicemen were reputedly more interested in close-harmony singing than in theatre, and although many US troops were famously issued with copies of *Henry V* during the build-up to the invasion of Iraq in 2003 there was no expectation that any of them would stage it. Even among British military and colonial personnel the percentage of Shakespeare offered in garrison and camp performances definitely fell over the course of the nineteenth century. In India, for example, although Lieutenant-Colonel Newnham could record in 1898 that 'all over India, notably at Poonah, Mhow, Meerut, Calcutta and Lucknow there are centres of attraction for amateurs', and that 'Simla is the Mecca of amateur actors abroad, and the Simla Amateur Dramatic Club is probably the best-equipped amateur club in the world',[61] his account of the amateur theatricals mounted across the sub-continent by colonial officers and their wives is dominated by farce, Gilbert and Sullivan, Arthur Wing Pinero and Haddon Chambers. The sole Shakespearean play he mentions seems to have been chosen primarily for its local topicality. At one point in the mid-1890s the highlight of the season at Simla – the hill-station to which the viceregal court transferred from Delhi to avoid the summer heat – was to have been a performance of *A Midsummer Night's Dream* actually performed 'in the spicèd Indian air by night' (2.1.124), in aid of 'Lady Roberts' pet charity, the homes in the hills for nurses and hospitals for sick officers', but in the event the monsoon rains came inopportunely early and the production had to be played in the cavernous Town Hall ballroom.[62]

In an area of the Empire rich in memsahibs, where amateur theatricals had been rendered respectable and even fashionable by the shows mounted at the viceregal residence by Lady Lytton and Lady Mansfield, *A Midsummer Night's Dream* provided a pleasant occasion on which Englishwomen might dress elaborately as fairies and remember the wild-flowers of home (see Figure 14), but among all-male communities farce and burlesque were far more to the point.[63] As we have already seen, these genres had always been prominent even among military thespians as earnest as the 7th New York Regiment Amusement Association, and by the 1880s the Guards, for example, had their own 'very comfortable little private playhouse' at their barracks in Chelsea devoted entirely to the efforts of 'The Guards' Burlesque'.[64] In the twentieth century such performances continued to dominate the repertory of amateur drama performed by soldiers and sailors.[65] Among sailors in particular, kept together in isolated single-sexed communities at far greater length than their army counterparts, cross-dressing was now undertaken much more frequently for comedic ends than in the service of Shakespeare's tragic muse,[66] and when allusions to his canon featured in shipboard entertainments at all it was in the jokily mock-homoerotic context of what is still known as the 'sods' opera' – a term for any performance mounted by sailors for sailors, always featuring both music and drag.

Figure 14. In the spicèd Indian air by night: *A Midsummer Night's Dream* performed by the
Amateur Dramatic Club of Simla in the 1890s.

PRISONERS

The question of whether all-male groups of expatriate and military
personnel should play burlesque, Shakespeare, or both arose most pointedly during the first half of the twentieth century. Military service had
always involved hours of tedious waiting which, if dedicated to the pursuit
of theatrical glory, might be transformed into something experienced as
gentlemanly leisure, but the number of idle man-hours needing to be
therapeutically structured by the social roles of performers and audience
members reached a new level during the two world wars. The opportunity
and the need for theatre was especially marked among those subjected to
internment, whether as civilians or as captured combatants, and behind
barbed wire Shakespeare's plays found themselves once more occupying a
contested position in a number of different all-male repertories.

The tension between Shakespeare and revue, for example, as Ton
Hoenselaars has shown, was played out dramatically at the all-male
Ruhleben civilian internment camp in Berlin during the First World

War. Here a group led by the actor Cecil Duncan-Jones and the designer Leigh Vaughan Henry produced *As You Like It* – pointedly, a play about exile – in 1915. These comparatively highbrow thespians, as well as offering *Twelfth Night* and *Othello* to mark the Shakespeare tercentenary of 1916, followed the practice of societies like the Stockport Garrick back home by offering serious modern plays too, but this repertory did not meet with the approval of all the camp's 4,000 internees. 'We read with regret that long-haired devils wish to pump Ibsen, further Shakespeare, etc. into this Lager', wrote one contributor to the camp magazine. 'We wish those people were anywhere but here.'[67] In practice, although the camp theatre remained much more popular than the less participatory cinema, many, as Hoenselaars explains, called instead for more 'light entertainment, in the form of variety shows and musical comedy'.[68] Duncan-Jones and his fellow Shakespeareans might have found themselves in more sympathy with the British conscientious objectors imprisoned back home at Dartmoor, who staged *A Midsummer Night's Dream* at some time between late December 1918 and April 1919, a play, as Clara Calvo points out, in which the choice between obeying a patriarchal injunction and being subjected either to perpetual single-sexed imprisonment or death is feelingly dramatized.[69]

As Chapter 2 showed, amateur drama was seized upon in Britain after the Armistice as one means of healing the social and psychological damage inflicted by the war, and one side-effect was that, when war broke out once more in 1939, the British army contained more practised theatrical performers, technicians and producers than ever before. The scale and speed of Allied defeats in the early stages of the war thus resulted in the capture of large numbers of enthusiastic and experienced amateur thespians. With seemingly unlimited time heavy on their hands and a particularly pressing need to keep their minds and bodies occupied in order to fend off despair and disease, such prisoners of war could dedicate themselves wholeheartedly to the theatre, and despite their apparently unpromising circumstances they often achieved production values rarely matched in civilian amateur drama. Transferred to the large Campo PG no. 70 PM 3300 in Italy in July 1943, for example, the theatre-loving Bombardier George Good put a brave face on his situation in a postcard sent home via the Red Cross:

Our play circle is giving 'Pygmalion' this week & I will be going [to audition for a subsequent production] tomorrow … in a camp of this size you are bound to get loads of talent & the acting & stage decorations of these plays are terrific. Of course lots of the fellows have done this stuff previous to the war & we have some celebrities to be sure![70]

Theatrical 'celebrities' were even thicker on the ground in Germany, as John Mansel realized after his transfer to Oflag VIB at Warburg late in 1941:

Here at VIB . . . is found the full talent of all British officers and prisoners of war at the moment and a considerable number of R.A.F. From 3,500 one would expect to find acting and musical talent and we are not disappointed. With a few professionals to guide and participate, the shows have been of a very high standard.[71]

'There were a number of professional and semi-professional actors in the camp,' remembered M. N. McKibbin, similarly, of the prisoner-of-war camp to which he was sent in Bavaria, 'and these men not only gave of the best themselves, but were tireless in their coaching of talented amateurs, of whom there was no shortage in a camp of six thousand men.'[72] Just as at home, where societies like the Stockport Garrick had hired full-time producers to teach elocution and direct their shows, these camps settled into a pattern by which large numbers of amateurs were guided by a small number of professionals.

It is characteristic of the way in which these camp theatres continued the work of the inter-war amateur dramatic movement that one of the two performance spaces at Stalag 383 in Hohenfels in Bavaria was christened, proudly beating London to it, the 'National Theatre' – albeit, self-mockingly, 'the National Theatre of Hohenfels'. The theatre at the Eichstätt camp, indeed, pioneered a form of subsidized drama: 'Theatre and other communal expenses were met from a fund into which each officer paid one-third of his pay, and for which activities in the other ranks' compound were also financed.'[73] As a result it would be just possible to cite one particularly fine prisoner-of-war production as a milestone in the emergence of subsidized Shakespeare. This was the production of *Hamlet*, elegantly dressed and superbly photographed, which was welcomed by eager capacity audiences at every single one of its performances at Oflag VIIIB in Tittmoning, Bavaria, in early 1941, and which provoked such demand when it was repeated with a different supporting cast after its Hamlet, Michael Goodliffe, was transferred to Oflag VIIC at Eichstätt later in the war that its run had to be extended by ten days. As at Kilkenny, its star even had his portrait painted in his Hamlet costume (by his fellow prisoner Major Aubrey Davidson Houston).[74] Goodliffe, who directed as well as taking the title role, had formerly been a professional actor, who had appeared with Laurence Olivier in Tyrone Guthrie's production of *Othello* at the Old Vic. He had also seen Olivier play Hamlet there for Guthrie in 1937, and something of Olivier's celebrated feeling for visual line is surely imitated in the careful poise of Goodliffe's silhouetted fingers in one photograph depicting Hamlet's audience with the Ghost. Goodliffe's Ophelia, more typically, had no professional stage experience at all: he was a junior British army officer called John Dixon.

Although this is one aspect of prisoner-of-war life which has been kept out of British popular memory, Axis camps like these in occupied Europe thus played host between 1940 and 1945 to what was easily the largest flowering of English single-sex theatre since Shakespeare's own time. Nor should this particularly surprise us. Even if the recent conscripts and volunteers who found themselves in captivity after Dunkirk hadn't included so many experienced amateur and professional actors, many imprisoned servicemen would probably have picked up a taste for dressing up anyway from the seasoned career officers in their midst, who preserved a strong cultural memory of the traditions of the Guards' Burlesque. In this single-sexed thespian army it is no wonder that in 1940 Michael Goodliffe, as the only fully qualified actor in the camp to which he was sent after being captured during the fall of France, should have been seized upon at once by its senior British officer, General Victor Fortune, who in the interests of morale ordered him to 'Put on some shows as soon as you can.'[75] Even with clothing in desperately short supply as the winter of 1940 set in, the quest for promising cross-dressers was on.

What might surprise us more than its scale or its enforced transvestism is that in an age of mass entertainment and mass conscription any of these captive military theatricals should have involved Shakespeare, a writer who had elicited such groans at Ruhleben during the previous conflict. Even the ambitiously high-minded Goodliffe produced sketch shows and a Christmas pantomime before undertaking his *Hamlet* in 1941, and, as a number of military archives show, that is much more the sort of material that PoWs generally staged, when left to their own devices: revues and pantos, with occasional forays into recent middlebrow plays and popular musicals, much as Captain Sock Buskin would have recommended. A whole troupe of brassiered Geordies, the 'Northern Lights' company, performed an item called 'Perchance in Greece' in one of their revues at Stalag 383, where they were by no means the only purveyors of such entertainment, and the camp's Christmas pantomime for 1942, *Aladdin*, contained even more male-to-female cross-dressing than did its counterparts in the commercial theatre at home. (The following Christmas the same team put on *Dick Whittington*, complete with added mermaids.) The same fat photograph album in the National Army Museum in

London which documents these shows, compiled by one R. J. Duncan, records that this theatre's finest hour was its production of Gilbert and Sullivan's *The Mikado*, which apparently so delighted the camp's operetta-loving commandant that he cancelled roll-call for three days as a reward.[76] Other such establishments too, even those reserved for hardened would-be escapees, showed similar theatrical tastes. The first show mounted at Colditz, in November 1941, was a revue called *Ballet Nonsense*, dominated by the display of home-made tutus,[77] and the establishment's thespians rarely ventured into anything more highbrow than Noël Coward thereafter.

The style of cross-dressed performance required by a successful male Gertrude or male Gertrude Lawrence, however, is obviously different to the burlesque drag manner favoured in a sketch show like *Ballet Nonsense*, and Goodliffe for one recognized that if he was to produce 'straight' drama at all with all-male casts his audiences were going to have to unlearn their modern understanding of what stage cross-dressing meant. In the face of a conditioned reflex of giggling, he later remembered, 'we soon found that unless the presentation of female roles was intelligently tackled, any serious productions were impossible'. When he produced *Hamlet* for the second time, Goodliffe greatly shortened the role of Ophelia, cutting the nunnery scene entirely, and it may be significant that, despite staging two *Hamlet*s and a *King Lear*, among many other shows, Goodliffe's most elaborate Shakespearean revival was the *Comedy of Errors* he mounted at Eichstätt in December 1943.[78] Although in this PoW context the frame-narrative of the play must have been especially poignant – dramatizing as it does Egeon's captivity in a hostile country and his ultimate release and reunion with his family – the main plot was handled very lightly, with the cast dressed in comic and sometimes mildly salacious Regency costumes which included a split red satin skirt for the Courtesan capable of being detached from her dress to reveal elaborate lingerie. The play was entirely set to music, like a Viennese operetta, and was billed as the annual light entertainment for Christmas: 'This evening we all went to see this year's Pantomime,' wrote John Mansel, by now also at the same camp,

a severely pantomimed version of 'A Comedy of Errors'. It was superbly done and produced by Michael Goodliffe, our Shakespearian actor. I regret to say that I have neither seen or read the play, but the way it was done was more like a ballet.[79]

Despite this concession to the panto tradition, however, Goodliffe claimed after the war that in his serious productions, especially his

Shakespeares, the cross-dressing conventions of the Renaissance had been fully recovered: 'Two or three clever actors solved this problem [with the female roles], so that our audiences accepted them exactly as the Elizabethans accepted their boy-actors.'

In certain respects, the subculture which grew up around these prisoner-of-war playhouses did indeed hark back to Shakespeare's own theatrical world. As Stephen Orgel has shown, one of the reasons the early modern English had all-male theatre companies was a belief that males were simply better at performing, including performing as women;[80] and this belief surfaced once more during the war. Describing the 1942 Eichstätt pantomime in his diary, for example, John Mansel was especially impressed by Brian McIrvine, who had played Gertrude for Michael Goodliffe:

Citronella (Brian McIrvine) is staggering and in a dance with the Prince, himself quite excellent, performs a dance at which the average girl would make a poor attempt. There is graceful movement accompanied by perfect control ...[81]

Such specialists in female roles, moreover, like Stalag 383's 'Pinkie' Smith, attracted cult followings of which seventeenth-century boy-players like Solomon Pavey or Edward Kynaston would have been proud: according to one prisoner, they 'really needed protection going "home" to their barracks after the shows'.[82] 'Of course some of the fellows have to take girls' parts,' wrote Bombardier Good, '& they are real knockouts ...'[83] Adulation of the beardless-ensign-cum-boy-actor seems to have been especially marked at Stalag VIIIB, at Lamsdorf in Silesia, where an impressive *Twelfth Night* was staged in 1943 (Figure 15).

This group picture was taken at the dress rehearsal, with a home-made camera. On the left, playing Sebastian, is Corporal Peter Peel, who saved this photo; and on the right, playing Viola, is a young RAF wireless operator called Denholm Elliott. (Keeping closely to the kind of repertory favoured in amateur societies back home, this cast alternated *Twelfth Night* with Shaw's *Pygmalion*, in which Elliott played Eliza Doolittle.) Elliott seems to have enjoyed a level of idolization at Lamsdorf after which his post-war stage and screen career could only be an anticlimax. 'Any person who played the [female] lead role in the camp theatre was considered to be a heart-throb,' remembered his fellow-inmate George Moreton. '"She" had more fans and more people dreaming about "her" than "she" would ever imagine. When "she" walked down the road, eyes would follow "her" adoringly.'[84] This is borne out by a sailor called Andrew Macdonald-Bell, who recalled Elliott's Viola with the understated lyricism of the time:

Figure 15. *Twelfth Night* at Stalag VIIIB, Lamsdorf, Silesia, 1943: with Corporal Peter Peel
(Sebastian, left) and Denholm Elliott (Viola, right).

Spellbound, we watched and listened as first he presented as a girl, then as a girl
pretending to be a youth, then again as a girl ... [The following morning], [q]
uite on impulse, I walked over to the slim lad who had been Viola, and
I thanked him for his marvellous performance. Denholm smiled, a long-lipped
Irish sort of smile. 'Glad you liked it,' he said, while his quiet eyes drifted
shyly away from mine and his hand went up to finger back a flopping wing
of dark hair.[85]

As in the Elizabethan age, too, these latterday boy-players attracted some
equally passionate anti-theatrical sentiment, both secular and religious.
The Lamsdorf camp newsletter *Stimmt*, for instance, ran a sustained
editorial campaign against 'theatre "pansies" and their bitchy admirers',[86]
while the diary of Ellison Platt, the Methodist padre at Colditz, is full of
more pious outrage about the criminally tempting defiance of God's
prohibition against cross-dressing, Deuteronomy 22:5, which he was compelled to witness in *Ballet Nonsense* and its successors.[87]

As Marjorie Garber has pointed out, however, troubled attention to the
transgression of gender boundaries represented by cross-dressing is always
liable to represent the displacement of anxieties about different border
transgressions entirely.[88] In the case of the born-again Renaissance boy-
players of the Oflags and Stalags, what may have been much more

disturbing than their potential for sexual ambiguity was an ambiguity as to whose larger cultural and national agenda their transvestite performances were really serving. After all, these theatres were actually German, and even the revues mounted in them sometimes betrayed as vivid an engagement with German culture as with British. In Stalag 383, for instance, the revue *Bally Who* included a skit on Goethe called 'Soust'.[89] Did such Allied actors as these really perform strictly as homesick warriors, bravely sustaining their comrades' national identity in the interests of combatant morale, or were they for the time being good puppet citizens of Fortress Europe, entertaining their captors and keeping their colleagues from more belligerent thoughts? Theatre as elaborate as this would have been impossible without at the very least the toleration of the Nazi authorities, and this toleration often extended to actual assistance when it came to procuring make-up, lighting equipment, photographic facilities, printed programmes and so on. At Eichstätt, Goodliffe and his fellow actors – who at different times included Robert Loder, Dan Cunningham, Wallace Finlayson and Desmond Llewelyn[90] – were by 1945 running 'an organised theatre with a permanent stage staff of carpenters and electricians, a nucleus of about two dozen very competent actors – professional and amateur – and three or four scenic designers'.[91] 'Probably we were even better equipped than our own English stage', Llewelyn remarked of the similar organization at Rotenberg, to which he was subsequently transferred, while Mansel thought that on entering the camp theatre at Warburg 'one might almost be in the auditorium of a small theatre at home ... The lighting is extremely good and again most professional, dimmers being used and all conceivable effects.'[92] Although some materials for this sort of substantial thespian operation could be improvised ('we found that excellent three-ply scenery flats could be constructed from Red Cross parcel crates')[93] and some obtained from sentries in return for bribes of cigarettes, many could not have been obtained without the active cooperation of the camp authorities, who arranged for programmes to be manufactured by local printers and helped to obtain costumes. ('All the costumes were hired from Kassel,' observed Mansel of the 1941–2 *Citronella*, 'and these of course put the finishing touches to a thoroughly good pantomime.')[94] At Eichstätt the Germans provided a library containing some 12,000 volumes, including playscripts, and would punish the prisoners when an escape attempt was discovered by cancelling performances.[95]

In fact the German prison authorities were not only monitors and censors of these shows, but also represented a substantial proportion of

their audiences, taking the best seats in the stalls for every performance (so
that the prisoners, however escapist the entertainment, would never forget
that the Germans were the masters in this situation and actual escape was
impossible). Sometimes, as in the case of the Dr Jung who took photographs of Goodliffe's *Hamlet,* they admitted civilian spectators too.[96] At
Rotenberg – where he acted in, among other plays, *A Midsummer Night's
Dream* – Desmond Llewelyn remembered that 'The Germans, particularly one who'd been a theatre critic in Berlin, always watched the plays,
taking photos and providing us with civilian costumes, wigs, and Leichner
make-up.'[97] As long as prisoners did not attempt to abscond in the
civilian clothes they were allowed to wear in modern plays,[98] camp guards
were generally more than happy to see their charges occupied with
theatricals, not only because such activities kept the Red Cross happy
too,[99] but because they usefully distracted many inmates from their
professed military duty to escape. Given good enough productions of
Hamlet, it appears, some prisoners could have been bounded in a nutshell
and counted themselves kings of infinite space. 'The entertainments as a
whole, after [escape attempts], were the most important part of Camp
life,' recalled one of Goodliffe's actors, Robert Loder. 'Some officers, not
interested in escape work, used to get exceptionally annoyed if their
regular entertainment was disrupted [by escape alerts].'[100]

   General, pragmatic toleration extended to definite patronage, however,
when it came to camp performances of Shakespeare. As far as all the
surviving evidence I have been able to locate is concerned, whenever
Allied prisoners of war staged Shakespeare in Europe they did so with
the active sponsorship and encouragement of the German authorities. Just
as Shakespeare's company had operated under conditions provided and
dictated by the Master of the Revels, so Goodliffe and his peers were
ultimately working for the Master Race. It cannot be accidental that
Goodliffe did not produce *Henry IV* as his first Shakespeare play, never
mind *Henry V*; instead he offered a play in which his colleagues might
find a painfully topical depiction of impotence and inaction, but which
his captors regarded primarily as a supreme triumph of Aryan high art.[101]
Hamlet had of course been the most important Shakespearean play for any
self-respecting German since before young Werther became sorrowful
(the Nazis' chief legal theorist, Carl Schmitt, would even publish a whole
monograph about it after being deprived of his Berlin professorship
in 1945),[102] and Goodliffe's two productions were duly provided with
costumes specially obtained for him from the Munich opera house: so was
his Strauss-like *Comedy of Errors.* In a regime otherwise committed to

extirpating all signs of sexual deviation in the interests of heterosexual reproduction, cross-dressing by Englishmen performing in Shakespeare could apparently be permitted and even encouraged. Perhaps for the camp authorities the practice offered antiquarian glimpses of that odd offshore pre-history Shakespeare had enjoyed in the bad old days before he became German.

Professionally made costumes were also procured, from the Breslau opera house, for the Lamsdorf *Twelfth Night* – not coincidentally, the Shakespearean comedy revived most frequently in Germany during the 1930s, when a ban on decadent modern drama made Shakespeare more prominent than ever in the already generously state-funded playhouses. The Germans, amazingly, even took this *Twelfth Night* on tour to other camps, transporting its cast around the country in Wehrmacht lorries which might otherwise have been moving supplies to the Eastern front. But then the Third Reich was serious about Shakespeare. In 1830 Brydges had seen Shakespeare as part of the genetic make-up of the English, and by 1911 Arthur Buckley could describe Stratford as 'a temple dedicated to the genius of the Anglo-Celtic race'.[103] In 1940 the German writer Hermann Burte, delivering a lecture in Weimar on the eve of the Battle of Britain, similarly saw Shakespeare as part of an ethnic inheritance, albeit one which in his erstwhile homeland had now been fatally contaminated:

Shakespeare ist der Unsere so gut wie der seiner Engländer ... wir als Deutsche von 1940 dem Geist der elisabethanischen Engländer und ihrem Genius William in Warheit näherstehen als die Englischen von heute, hinter deren Thron jener Shylock steckt und herrscht, den Shakespeare erkannte und – verwarf!

[Shakespeare belongs as much to us as he does to the English ... We Germans of 1940 are in truth closer to the spirit of the Elizabethan English and their genius William than the Englishmen of today, behind whose throne lurks and rules that Shylock whom Shakespeare recognized and – rejected!][104]

This remark provides a useful gloss on one incongruous item in Stalag 383's otherwise studiously undemanding repertory. It is the sole Shakespeare play this theatre ever attempted, and one of the only plays on the list R. J. Duncan preserved of its productions from which no photographs are displayed in his album (Figure 16): *The Merchant of Venice*. It would be nice to be able to pretend that what was still at the time the most often revived Shakespearean comedy among English professionals and amateurs alike had been chosen for revival at this camp in sheer crass obliviousness as to what ideological charge the play might carry in Hitler's Bavaria.[105]

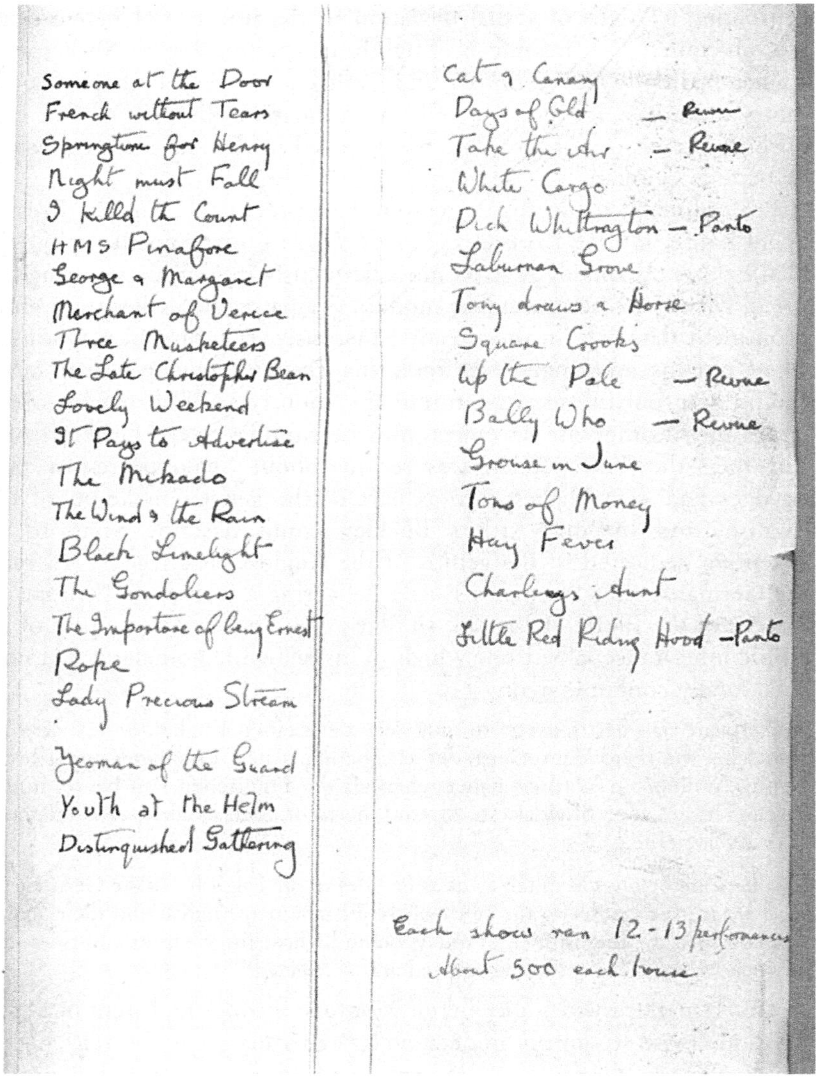

Some one at the Door
French without Tears
Springtime for Henry
Night must Fall
I killed the Count
HMS Pinafore
George & Margaret
Merchant of Venice
Three Musketeers
The Late Christopher Bean
Lovely Weekend
It Pays to Advertise
The Mikado
The Wind & the Rain
Black Limelight
The Gondoliers
The Importance of being Ernest
Rope
Lady Precious Stream

Yeoman of the Guard
Youth at the Helm
Distinguished Gathering

Cat & Canary
Days of Old   — Revue
Take the air   — Revue
White Cargo
Dick Whittington — Panto
Laburnam Grove
Tony draws a Horse
Square Crooks
Up the Pole   — Revue
Bally Who   — Revue
Grouse in June
Tons of Money
Hay Fever
Charleys Aunt
Little Red Riding Hood —Panto

Each show ran 12-13 performances
About 500 each house

Figure 16. R. J. Duncan's list of the repertory of the Stalag 383 camp theatre, Hohenfels, Bavaria.

But the cheerful account of life at Stalag 383 published after the war by N. M. McKibbin sadly makes this impossible:

One useful gesture the Jerries did make was to loan us the complete costumes for *The Merchant of Venice* from the State Theatre of Berlin; and though this was done simply because they considered it an anti-Jewish play, it was none the less welcome. A grand production was most enthusiastically received ...[106]

It is true that McKibbin, writing in 1947, after the doings of Stalag 383 had been rather upstaged by revelations about what had been happening at another camp only fifty miles away, Dachau, was at pains to remember this production as having challenged Nazism rather than collaborated with it. 'I remember few more impressive performances,' he continues, 'than that of Bob Jarvis, an Australian professional, who gave Shylock a fine dignity rather disturbing to the Germans in the stalls.' But he seems unnaturally keen, just as Garber might predict, to change the subject immediately to that of the camp's 'fellows who could make up to look like girls – glamorous and sophisticated girls', our 'female impersonators', or rather 'actors taking female parts, which is quite a different thing'. 'Shylock's daughter,' he recalls, 'was played by a sergeant whose name escapes me ...' It does not appear, then, that this production adopted the change to Shakespeare's script followed by National Socialist dramaturgs, whereby Jessica became an adopted Gentile so that Lorenzo could enjoy a miscegenation-free elopement, but for McKibbin the point here is not the defence of inter-racial marriage but the vindication of cross-gender casting: 'under the magic of the Theatre the character was just Jessica and it was as easy to accept her beauty as to accept Lorenzo and the moonlit bank the lovers sat upon'.[107] According to McKibbin, it appears, thousand-year Reichs may come and go, but world-beating British military cross-dressing goes on forever. But which factor was uppermost in determining what this performance, and others like it, could mean – the transvestite skills of its cast, or the vested interests of its sponsors? Despite being staged in English to a mainly Anglophone audience, this surely was a genuinely European Shakespeare, serving a vision of a pan-European literary canon. Unfortunately, it was a vision which understood European cultural identity in racial terms, and which found in Shakespeare's Venetian comedy an endorsement of genocide.

The troubled semi-internationalism represented by Shakespeare's presence in the theatrical repertories of prisoner-of-war camps in Nazi Germany is highlighted by the very different fortunes enjoyed by his plays in parallel circumstances in Asia. While accounts of prisoner-of-war theatricals in Japanese camps are often just as preoccupied with the difficulties and opportunities of female impersonation, the extraordinary and troubling incidence of inter-cultural Shakespeare represented by the Stalag 383 *Merchant of Venice* had no parallel in the Far East, where the lack of any common culture between captors and captives produced other problems entirely. The attitude of Japanese camp governors to prisoner-of-war theatre was less enthusiastic, although here again Shakespeare seemed at least tolerable, and once more the British would turn to *Hamlet* – though this time more in the spirit of the sods' opera than that of the elaborate high-culture productions mounted at German camps like Tittmoning and Eichstätt. In Japanese camps, prisoners were even less well fed than were their counterparts in Europe, never mind being granted access to materials they might use for thespian purposes, and their time was frequently spent in slave labour, but miraculously some still managed to find the additional physical and mental fortitude demanded under such circumstances by amateur theatricals. If anything, the especially dispiriting nature of prison-camp life in the Pacific made theatre all the more urgently necessary, as Frank Twiss, a Royal Navy lieutenant captured after HMS *Exeter* was sunk during the battle of the Java Sea in 1942, remembered:

When we first arrived at Zentsuji, we were rather depressed. There was no entertainment at all. To that extent there wasn't anything to boost one's morale, but the British group that came down from Ofuna, and those who came up from Malaya, did contain some quite able people, and before very long the British organised a regular display of theatrical or pantomime-type performances.[108]

These took place in a former barracks canteen which could hardly have compared with the facilities offered at Stalag 383 as a promising venue for drama: the acting area was separated from the spectators by a four-foot-high serving counter so that 'the audience only saw the top half of people', though on the positive side this 'gave scope for an immense amount of fun and games in the way of scenery changes and tricks of one sort or another'.[109] Zentsuji included Dutch and American prisoners as well as British and Australian, and an element of national rivalry in the performing arts soon developed among the allies:

Theatrics were also taken up by the Dutch, who were extremely clever at it, and the Australians joined us as well. The Americans didn't go so much on theatre but they were very much better at a thing like barber shop singing . . . In Zentsuji, we eventually put on a performance every week, one nation or another, the Americans, the Dutch and the British, one after the other . . . the British theatre was reasonably high class.

With the true British vagrants of the Thespian race naturally taking the lead in amateur drama, the Senior Service just as naturally took the lead in cross-dressing, with the beardless ensign Lieutenant Twiss showing the way: 'The very first one was a pantomime. I was the princess who lost her shoe, or whoever it was in Cinderella.'[110] Other Christmas shows followed – at the end of 1943, for example, the Anglo-Australian group performed both *Ali Baba* (with a script rich in catchphrases such as 'Sic Transit Gloria Swanson' and 'Pro Bono Public Houso') and a version of *A Christmas Carol*[111] – but Shakespeare played a crucial role in the Zentsuji repertory too. As in the old days of the Theatres Royal, however, the invocation of his canonical texts might serve to legitimate rather less elevated entertainments:

Every now and then we'd get into trouble with the Japanese because, of course, every show had to be censored. We therefore had to supply the script, which was extremely difficult because we had practically no paper or pencils or anything like that. We eventually hit upon the idea of copying out two or three of Shakespeare's plays because we'd got hold of a book of them from somewhere, some prisoner had brought it up with him. We used to put in a Shakespeare play and every week we had a performance and did something quite different, not related to it at all. But the Japanese never hoisted that in. They didn't understand the reading; they didn't understand English, let alone Shakespeare's English, and we'd obeyed the rules. We'd put in something to show what we were supposed to be doing and that satisfied the rules.[112]

In fact, far less well-supplied with play-books than their counterparts in Europe, the British prisoners mainly performed their own vaudevillean revues, together with memorial reconstructions of the Aldwych farces that had been a common denominator in the prisoners' theatregoing back home. ('We put on most of the Ralph Lynn and Tom Walls shows because people would get together and go over the play, as they remembered it, and we would reconstitute it, reconstruct it rather, and replay it within the limits of our staging'.)[113] An actual copy of the Complete Works, however, was far too valuable an asset to use solely for the purposes of fobbing off the censor, and at some point after Lieutenant Colonel E. J. Hazell and Alan Dant arrived at Zentsuji in 1943 the patriotically named 'St. George's Players' set about performing full-scale productions of Shakespeare in as close an approximation as they could manage to the customary full-historical-dress manner. Among Hazell's papers in the Imperial War Museum – which include meticulously hand-made Christmas cards exchanged between prisoners wistfully depicting half-timbered pubs called The Soldier's Return, and post-war letters bearing witness to Japanese atrocities – is the fragile typed playbill to one of these shows, *Macbeth*, in which Hazell played the First Witch. With its 'crowns, swords, shields, daggers, etc.' and its attempt at early medieval costuming, this production represented an extraordinary investment of resources for these half-starved men, and this bill provides a vivid index of how vitally the work of Shakespeare might serve as a rallying point for those who (like Malcolm) could not even obtain reliable news of their homeland and often despaired of ever seeing it again.

Single-sexed Shakespeare took its place in the repertory at another Japanese camp too, Yasumi (ironically named after the Japanese word for rest or holiday, in the manner of Ruhleben), albeit in a rather less heroic and straightforward style. Yasumi's more educated inmates included a future Director of the National Portrait Gallery who would in time become an expert on Shakespearean portraiture, the young Lieutenant David (later Sir David) Piper.[114] Intellectual and diffident (inclined to feel, as he confided to his diary, that he was 'making a failure even of being a prisoner-of-war'), Piper was put in charge of the camp's library – by comparison with the literary riches available at Eichstätt, a tiny and miscellaneous collection of novels, language textbooks and other works either saved among personal possessions on capture or sent in such Red Cross parcels as the prisoners received.[115] As a known writer of poems, richly detailed diary entries, meditations and passionately imagined post-war menus, furthermore, Piper was inevitably conscripted into Yasumi's theatrical productions too. These, though less frequent than at Zentsuji (monthly rather than weekly), were again predominantly of revues, together with pantomimes (Piper was especially cheered by *Dick Whittington* at Christmas 1944).[116] In keeping with this repertoire, Piper's masterpiece, yet another instance of modern military theatricals' usual preference for comic cross-dressed versions of Shakespeare in place of serious ones, is a one-act burlesque called *Shamlet: A Drammer* [sic], performed on 3 June 1944. Here at last Shakespeare and the sods' opera came together, and Ophelia, instead of being substantially cut, came into her own.

The typescript of this late but perfect example of the Shakespearean burlesque is preserved among Piper's wartime papers in the National Army Museum,[117] and as at Zentsuji it purports to offer Shakespeare as a legitimating and respectable backbone of the British expatriate theatrical repertory. On stage for much of the time is a Commentator, who plays much the same role as would be played a decade later by the compère Wallace Greenslade in *The Goon Show*. He opens the proceedings by explaining why the actors have on this occasion gone to Shakespeare's lov'd fount of magic:

> If there is any criticism of the quality of the entertainment we present to you each month, it is that there is a lack of meat – in other words, 'straight stuff', honest drama. To whom could we turn more appropriately than to the Immortal Bawd, sorry, – Bard, William Shakespeare. Bill's name, by the way, is spelt in at least a dozen different ways, all of them pronounced Bacon.

The Immortal Bawd – as good a term as any for Shakespeare in his capacity as patron saint of the transvestite theatre – is in this instance represented by his most famous tragedy, albeit as surreally and sometimes salaciously adapted:

> We have chosen to present you – Hamlet. Not without some difficulty, of course – William takes 3½ hours over it, deploying X characters (not including alarms and excursions) – 3½ hours to disentangle the very simple case of our hero, who, however, complicates the whole thing by going all introspective (broody). So we had to change it a bit, & I hope you'll agree it peps the whole thing up ...

The Commentator, who is frequently interrupted and asked for further explanations by an interloper known simply as the Little Man, supplies ludicrous segments of plot summary between scenes, and sometimes obstructs the play proper, especially when Hamlet is attempting to recite his most famous soliloquies. The skit's comic intolerance for these speeches is probably modelled on that of W. S. Gilbert's burlesque *Rosencrantz and Guildenstern* (1874), in which all the play's minor characters conspire to interrupt Hamlet's soliloquies and have him sent to England so that they can live out their lives in peace. But as well as liking to speak to himself while getting all introspective (broody), Piper's Hamlet is also addicted to golf: in the final scene he kills almost all the other characters in turn with a golf club, including, miraculously, the Ghost. This detail may have been inspired by a knowledge of Barry Jackson's controversial modern-dress production of 1925, which had famously been dubbed '*Hamlet* in plus-fours', but in any case this niblick-wielding Prince is for once far less intellectual than Laertes, a languid and effete fop impersonated by Piper himself. The real star of the show, however, is Ophelia, played by Iver Borton, 'in bathing trunks and bogus bosom etc',[118] as a pungent reminder of some of what the prisoners were missing. Before her first entrance, Hamlet is once more trying to make a soliloquy, despite being so distracted by the Commentator and the Little Man that he garbles even his most famous lines:

H[AMLET]. Shut up! You've got me all boxed up ... ah!
   Woman, thy name is frailty.
C[OMMENTATOR]. Nope. Haven't met her.
L[ITTLE] M[AN]. But what is woman?
C[OMMENTATOR]. Well, well. Where've you been all these years?
   Woman? Well, now: it's hard to explain ... Like you and me,
   but different (makes appropriate gesture). See?
L[ITTLE] M[AN]. O yes. I remember now ... a long, long time ago.
   Nice.

It all comes back to the Little Man in time, much as it does to Gilbert's
Rosencrantz (who finally gets Hamlet out of the way in order to claim the
hand of his childhood sweetheart, Ophelia). Shown what woman is rather
more vividly by Ophelia's appearance in a comically rather than neurotic-
ally hysterical version of the nunnery scene, the Little Man leaves the stage
in order to take an ostensibly protective interest in her after hearing a
revised version of 'There is a willow grows aslant a brook' to the effect that
Hamlet has drowned her in order to avoid marriage. At the end of the
play, after all the other characters in *Hamlet* are nominally dead too, the
Little Man and she run across the stage in a flurry of confetti, carrying
suitcases labelled 'Just Married'. This unexpectedly happy ending would
mercifully be echoed by the one that awaited Piper himself a little over a
year later. Reunited after the war's end with the girlfriend he had not seen
since 1940, he immediately married her, and it would be she who
eventually published a memoir of his captivity (which he composed in
1965, drawing on his Yasumi journals) after his death in 1990.[119]
   Both the question of what woman is and the question of what
Shakespeare is haunt all of these examples of prisoner-of-war performance. The social situation constituted by theatres in which all-male casts of
prisoners played to audiences consisting not only of fellow prisoners but
of captors is perhaps the most extreme of those in which Shakespeare's
plays have been acted outside the professional theatre over the last four
centuries. In these circumstances, servicemen could be transformed by the
sheer collective willpower of their colleagues into tragic and comic heroines, while the playwright himself might be construed either as a figure
for patriotic celebration, as an international icon of high culture equally
available to Allies and to Axis, or as a slightly burdensome, highbrow
Immortal Bawd best subjected to lowbrow officer-class burlesque. It is
one of the stranger aspects of the post-war Shakespearean theatre that the
all-male casting cruelly enforced on these resourceful, determined and
unfortunate prisoners-of-war – their productions conditioned not by
domesticity, but by a yearning for it – has in our time been seen less in

the military theatre than in the professional. Here, amazingly, whole troupes such as Propeller have voluntarily gone without onstage women, and whole paying, non-captive audiences have been prepared to accept professional equivalents of Iver Borton in Shakespeare's female roles.

In the amateur Shakespearean theatre, meanwhile, although female-to-male cross-gender casting has been quite common for small roles where the demographics of available casts have not corresponded with those of Shakespeare's cast lists, the all-male tradition of the Victorian officers' mess forcibly revived in the Oflags and Stalags has disappeared. The questions of national identity which shaped expatriate performances by military personnel, colonists and diplomats alike down to 1945, however, remain centrally important to the ways in which Shakespeare's plays are now produced non-professionally within Britain itself. If Shakespeare's audiences at Hohenfels and Eichstätt were problematically composed of Anglophone prisoners, non-Anglophone captors and non-Anglophone locals, typical audiences for the mode of amateur Shakespeare which has been most conspicuous in post-war Britain have been composed, albeit to rather blander and more relaxed effect, of locals, domestic holidaymakers and foreign tourists. As my next chapter will show, the international, national and class status of Shakespeare's plays are still being negotiated against one another, even in the outdoor theatres in which amateur Shakespeare is increasingly felt to belong.

CHAPTER 4

Shakespeare in the open: outdoor performance

QUINCE Pat, pat; and here's a marvellous convenient place for our rehearsal. This green plot shall be our stage, this hawthorn brake our tiring-house ...

(*A Midsummer Night's Dream*, 3.1.2–4)

It would not be fair to say that the collective idealism which filled Britain with amateur dramatic societies in the 1920s and 1930s and sustained such enterprises as the National Theatre of Hohenfels in the early 1940s has completely dissipated since the end of the Second World War. It might be accurate, however, to suggest that it has found different channels of expression, and that these have often by-passed the non-professional stage. Since the passage of the National Theatre Act in 1949, the establishment of the Royal Shakespeare Company in 1960 and the belated inauguration of the National Theatre Company at the Old Vic in 1963, amateur societies and specialist clubs have no longer had a near-monopoly on the performance of plays which could not be guaranteed a commercially viable run in the West End, especially those of Shakespeare. The post-war expansion of universities (some with new-fangled drama departments, such as the country's first, at Bristol, founded in 1946) provided an outlet for much young talent which might otherwise have gone into local amateur groups, while the establishment of the Fringe alongside the first Edinburgh Festival in 1947 offered a new forum for avant-garde theatre on the borderline between student drama and the profession. From being the home of emergent theatre before the war, amateur drama has been more commonly regarded since as the last refuge of the residual. However accurate the perception may be, the non-professional stage is now usually seen as a place where the middle-aged can still go to perform and to see the sorts of minor plays and the styles of revivals of classics that are now felt to be too dated and too tame for either the West End or the subsidized companies.

Figure 17. What one local newspaper described as 'Shakespeare – 1970 style!': *The Merchant of Venice*, Bolton Little Theatre, 1970. Allan Sharples (Lorenzo), Frances Clemmitt (Jessica), Robin Alexander (Bassanio) and Ann Mathieson (Portia).

While this chapter will be setting out to correct or at very least qualify this impression, it is true that most of the amateur societies founded before 1939 have produced much less Shakespeare since the establishment of the RSC and the National. At the same time, their Shakespeare has tended to look more old-fashioned than that of the contemporary professional stage. The excellent Bolton Little Theatre, for instance, where Sir Ian McKellen (now its patron) performed as a schoolboy, was well ahead of many of its amateur peers when it staged its first modern-dress production of Shakespeare, *The Merchant of Venice* (Figure 17). But this event only took place in 1970, almost fifty years after Barry Jackson had first initiated the trend at the Birmingham Repertory; and by then the position of Shakespeare within the Bolton repertory, however his plays were costumed, was beginning to look precarious. A decade later the society had dropped his work entirely as part of a steady and ineluctable movement down-market. 'While [Mike Harding's] *Fur Coat and No Knickers* (1983) played to nearly 100% capacity,' wrote Michael Shipley in 2006, '[Ibsen's] *The Lady from the Sea* (1983) was a total box office disaster,' and he went on to lament the fact that the society had performed no Shakespeare at all since their last *A Midsummer Night's Dream* in 1979.[1] This was not quite true: in their 2002–3 season, relapsing into an earlier tradition of staging Shakespeare only in light-hearted excerpts and spin-offs, they had produced Christopher Luscombe's *The Shakespeare Revue*,[2] but when they played *A Midsummer Night's Dream* again in 2009 it was their first attempt at a full-length Shakespeare play for thirty years.[3] A comparable malaise afflicted even the artistically ambitious Questors in Ealing, who in the post-war period also revived a Victorian drawing-room tradition of dealing with Shakespeare without embarrassing serious-ness. Although this society continues to perform a full-length Shakespeare play in most seasons, they have also, since the success of their member Michael Green's *The Art of Coarse Acting: or, How to Destroy an Amateur Dramatic Society* in 1964, indulged a vein of cosy self-parody. Under Green's direction, from 1970 onwards the society took to staging comic instances of bad acting and stagecraft, some of them in the form of Shakespearean parodies (heavily indebted to the sketch 'So That's The Way You Like It' in *Beyond the Fringe* and the burlesque tradition that lies behind it), under titles such as *All's Well That Ends As You Like It* and *Henry the Tenth, Part Seven*.[4] Elsewhere too, amateur Shakespeare seemed to have ceased to matter by comparison with what was happening in the professional theatre. When in 1972 a former member of Nugent Monck's company at the Maddermarket, the dentist K. Edmonds Gateley, achieved the feat of becoming the first person ever to have acted in, directed and designed sets for the entire Shakespeare canon, with his own amateur company, the Southsea Shakespeare Actors, he may have been rewarded with an MBE, but he missed out on the sort of accolades about his lasting influence on the classical theatre that had been showered on Monck on his completion of a similar feat forty years earlier.[5]

It would nonetheless be misleading to describe the post-war period as one of unmitigated decline in amateur Shakespeare in Britain. Conven-tional Little Theatre productions, it is true, may have fallen in number since the 1930s, but a different mode of Shakespearean performance has grown exponentially in popularity. While indoor amateur stages are now more often associated with Agatha Christie or Alan Ayckbourn than with anything Elizabethan, there remain other venues, many of them inaugurated since 1945, which are associated almost entirely with the performance of Shakespeare: places like Brownsea Island in Poole Harbour, in Dorset, home of the Brownsea Open-Air Theatre (established in 1964), or the grounds of Tolethorpe Hall in Rutland, home of the Stamford Shakespeare Festival (established in 1968). Physically, these venues have less in common with the theatres described in my previous chapters than with the green plot where Quince and his fellows rehearse in *A Midsummer Night's Dream*. So far from disappearing since the war, amateur Shakespeare has come spectacularly out into the open.

For many performers and spectators, indeed, outdoor performance and Shakespeare are now practically synonymous, whether the actors involved are amateur or professional, and this overwhelming movement towards open-air performance is one in which the non-professionals have often led the way. However counter-intuitively, given the vagaries of the British climate, this vogue for outdoor Shakespeare continues to intensify: even after a succession of disastrously wet summers from 2007 onwards, from June to August it is still practically impossible to be more than twenty miles from an open-air Shakespearean venue in mainland Britain without fleeing to the moorlands of Scotland. The theatrical organizations involved range from large professional set-ups like the New Shakespeare Company, based at the Open-Air Theatre in Regent's Park in London (described by its former artistic director and historian as 'the national theatre of the open air'),[6] down to amateur groups as small as The Villagers, near Gosport in Hampshire (who describe themselves on their website as 'a group of friends who accidentally put on a Shakespeare play every July').[7] Some places receive only a visit of a night or a week from one of a number of restlessly vigorous small professional touring companies, such as Illyria or Chapterhouse, both of whom specialize in performing in the grounds of country houses and castles.[8] Others are the sites of entire summer seasons of outdoor amateur Shakespeare, such as the Stamford festival, and some of these can even spread across a number of venues, as in the case of the Cambridge Shakespeare Festival.[9] It is likely, in fact, that even if one counts in the activities of the RSC the total number of performances of Shakespeare given outdoors in England every year now exceeds the number given indoors. This penultimate chapter will examine the phenomenon of outdoor Shakespeare, charting its long and under-explored history, and considering why this potentially uncomfortable form of entertainment should be the principal way in which theatre audiences in Britain still want their amateur Shakespeare. Taking outdoor Shakespeare seriously, I will argue, can transform the received narrative of how the amateur performance of his plays has dwindled into insignificance over the last half-century: as places in which Shakespeare means, the open-air theatres that have been proliferating since the early twentieth century are now as powerful and important as any of the indoor, subsidized playhouses. Before charting their neglected past and present, however, it may be helpful to look more closely at a single case-history in how and why indoor Shakespeare came to be overtaken artistically in the post-war years, that of one of the societies whose foundation in the boom years was noted in Chapter 2, the Middlesbrough Little Theatre.

STAYING INDOORS

The Middlesbrough Little Theatre, which was founded in 1930 and which remained active throughout the war, entered the post-war period with renewed commitment and optimism,[10] and to fanfares of national publicity. In the midst of rationing and austerity, this society, which had hitherto performed in rented church halls, boldly set out to raise funds with which to acquire its own auditorium. This new home, moreover, was to be no mere converted warehouse or deconsecrated chapel but a purpose-built, architect-designed, up-to-the-minute modern playhouse, embodying the highest ideals of the amateur movement. In a series of programme notes issued during its immediate post-war seasons, the Middlesbrough Little Theatre recalled its original mission and articulated a proud vision for the future. The organization had come into being, recalled an essay in the programme for *Our Town*, after the conversion of the old Middlesbrough opera house into a Gaumont cinema had deprived Teesside of its last venue for serious live theatre, an event which had moved the actress Leah Bateman, a member of Charles Macdona's Shavian touring company, to a ringing exhortation:

Keep the legitimate stage alive in your town by every means in your power. The stage is not yet dead, it is temporarily submerged by a wave of celluloid from the west. With the help of good, well-managed amateur societies the torch can be kept burning until such time as the theatre will once more take its rightful place in a society of thinking people.[11]

The good, well-managed society that had been keeping the torch burning ever since now longed to do so in a temple worthy of its highest aspirations. An essay headed 'Our toil shall strive to mend' in the programme for the society's 1946 production of *Romeo and Juliet* zealously outlined the nature and purpose of the proposed new building:

The theatre ideal has a very definite relation to theatre architecture: and we cannot insist too strongly upon the necessity of a noble building in which to present our plays ... There must be in it the dignity which breeds solemnity – that dignity which heretofore has been reserved almost exclusively for the church.

As for the size of this noble auditorium,

The house seating two thousand or more people is going out of fashion, because its dimensions are such that the intimacy demanded by the new ideal is impossible. On the other hand, there is a tendency on the part of some to make their auditoriums too small, even where space and expense do not dictate a limit.

Instead the essay envisages a main house seating some 700 or 800, complemented by a much smaller space with flexible seating, 'for very intimate plays and for experiments'. This utopian playhouse would have to be designed by someone already experienced in contemporary theatre design and the latest innovations in lighting and backstage technology, since 'reform in stagecraft has been developing so rapidly that only those working continually in the more progressive theatres know which of the new inventions are practical'. The architect's overall brief, however, in accordance with the society's ambition to offer both intellectual stimulation and physical comfort to every stratum of Teesside society, would be clear:

Our theatre must be democratic: it will offer a complete and satisfying view of the stage from every seat: the auditorium shall be of the simple fan-shaped form adopted by the more progressive architects: the rows shall be well spaced and the seats deeply cushioned in every part of the house.[12]

While this ambitious project was being put into effect, the Middlesbrough Little Theatre reached another milestone, its 100th production, and it did so in the year of the Festival of Britain, 1951. Determined that its continuing if now finite tenancy of the St John's Hall on Marton Road should not inhibit either its artistic ambitions or its commitment to the works of the national playwright, the MLT decided to stage *Hamlet*. Between helping to manage the onerous financial affairs of the new building project, a local accountant, John Berriman (who twenty-one years earlier had acted in the MLT's first ever production), appeared as the Ghost; Lennard Douglas of the Halifax Building Society, another veteran with twenty years' experience in the society, played Hamlet; and the role of Ophelia was played by a newcomer, a sixteen-year-old Yarm grammar-school girl called Wendy Craig (Figures 18, 19). The production is documented by an entire souvenir edition

'Whither wilt
thou lead
me?'

Hamlet's first encounter
with the ghost of his
father (John Berriman)

'And will a' not come again?'

Ophelia, driven insane by the stresses in which she becomes involved, mourns the death
of her father, Polonius, in mad snatches of song.

Figure 18. *Hamlet*, Middlesbrough Little Theatre, 1951. Hamlet (Lennard Douglas) and
the Ghost (John Berriman). *North-Eastern Weekly News*, 27 April 1951.

Figure 19. *Hamlet*, Middlesbrough Little Theatre, 1951. Ophelia (Wendy Craig).

of the *North-Eastern Weekly News* (27 April 1951), which makes it clear that, however progressive the society aspired to be in its architecture, it wanted as little innovation as possible when it came to playing Shakespeare. The director, Lawrence Hayes, would not be drawn, for instance, on the question of whether his production was informed by particular ideas. 'Producing "Hamlet" as with any other play is essentially a practical job of work,' he told the *North-Eastern Weekly News*. 'The setting, costumes and wigs, and properties, require considerable organization.' A supportive local theatre critic, Terence Feely, is very much on his side, preferring the pragmatism of the amateur stage to the gimmickry of its professional counterpart. 'Each generation, they say, gets the "Hamlet" it deserves, but one wonders what this one has done to deserve some of the "Hamlets" it has been given of recent years . . .' He goes on to write off modern literary criticism entirely ('One can read anything into Shakespeare if one studies him in sufficient isolation for the right length of time'), and then dismisses a long succession of well-regarded theatrical interpretations of *Hamlet* from Henry Irving to his own time, finishing with Michael Benthall's 1948 Stratford production, in which Paul Scofield and Robert Helpmann alternated in the title role. To Feely, this show had merely exemplified the sort of self-indulgent questing after novelty and self-display characteristic of the theatrical profession in general, and the only professional *Hamlet* he admits to admiring at all is the one by which Hayes' interpretation, as the photographs attest, was most obviously influenced: 'Perhaps Olivier's film Hamlet came nearest to a Prince of Denmark who was not simply a 20th century neurotic actor.' Feely concludes, tellingly, by praising the amateur stage not as the cutting-edge of experimental Shakespeare but as the last refuge of safe Shakespearean tradition, a space where actorly imagination is properly curtailed:

In a society like the Little Theatre however one is more likely to get an objective interpretation than on the professional stage. Amateurs must submit themselves more to the surgeon's knife of the producer: they are not so intent on personal propaganda: they are nearer to everyday life than those in the professional theatrical hothouse. They are more likely to produce a 'Hamlet' which will keep Shakespeare static in his grave although critics may whirl like dervishes.

Despite this production's evident conservatism, the programme for the 1951 *Hamlet* came complete with an encouraging letter from the Middlesbrough Little Theatre's honorary president, someone whose own career as an actor and director had already been marked by some radical changes of direction: Tyrone Guthrie. Just two years before another such change – his acceptance of the founding artistic directorship of the Stratford Shakespeare Festival in

Ontario – Guthrie praises the society's taste, ambition and catholicity. To him, these are all embodied in their choice of *Hamlet*, 'one of the great masterpieces of expression of the human spirit', as MLT's 100th production, an achievement which in itself speaks volumes for their 'dogged persistence – a quality, incidentally, which must not be underestimated'.

Notwithstanding his support for the Middlesbrough amateurs, however, Guthrie was about to render their new auditorium obsolete as a venue for Shakespeare almost before it had opened. The beautifully simple and well-proportioned theatre which the architects Elder and Pierro designed for Middlesbrough was in the event not quite as large as the society had at first envisaged – seating 500 rather than 800, and with no adjoining studio space – but more importantly it was (and is) completely end-on in configuration. The seating, on both stalls and circle level, does taper slightly towards the stage in the 'fan-like' configuration the MLT specified, but the building is otherwise perfectly box-shaped. The rows of seats all run parallel to a 26 × 14 feet proscenium arch (the first few can be removed to form an orchestra pit), and although the stage was innovative for its time in boasting a large backstage area into which scenery flats could be run sideways on tracks instead of needing to be hoisted into a fly-tower, the Middlesbrough Little Theatre is in every other respect a textbook example of the 'fourth wall', peepshow theatre appropriate to nineteenth-century realism. It was officially opened in 1957 by Sir John Gielgud, and as the first purpose-built new theatre to open in Britain since the war it attracted considerable attention: Kenneth Tynan wrote about it in the *Observer* (3 November 1957), a publication which had already run an article with a photograph the previous week, and the *Daily Telegraph* reviewed the MLT's first production there too (22 October 1957). Significantly, that production was not of a Shakespeare play but of George Bernard Shaw's *Caesar and Cleopatra*, a specimen of a kind of drama – calling for large, decorative, realistic sets and historical costumes – to which this shape of auditorium is far better suited.

At almost exactly the same moment in 1957 when the MLT was opening its doors, a very different theatre was being inaugurated on the far side of the Atlantic: the auditorium which Guthrie had commissioned from Tanya Moiseiwitsch for the Stratford Festival in Ontario, newly given a permanent shell (by Robert Fairfield) to replace the canvas of its original circus-sized tent. Seating 1,830 people on three sides of a thrust stage (from which no spectator is more than 19.8 metres distant, so as to preserve the intimacy demanded by the new ideal without sacrificing scale), this roofed modernist hybrid between a Greek amphitheatre and an Elizabethan public playhouse could not be more unlike the theatre to which Guthrie stood as absentee godfather in Middlesbrough. It was this building more than any other which would set the dominant style for post-war Shakespearean production, at a stroke rendering the MLT's proscenium quaintly archaic. Guthrie's thrust-stage amphitheatre would be imitated by most of the venues purpose-built with Shakespeare in mind across Britain over the next forty years and more: the Chichester Festival Theatre (1962), the Crucible in Sheffield (1971), the Olivier auditorium of the National (1976), the main house at the Barbican (1982), the Courtyard in Stratford (2006) and the remodelled Royal Shakespeare Theatre interior for which the Courtyard provided the working model (2011). In terms of Shakespearean production, the Little Theatres, meanwhile, appeared to have been sidelined: as far as the trend towards open-stage, concept-driven productions was concerned, which John Styan influentially traced in his major study *The Shakespeare Revolution* in 1977, the revolution seemed to have started without them.[13] Thus overtaken by the subsidized sector, the Middlesbrough Little Theatre eventually joined it. Although it remains the home venue of the amateur dramatic society still known as the Middlesbrough Little Theatre, which continues to stage productions of a very high standard, the building itself was taken into public ownership in 1974, and it is now simply Teesside's chief municipal venue for touring theatre and musicals, rechristened in 1996 as the Middlesbrough Theatre.[14] At a 2007 gala performance to mark the fiftieth anniversary of the building's opening, Shakespeare was represented solely by the playing of two recordings, an audio tape of Sidney Giles reciting the first chorus from *Henry V* at an MLT performance in 1959, and a video of Sir John Gielgud reciting the epilogue to *The Tempest* from Peter Greenaway's film *Prospero's Books*. The wave of celluloid, evidently, had yet to recede.

GOING OUTSIDE

This account of how the evolution of the post-war professional Shakespearean stage left the amateurs wholly behind, however, leaves out two very different venues which pre-date Guthrie's open-stage experiment in Ontario by decades. One is the tiny Maddermarket in Norwich, described in Chapter 3, which, with a professional director but amateur actors, had provided Guthrie with his first experience of watching Shakespeare performed on a thrust stage without interruptions for changing scenery. The other is an amphitheatre on a similar scale to Moiseiwitsch's tent, and similarly purpose-built for the performance of Shakespeare, which had already been drawing capacity crowds for twenty years before Guthrie went to Canada; a theatre which not only boasted amateur actors but an amateur architect,

Shakespeare in the open

Figure 20. The auditorium at Minack, *c.* 1933.

builder and manager too. Its non-professional status is doubtless a prime reason why it has been substantially left out of the history of twentieth-century theatre design to date, but the other reason is structural: unlike the Stratford Festival Theatre, or the Guthrie in Minneapolis, or the Olivier in London, it has no roof. Despite this potential disadvantage, it continues to offer an immensely popular seventeen-week season every summer, consisting primarily of amateur Shakespearean productions rehearsed elsewhere. It is situated at the extreme south-westerly tip of the English mainland: it is, of course, the very shrine of British non-professional Shakespeare, the Minack (Figure 20). This theatre is built into a precipitous Cornish cliffside close to Land's End: it boasts the Atlantic itself as a backdrop, and it is aptly and apocalyptically described by one commentator as 'England's first and last theatre'.[15] Its founder, Rowena Cade, meanwhile, is depicted by the theatre's official mythology (in characteristically English fashion) as a pragmatic amateur who simply made the whole project up as she went along without any ideas being involved at all.

The notion that the Minack is simply the expression of one isolated woman's eccentricity, however, will not survive an examination of this theatre's place in the longer histories of outdoor Shakespeare and of twentieth-century outdoor performance more widely. Over the half-century leading up to its inauguration in 1932, a fashion for hosting charity garden parties featuring Shakespearean performances, an academic interest in staging Greek tragedy under something approximating to its original conditions of performance, the immense popularity of outdoor historical pageants and the energetic promulgation of open-air Shakespeare by touring actor-managers together provide a context in which the Minack – for all its wild impracticality and the sheer improbability of its setting – looks almost mainstream. Indeed, the neo-classical auditorium on the cliff at Porthcurno belongs within a longer cultural history still, since the post-Renaissance return to the open-air performance of Shakespeare of which the Minack is the most conspicuous expression had its first stirrings (as with so much else in the modern reception of the plays) with David Garrick. At the climax of the Jubilee in Stratford-on-Avon in August 1769, Garrick had intended to bring Shakespeare's imaginary characters onto the streets of Shakespeare's real home town: but his culminating pageant, a procession of Drury Lane actors presenting mobile *tableaux vivants* from the plays, was in the event cancelled due to torrential rain. This event, or non-event, is nowadays mainly remembered, if at all, in the context of Enlightenment Bardolatry and Stratford tourism.[16] But Garrick's impulse to take Shakespeare's characters outside into the fresh English air, to identify the works of the newly crowned national poet with the rural heartland of his country, is an impulse which for the last century and more has haunted the British performance history of the canon to a vast and hitherto unacknowledged extent. Outdoor Shakespeare is now a phenomenon which traverses the categories of professional and amateur, and it always has done: the histories of commercial and non-professional open-air production are inextricably bound together, and any account of the Minack and its successors which fails to discuss the activities of, for example, Ben Greet and the open-air theatre in Regent's Park can only be incomplete. Between them, the socialites, the academics and the showbusiness professionals who pioneered outdoor performance have provided non-professional Shakespeare with the particular niche in modern British culture in which nowadays, rain or shine, it seems most comfortable.

PRIVATE THEATRICALS 'AL FRESCO'

Among amateur players, outdoor performance has been associated both with the aristocratic, single-class traditions of private theatricals and the more democratic model of voluntary theatre offered by the civic amateur dramatic society. After Garrick's Jubilee procession, the most striking anticipation of the twentieth-century vogue for outdoor Shakespeare belongs very much to the aristocratic camp, namely the fictitious production of *A Midsummer Night's Dream* arranged by Lady Penelope Penfeather in the grounds of Shaw's Castle in Sir Walter Scott's novel *St Ronan's Well* (1823). This was Scott's only novel to be set in the present day, and characteristically for a performance of Shakespeare by the gentry in the 1820s the *Dream* it depicts is abbreviated to a series of wordless tableaux.[17] The real-life production which would finally initiate the Shakespearean theatre's rediscovery of the great outdoors sixty years later was more interested in the self-consciously artistic and avant-garde than it was in achieving social cachet, but in its mode of funding it was nonetheless another specimen of élite private theatricals: the *As You Like It* staged in woodlands at Coombe Warren in Surrey in the summer of 1884, and repeated in 1885.

   This was the first effort by a group called the Pastoral Players, who were essentially the theatre club of the Aesthetic Movement. Their *As You Like It* was entirely supported by aristocratic patronage, its audience including the Prince of Wales himself, and though many of the cast were hired professionals, the role of Orlando was played by the Aesthetic hostess Lady Archibald Campbell. (Hence surviving photographs of the love scenes slightly resemble those of Florizel and Perdita in the Stockport Garrick's *Winter's Tale* twenty years later.)[18] Like the Kilkenny Theatrical Society, the Pastoral Players aspired to perform Shakespeare with a level of refinement beyond that to be expected from any vulgar public playhouse; one of their moving spirits was Oscar Wilde, who described the costume worn by Phoebe as 'a sort of panegyric on a pansy'.[19] This comment's emphasis on the look and dress of the production is appropriate, since its prime *raison d'être* was the temporary emancipation of its designer, E. W. Godwin, from the tinselly constraints of the West End. Godwin enjoyed absolute artistic control over every detail of the play's mise-en-scène, to an extent impossible in the commercial theatre of the time, and, while professional theatre critics commented approvingly on the production's realism, the Aesthetes themselves waxed lyrical about the exquisite and complete coordination of its colour scheme.[20] Artistic breakthrough or not, this production was soon imitated by the Lady Penelope Penfeathers of the time, who recognized in outdoor Shakespeare an attractive mode of staging their own status as hosts, cultural patrons and social benefactors at the same time as showing off their own grounds. In the middle of Poole Harbour in Dorset a decade later, for example, one group of well-bred non-professionals were content with making *As You Like It* if not aesthetically cutting-edge then at least audible, in a context of generalized Elizabethanism:

Through the kindness of Captain and Mrs Kenneth Balfour, their beautiful home, [the Castle] on Brownsea Island, was thrown open to the public on the afternoon of August 8th. Nothing could have been more enjoyable than to witness, on such an enchanted spot, revels and dances of the olden times, and to see *As You Like It* played by a charming band of actors and actresses. The rain kept off, and steamboats were kept busy between the mainland and the island from one till past eight o'clock, bringing crowds to witness the play, the dances, and the sports. Lord and Lady Wimborne brought a large party, and the county was well represented. The audience received the characters very cordially. Without being invidious, it is fair to notice Rosalind (Miss Eva Fairfax) and Orlando (the Honourable Frederick Guest), who rendered their long and difficult parts with great spirit, speaking clearly – no easy task in the open air with a strong wind blowing. It is hoped that a substantial sum will be realised for the Cornelia Hospital in Poole, in aid of which the entertainment was got up.

Like the Pastoral Players' production, this *As You Like It* too was mounted with professional assistance, though admittedly the director involved was less well connected than E. W. Godwin: 'Mr H. Nash, of the Bournemouth Theatre, gave his services most kindly, helping to select a suitable spot for the performance, and coming over to make the final arrangements and superintend the play.'[21]

SHAKESPEARE AMONG THE GREEKS

If outdoor Shakespeare at first took root at the end of the nineteenth century in private soil – among those who owned sufficiently large pieces of land on which to host full-scale theatrical performances – then it was sustained by something equally élitist, the interest in performing Greek tragedy fostered at late nineteenth-century universities and private schools. The fact that the Pastoral Players' *As You Like It*, a landmark in the emergence of the modern director, took place outdoors was partly dictated by a painterly preference for seeing colours by natural light, but it also chimed happily with Godwin's intellectual commitment to the ancient theatre and indeed the classical past more generally. As well as providing lavish Alma-Tadema-style designs for West End plays on classical themes (such as John Todhunter's *Helena in Troas*, for which he built an imitation Greek auditorium inside Hengler's Circus in 1886), he published extensive essays on classical dress, including a whole series on the costumes that ought to be used in productions of those Shakespeare plays with ancient Greek settings, such as *Troilus and Cressida* and

A Midsummer Night's Dream.[22] Godwin's twin interests, in a single artist's complete control of the theatrical event and in ancient drama, would become more visibly central to theatrical modernism in the next generation, most obviously in the work of his illegitimate son by Ellen Terry, Edward Gordon Craig, whose 1911 manifesto for a drama school (in *The Art of the Theatre: Second Dialogue*) would famously demand both masks and 'two theatres, one open-air, one indoors'.[23] But meanwhile a neo-classical revival of unroofed theatre was in the air already. It isn't merely coincidental that the revival of English outdoor theatre should have taken place during the heroic age of classical archaeology, from Schliemann's work at Hissarlik (Troy) (1871–90) to Arthur Evans' at Knossos (1899–1935). The pursuit of reforms to the classics syllabi at Oxford and Cambridge, downplaying philology in favour of a broader attempt to reconstruct ancient cultures, had finally persuaded the university authorities to relax a Victorian ban on student performances, and in 1880 English undergraduate drama had its rebirth, in the form of an all-male production of Euripides' *Agamemnon* at Balliol College, Oxford, in the original Greek, starring a young Frank Benson as Clytemnestra. Three years later, Girton College, Cambridge, staged an all-female production of Sophocles' *Electra*, and in 1887 the newly established Oxford University Dramatic Society staged a lavish *Alcestis*, for which they simply bought the leftover auditorium, set and costumes which Godwin had designed for Todhunter's *Helena in Troas* the previous year. The fact that the founding charter of the Oxford University Dramatic Society restricted its members to producing either classical drama or Shakespeare would have a lasting influence on the converging ways in which both were produced in the open air over the coming years.[24]

It was abundantly clear from the outset that any private school interested in continuing to produce Oxford and Cambridge classicists needed to stay abreast of all this: Eton, Harrow and Winchester, for example, all paid for visiting performances of the 1880 *Agamemnon*, and in 1882 the headmaster of Bradfield College in Berkshire, Herbert Branston Gray, invited Benson to stage an *Alcestis* there.[25] All these shows took place indoors, but Gray, supported by an energetic young classics master called Lepper, was determined to give Bradfield a pre-eminence in educational revivals of Greek drama which it has never lost. Armed with the measurements of the auditorium at Epidauros, Lepper set teams of schoolboys to work with shovels in an abandoned chalk pit in the school grounds, and they duly proved that clean-limbed sons of the Empire could be fit successors to the conquering heroes of antiquity. By 1890 the first purpose-built unroofed theatre to be constructed in England since the Renaissance was complete. An expression, and indeed a product, of the same muscular Hellenism which in 1896 would inform the first modern Olympic Games, this theatre is still in use: it has now been the venue for a triennial performance of a Greek play in the original for a century and a quarter.[26] Other schools and colleges followed suit, and have continued to do so; in Dorset alone Canford built its own Greek theatre during the 1920s, while Bryanston dug theirs to mark the Festival of Britain in 1951. Even as recently as 1964 the designers of the most futuristic educational building of the post-war period, the all-new St Catherine's College in Oxford, felt obliged to include a small Greek theatre in its grounds. As a result of the interest in outdoor Shakespeare which has largely overtaken the classicism which at first inspired them, each of these damp and unlikely venues has been used as a stage for Shakespeare almost as often as for Sophocles or Euripides. In the same tradition, the Saïd Business School building at Oxford, designed by Edward Jones and Sir Jeremy Dixon and opened in 2001, has an amphitheatre on its roof, which so far has been used almost entirely for summer performances of Shakespeare.

SHAKESPEARE AS PAGEANT

If the late nineteenth-century revival of live classical drama provided one precondition for the emergence of outdoor Shakespeare, assuring that many of the privately educated would emerge into adulthood after character-forming and potentially habit-forming experiences of sitting on damp terraces watching their peers recite poetry in togas, from the 1900s onwards a very different form of open-air performance was equally important to the popularization of outdoor playing, especially among amateurs. By contrast to the activities of the Pastoral Players or the students of Bradfield, this was a form committed, like the civic amateur dramatic societies founded at the same time, to the participation of all classes in the national culture, and like them it was profoundly engaged with Shakespeare as both a symbol and an expression of that culture. One other school to take an interest in the educational performance of Greek tragedy was Sherborne, also in Dorset, and it was here in 1905 that a music master, composer and playwright called Louis Napoleon Parker would invent a kind of modern drama which still haunts the consciousness of outdoor Shakespeare: the historical pageant.[27] Nominally celebrating the 1,200th anniversary of the founding of Sherborne Abbey, Parker's first pageant deployed poetry, costumed processions, music and episodes dramatizing key events in local history from the ancient Britons to the Tudors, all in the service of a bustling, colourful vision of local identity across the centuries. Among much else, Parker was one of the leading English disciples of Richard Wagner, and communal theatrical spectacles like this one, which he spent much of the remainder of his career devising, share something of Wagner's grandiose dream of a total theatre capable of embodying the consciousness of a people. However, if they were Wagnerian in scale (and sometimes in details too – at the conclusion of the Sherborne pageant, for example, all the participants assembled to the strains of the march from *Tannhauser* and shouted 'Hail!' in unison), the pageants which flourished from 1905 down to the late 1930s were also pervasively Shakespearean, both formally and in their incidentals.

Too big to be staged indoors, even were the proud contemplation of their historic venues not half of their point, these events accustomed enormous numbers of people right across the country to sitting in outdoor grandstands watching their fellow citizens wearing historical fancy dress. The Sherborne pageant of 1905 was mounted among the ruins of the town's Norman castle by a cast of almost 900 local volunteers, with all the profits from its 2,000 ticket sales per show donated to local charities.[28] Attracting extensive national press coverage, it immediately caught the public imagination. Parker was promptly commissioned to devise another such show to be performed at Warwick Castle the following summer, this one employing a cast of 2,000 and seating 5,000 spectators per show, and his ensuing Dover pageant of 1908 was on a similar scale.[29] By the end of 1909 Parker had also produced pageants for Bury St Edmunds, Colchester and York. Liverpool, Potter Heigham, Oxford and St Albans, among many smaller towns, staged their own in 1907; Chelsea, Cheltenham, Winchester and Pevensey theirs in 1908.[30] During the ensuing few years the vogue spread to ever further reaches of the kingdom. On 10–13 August 1910, for instance, a pageant mainly scripted by one Gilbert Hudson was staged 'in the historic ruins of Pickering Castle' in North Yorkshire, in what the published script-cum-programme makes clear was a concerted bid to attract more visitors to this little-known market town.[31] Such pageants continued to be staged down to the outbreak of the Second World War: E. M. Forster scripted two, *Abinger Pageant* (1934) and *England's Pleasant Land* (1938), which would provide part of the inspiration for the Poyntz Hall pageant at the heart of Virginia Woolf's novel *Between the Acts* (1941).[32]

In essence, as Roger Simpson has observed, the pageant as created by Parker is 'a chronicle play in which a social body rather than an individual is the hero'.[33] As such it is heavily indebted to Shakespeare's histories, which are consciously invoked as a precedent, for example, in Frank Lascelles' prefatory note to the published text of the Oxford pageant of 1907: 'a modern Pageant, like a historical play of Shakespeare, is often compelled, by reasons of space, time, and suitability for representation, to foreshorten history'.[34] However pageants may have foreshortened history within their individual episodes, though, they extended the chronological reach of the Shakespearean history play to something getting back towards that of the medieval mysteries, which had covered the entire story of the universe from the Creation to the Last Judgement. The ten episodes of the Warwick pageant, for instance, cover 2,000 years instead of the mere ninety or so dramatized in Shakespeare's two tetralogies. The pageant narrows Shakespeare's scope geographically, however, dealing not with the tribulations of the English monarchy and its discontents but solely with a single town or city, which, in Mick Wallis' piquant critique of the form, is not so much revealed as the locus for real historical conflict and change as simply transformed into 'a monument to itself'.[35] It is transformed, too, into an advertisement for itself: these events were designed not only for the performance of local history by the locals to the locals, but for attracting the attention of paying spectators from further afield too. The organizers of the Sherborne pageant, for instance, deliberately established contact with the citizens of Sherborn, Massachusetts, and their emulators were advised that 'The interest in pageants is particularly great in America, and it is well worth advertising in the American shipping lines.'[36] The Pickering pageant of 1910 was less optimistic about the reach of its appeal, but the White Swan Hotel advertised special rates for 'Pageant Week', and its proprietors assured potential out-of-town visitors to the event that 'Carriages meet all Trains to convey Visitors to the Grounds at reasonable charges.'[37]

By their very nature, pageants necessarily involved the recruitment, drilling and dressing of enormous amateur casts drawn – in a conscious emulation of the medieval tradition by which different guilds were responsible for different individual episodes in the mystery plays – from cooperating local organizations with an investment in asserting the continuing vitality of their community and its social order. These ranged from the local gentry (usually cast as successive generations of their own ancestors) to local primary schools.[38] Mary Kelly of the Village Drama Association, herself the deviser of numerous such events and the author of *How to Make a Pageant* (1936), aptly describes the pattern which tended to result. To her, the conventional pageant represented a combination of sub-Shakespearean historical drama with the miscellaneous exhibitionism of ill-assorted local civic bodies, all held together under a general umbrella of self-aggrandizing patriotism:

The majority of pageants resemble each other as closely as peas. There is the Spirit of the Ages dressed in grey-blue, or Father Time, or some character, who 'narrates' (usually in rather halting blank verse) between the episodes, to explain what they are about. There are the Episodes: The Romans occupying Britain, The Founding of an Abbey, An Olde Englyshe Fayre, The Visit of Good Queen Bess, the Arrival of Charles I on the Eve of a Battle, and so on; ending with a great round-up of Spirits, of Peace, of Harmony, of the District Nursing Association, the Boy Scouts, the Women's Institutes, the British Legion, and a number of other associations, followed by all the performers, all singing 'Land of Hope and Glory'.[39]

Kelly is criticizing the model pioneered by Parker here – she herself dreamed of a more forward-looking, Hegelian dramatic form capable of illustrating 'the gradual growth of the human mind'[40] – but whether supplied with a script by Parker, Kelly, Forster, Frank Lascelles or any of the others who tried their hand at the pageant over the thirty-odd years of its useful life, the essence of the thing, however self-important the separate local organizations involved, was the massed participation of a whole community. Superior to any professionally produced chronicle play indoors, to quote Parker's American disciple Percy Mackaye, pageants constituted 'drama *of* and *by* the people, not merely *for* the people':[41] the reanimation of the local past, on the very spot where it had happened, through collective amateur spectacle.

Framed in pseudo-Shakespearean blank verse, these shows frequently borrowed whole sections of their scripts directly from Shakespeare's histories, constituting some of the largest amateur productions ever staged of particular scenes, indoors or out. Parker cheerfully acknowledges his debts in the published text of the 1906 Warwick pageant, which incorporates Warwick the Kingmaker's change of allegiance during and after his visit to King Louis of France (from *3 Henry VI*, 3.3 and 3.4), here placed as the next scene after a depiction of the arraignment at Warwick of Piers Gaveston (from Marlowe's *Edward II*): 'I wish to express my very particular thanks to the authors of Episodes VI and VII – Kit Marlowe and William Shakespeare.'[42] Gilbert Hudson had to adapt Shakespeare a little more freely than this to persuade him to dramatize Pickering, but fortunately the castle that provided his pageant's backdrop had once confined Richard II, so that the deposed king's local representative was able to recite long stretches of dialogue more usually associated with the Pomfret of 5.5. (In between, on this occasion, the unfortunate Plantagenet was also obliged to endure a local jester, and a choir of Yorkshire maidens who sang him 'Sumer is icumen in'.)[43] The 1919 *Oxford Pageant of Victory* used dialogue from the last scene of *Henry V* to frame a spectacular recreation, imitated from late Victorian stage productions, of the betrothal ceremony of Henry V and Katherine de Valois,[44] while less pacifically the 1930 Army tattoo at Aldershot incorporated passages from earlier in the same play during pageant-style re-enactments of the siege of Harfleur and the battle of Agincourt.[45] A more naval specimen of the genre, Arthur Bryant's 3,000-strong *Greenwich Night Pageant* of 1933, instead borrowed substantially from the last scene of *Henry VIII* for its depiction of the christening of Elizabeth I. The 1939 pageant staged at Kenilworth – with Parker's grandson Anthony in overall charge, but a few episodes in the script contributed by the ageing Louis Napoleon himself – used the castle as the locale for a condensed account of the relationship between Falstaff and Prince Hal drawn from both parts of *Henry IV.*[46]

Even when they did not employ Shakespeare as a scriptwriter, these pageants devoted much of their energy to the evocation of Shakespeare's England, often every bit as full of revels and dances of the olden time as the programme at Brownsea in 1893. As Kelly's account of the customary formula suggests, it is quite rare to find a pageant that does not include an appearance by Elizabeth I: she even arrives on a white horse, played by the usual beardless ensign, in the 1930 Aldershot tattoo, in order to recite her big speech at Tilbury. Many pageants, indeed, dramatize no historical events post-dating her reign (following the example of Parker's original at Sherborne, which ends with Sir Walter Raleigh having his tobacco-pipe extinguished by an alarmed servant the first time he attempts to smoke it at the manor he owned near the town). Their scriptwriters appeared to feel that after the Elizabethan era all of English history was banal and unpicturesque, unfit to be shown in a pageant, or that all questions of national and local identity were settled forever by the defeat of the Spanish Armada in 1588. (The arrival of news of this event provides the grand finale for a number of pageants, including Hudson's at northerly, non-coastal Pickering.) Even Mary Kelly reluctantly conceded that no styles of dress from later than the early seventeenth century showed to advantage out of doors, and she largely restricted her advice on casting to the perennial problem of how to get the right person for 'the familiar Queen Elizabeth scene'.[47]

The Age of Shakespeare which provides such a focus for nostalgia within the pageant as a whole is actually labelled as such within a few by a personal appearance from the playwright. He appears as a promising ten-year-old in Parker's Warwick pageant of 1906 (played by 'a Boy from Stratford'), who inevitably gets introduced to Queen Elizabeth during her visit to the castle; and, still a boy, he is introduced to her once again during her 1575 visit to Kenilworth in Parker junior's pageant of 1939.[48] It is not surprising, given all this Tudor dress, blank verse and borrowed Shakespearean dialogue, that the organizers of some local pageants brought in accredited Shakespearean producers to help stage them. Parker himself cooperated extensively with Herbert Beerbohm Tree, who loaned him lightweight stage armour from his supply at Her Majesty's Theatre for use in pageants in return for advice on mounting processions in his own spectacular productions there (which among supernumerary-crammed revivals of Shakespeare's histories included Parker's own *Drake of England: A Pageant Play*, 1912). Nugent Monck directed and organized a number of pageants in East Anglia from 1910 to 1930, continuing his theatrical attempts to recreate medieval and Renaissance modes of performance by other, outdoor means.[49] In 1924, similarly, the Shakespearean actor-manager Frank Benson collaborated with Frank Lascelles on a *Pageant of Empire*, mounted as part of the British Empire Exhibition, and featuring a poem by Alfred Noyes called 'Shakespeare's Kingdom', set to music by Edward Elgar.

BEN GREET AND REGENT'S PARK

With these immense theatrical events acclimatizing countless amateurs and a few professionals to the outdoor recreation of the spacious days of Queen Elizabeth; with generations of school and university students now used to the idea that unroofed amphitheatres might provide a fit venue for the performance of great drama; and with some patricians already experimenting with hosting Shakespearean performances in the grounds of their stately homes, it only needed a single vigorous propagandist to ensure that the outdoor performance of Shakespeare proper would become a mainstay of the national culture. In fact by the time Louis Napoleon Parker was galvanizing the people of north-west Dorset to don Tudor dress and cry hail to Sherborne, just such a proponent of open-air Shakespeare had already been touring from one green plot to another for almost twenty years: Sir Philip Barling Ben Greet.

Ben Greet was the single most important popularizer of outdoor Shakespeare, and though himself a hard-headed professional he continues to exert an enormous if largely unrecognized influence on the forms of

Shakespearean performance favoured by amateur players and their audiences. As one obituarist put it on his death in 1936, much of Greet's career was devoted to the proposition that 'under the greenwood tree or some semblance of it [Shakespeare's] pastoral plays should be best enjoyed'.[50] Whether or not Greet saw the Aesthetes' *As You Like It* at Coombe in 1884–5, he certainly heard about it and recognized its commercial potential: within a year of the Pastoral Players' final performance of the play, the first batch of Greet's copycat Woodland Players were on the road with their own outdoor *As You Like It*.[51] The amateur and the professional would continue to cross-fertilize one another throughout his career. Greet had a knack for bringing together elements from the avant-garde, academic and even religious stage (he had extensive contacts, for example, at Oberammergau)[52] and making them saleably mainstream. 'Mr Greet occupies a unique position in the dramatic world,' commented one admiring journalist in 1908, implicitly comparing him to his sometime colleague William Poel. 'He is anything but a literary and impractical "crank", but a highly successful actor and director and a man of affairs.'[53] As such commentators also recognized, his productions borrowed extensively from contemporary classicism ('Greet's open-air theatre recalls the Greek,' observed one),[54] not least in the shape of their improvised auditoriums. As one expert remarked when recommending Greet's methods to amateur dramatic societies in 1919,

in purely pastoral locations, the ideal [open-air theatre] is that which most closely approximates to the form of the Greek amphitheatres, a curving hillside with a level playing-space at the bottom and a screen of trees behind the actors.[55]

Where Greet could not find adequate trees in situ, incidentally, he simply filled out the existing vegetation using his own potted shrubs. His productions were Hellenic too in some of their costuming: the Athenian nobles in his many productions of *A Midsummer Night's Dream* always wore antique robes and tunics, just as Godwin would have recommended (even though, as Greet solemnly pointed out, 'The wearing of Greek and Roman draperies is an art and must be very carefully rehearsed').[56] His shows conflated the classical and the Shakespearean in other ways too: prescribing acting style in a note to his edition of *A Midsummer Night's Dream*, Greet makes the unlikely observation that 'This comedy is after the Greek style: repose and limited movement and gesture were always observed.'[57]

But Greet's shows borrowed from native Elizabethanism too, selling the 'authenticity' of seeing Shakespeare performed in the open air.

Sharing the same delight in site-specific re-enactment that informed the Edwardian pageant, he was especially pleased, for example, to be able to perform in the grounds of Wilton House in Wiltshire, rumoured to have been the venue of the première or even the composition of *As You Like It*,[58] where he billed his own production as 'the *second* performance of this play at Wilton'. The Woodland Players' advertisements for their 1887 performances at Barrett's Park in Henley-in-Arden, similarly, excitedly promised '*As You Like It* performed *for the first time* in *Shakespeare's native Forest of Arden*'.[59] Greet collaborated extensively with William Poel during the 1880s and 1890s, notably on the latter's revival of the morality play *Everyman*,[60] and though he was himself no doctrinaire neo-Elizabethan when it came to the shape of his stages or the provenance of his incidental music he did recognize the practical advantages of playing without elaborate and expensive sets. His acting editions of Shakespeare plays list three main ways of mounting them, apparently in descending order of preference: '(a) in the open air, (b) with a simple but artistic setting [in the Elizabethan manner], and (c) with all the pomp and circumstance of the modern public's requirements'.[61] The blocking and business which the editions recommend is described as identically suitable for (a) and for (b) – so that the Woodland Players' productions seem mainly to have offered a more accessible, outdoor version of what Poel's English Stage Society tried to offer in hired halls, a definitely Elizabethan Shakespeare rescued from scenic elaboration.[62] His obituarist took this point too: 'For Ben Greet the play was the thing, not the scenery. In that respect he was one with Shakespeare.'[63] The sense that acting Shakespeare outside provides direct access to the one true original method, indeed, has remained a recurrent motif of open-air producers: in 1934, for example, when the Richmond Shakespeare Society was established specifically to mount Greet-like amateur outdoor performances beside the Thames, an enthusiastic local journalist observed that

> if the society's interpretation of *Much Ado About Nothing* [with special Elizabethan dances] is to be taken as a foretaste of what we may expect in the future, then Richmond will be one of the few places where Shakespeare's works may be seen as they were intended to be seen – and heard.[64]

Throughout the 1880s and 1890s the Woodland Players took what Greet called Shakespeare's 'pastoral plays' (mainly *A Midsummer Night's Dream, As You Like It, Twelfth Night, The Tempest* and *Much Ado About Nothing*) to a variety of hitherto unexploited sylvan venues all over Britain. At first these were mainly Brownsea-like garden parties, for which the company advertised themselves for hire as 'The Latest Novelty and most charming entertainment'.[65] In 1888 alone, for example, they performed at Charlton Park, 'before H.R.H. The Marchioness of Lorne'; at Garrick's Villa at Hampton, 'before H.R.H. The Princess Fredericka'; in the gardens of Lady Frances Bushby's house in Broxbourne; and, 'by kind permission of The Rt. Hon. The Earl of Sandwich', in the grounds of Hinchingbrooke Park, Huntingdon, in aid of the Huntingdon County Hospital, under the patronage of The Earl of Sandwich, the Venerable the Archdeacon of Huntingdon, and the Worshipful the Mayor of Huntingdon.[66] They regularly performed, too, in the gardens of King's College, Cambridge and Worcester College, Oxford, and gave performances at other strongholds of outdoor academic performance such as the grounds of public schools including Rugby. Increasingly, however, their itineraries also included public municipal gardens, in towns such as Cheltenham, Edgbaston, Ipswich, Tonbridge, St Leonard's and Bournemouth. In London they performed in the Grove at Alexandra Palace, and in 1901 they made their first visit to a site then belonging to the Royal Botanical Society inside the Inner Circle in Regent's Park. In that year Greet's actors gave over a hundred outdoor Shakespearean performances, about as many as the English summer could possibly have permitted.[67]

By taking the plays to outdoor venues such as these, Greet was felt to be rescuing the Bard from the seedy taint of the West End, saving him, just as were the Stockport Garrick Society and their colleagues, from the debasement and vulgarity of the conventional commercial stage. As one spectator put it, Greet reclaimed Shakespeare from commercial, urban modernity for the timelessly natural: 'when the play was done and the audience dispersed over the soft grass, with the night sky above, spangled with stars, the lovely evening they had spent was unspoilt at the end by the glare of gaslight and shouts for cabs'.[68] Just as important as Greet's claim to Elizabethan authenticity, in fact, was the Woodland Players' skill at profiting from one of the same widespread attitudes that had enabled the Greek plays to happen at Oxford and Bradfield: a sense that outdoor performances of educationally valuable old plays could be exempted from normal moral prohibitions against live drama. There was something innately healthy about seeing Shakespeare's plays staged on a lawn rather than in surroundings of red plush, something which breathed the same true, invigorating air as amateur sport. What Greet had recognized was that thanks to the recent development of electric lighting[69] (and, in time, electric amplification) he could now offer lucrative evening performances of Shakespeare not only without the expense of hiring an indoor theatre but to audiences who might otherwise have refused to enter one. With anything that might bring a blush to the cheek of the young person discreetly removed from their acting texts, the Woodland Players offered Shakespeare in a form which might even be suitable for children. In fact, if the play was *A Midsummer Night's Dream*, Greet would carefully arrange for local infants to join the cast as supernumerary fairies: ideally, he specified, there should be twenty-four of them (who might between them bring as many as forty-eight parents into the audience).[70] As this practice and his bowdlerization of Shakespeare's scripts may suggest, the Woodland Players, in keeping with Greet's energetic membership of the Church and Stage Guild, deliberately offered Shakespeare as educational, morally safe family entertainment. As a result they were able to convene an enormous and hitherto largely untapped middlebrow audience for live Shakespeare which has continued to support open-air performances ever since. The high moral tone Greet insisted on maintaining with his companies even persuaded some respectable and otherwise untheatrical families to allow their daughters to enter the profession under his tutelage, among them Sybil Thorndyke. 'Study the humanity, the heart, the English of Shakespeare, as of the Bible,' Greet advised such aspirants, apparently convinced that his compatriots included God, 'study them, my young friends, inwardly digest your Bible and outwardly demonstrate your Shakespeare: you will then start in life pretty well equipped.'[71]

Wherever he went, Greet sought out enthusiastic local playgoers and musicians and the organizations, often amateur dramatic societies, to which they belonged. A glimpse of his success in popularizing his methods among this constituency is provided in the shape of a playscript published by his admirer the Reverend S. N. Sedgwick. *With Shakespeare's Fairies*, 'Being an adaptation of "The [sic] Midsummer Night's Dream," specially made for outdoor performance by amateur dramatic societies, village players, women's institutes and others', was first acted by the Bishopstoke Village Players in Hampshire in 1912. Sedgwick too was keen to encourage others to join the outdoor fun: the printed edition of his abbreviation promises that

Copies of the special music, arranged and composed for this play, together with suitable gramophone records for alternative use; a donkey's head, specially made for lightness of wear and audibility of the wearer, and the lion's mask, can be obtained from the author, The Rev. S. N. Sedgwick, c / o The Sheldon Press . . .[72]

In the same year Greet supplemented his own practical example of performing outdoors by publishing his set of pragmatically annotated acting texts of the Shakespeare plays most favoured by the Woodland Players. Entitled, with what may sound a slightly condescending attitude towards his non-professional colleagues, *The Ben Greet Shakespeare for Young Readers and Amateur Players*, this series provides minute advice on acting ('Do not imitate our star actors. Try to be natural, spontaneous, and original'), stage direction ('When the characters enter, the person speaking generally comes second'), deportment ('Don't fidget your hands and feet – forget them, and let them be where the good Lord has placed them'), etiquette ('As a general law do not emphasize the personal pronoun or make any gesture of pointing to yourself or others. It is bad manners, bad grammar, and bad art'), and pronunciation ('Do not imitate some of those professors, especially teachers of what is called Elocution and Expression, if by any chance they happen to pronounce it in up-to-date American or cockney British, or tell you it was conceived in any other brogue, accent, or pronunciation than the purest of pure English').[73] Like earlier, nineteenth-century acting texts of Shakespeare, Greet's editions even supply diagrams prescribing relative positionings for characters at different points in the action (Figures 21, 22). Greet himself seems to solve the plays' logistical problems and direct their rehearsals from the margins. In *As You Like It*, for example, when Orlando expresses surprise that Ganymede should speak in such an un-rustic manner (3.2.331–2), Greet provides some explanatory business by which Celia can enable her temporarily off-balance cousin to produce her next line: '*Rosalind, sitting, is puzzled what to say. Celia whispers to tell her she had an uncle once who possibly was a Bishop.*'[74] In the last act of *A Midsummer Night's Dream* he keeps an especially tight directorial rein on 'Pyramus and Thisbe': '*Note. – The performance of this tragedy is intended by its actors to be serious, the more serious they are the more humorous it becomes for the audience. There should be very little horseplay that is not in keeping with the situation, and hardly any alteration of the text.*'[75] Armed with these editions and an open space sloping down to some trees, it seems, anyone old enough to read could stage Shakespeare. 'I believe if children could see all the plays, and act all the plays written by this wonderful man, William Shakespeare,' he wrote,

there would be more joy in the world and more gratitude for the wonderful gift of books and literature. I have been fortunate enough to see some of his plays acted by quite young folks, and every time have been impressed by the remarkable understanding and grip they have had of the first meanings of his mind and actions.[76]

As Greet's strictures against modern American pronunciation suggest, by the time these editions appeared (in 1912) his tours were crossing North

¹*He begins to dance like an airy spirit; they come from each side.*

²*All kneel.*

³*They all rise and keep bobbing to the music.*

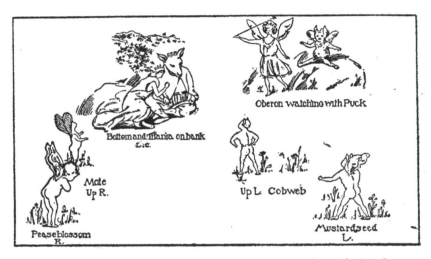

Figure 21. How to stage *A Midsummer Night's Dream*, 4.1: from *The Ben Greet Shakespeare for Young People and Amateur Players: A Midsummer Night's Dream* (New York: Doubleday, 1912).

America as well as Britain. Here he continued to benefit from the educational revival of classical theatre: in 1904, for example, his company played *Hamlet* and *As You Like It* at the new outdoor Greek theatre for which William Randolph Hearst had paid on the campus of the University of California at Berkeley. Here, too, the bracing moral and didactic tone of his publicity continued to attract new audiences to open-air productions of *Everyman* and *A Midsummer Night's Dream*, the latter of which, he claimed, owed its modern popularity to outdoor producers:

Open-air plays have been universally recognized as being at once unique, delightful and educational. They have been given at nearly every university and college in this country as well as in England. Surely a movement which has resulted in the revival of 'A Midsummer Night's Dream', one of the most glorious plays ever written, is worthy of public goodwill and support ...

Position of Characters at Epilogue

Note. The dance can be given after the epilogue, if desirable. It is quite picturesque to dance to the singing instead of to modern instruments

Figure 22. How to stage the epilogue to *As You Like It:* from *The Ben Greet Shakespeare for Young People and Amateur Players: As You Like It* (New York: Doubleday, 1912).

No other play lends itself better for outdoor performance. OUR TRUE INTENT IS ALL FOR YOUR DELIGHT.[77]

I will be returning to the claim that it was outdoor performance which made *A Midsummer Night's Dream* one of Shakespeare's most popular plays in my conclusion; but whether it did or not, it certainly made it the only Shakespeare play to have appeared at one particularly exclusive venue in Washington, DC. One of Greet's official envelopes from the pre-war years, sent from the Woodland Players' Broadway office in 1914 (to the Southwestern Louisiana Industrial Institute, presumably in pursuit of yet another booking on yet another massive transcontinental tour of campuses and parks), proudly records what must nowadays seem the most unlikely of all the venues to which the Woodland Players took their outdoor Shakespeare: the lawn of the White House, where the company performed before President Roosevelt on 14 November 1908 (Figure 23).[78] In North America as in Britain, as well as thus cultivating the acquaintance of powerful people whose gardens had theatrical potential, Greet deliberately sought out amateur actors, musicians and

Figure 23. Business stationery of the Ben Greet Woodland Players, 1914, depicting their performances on the White House lawn, 14 November 1908.

theatrically inclined children,[79] and he exerted lasting influence, some-times in unlikely places. Patty Lee Clark, for example, introducing the text of her whimsical Shakespearean playlet *The Admirable Miranda* in Westfield, Massachusetts in 1905, reported that its cast (of six women and one dog) had produced it 'in the simplicity of the Elizabethan period' so successfully that even those in the audience 'who had not seen Ben Greet's matchless, but simple, production of old time plays, saw after all that "the play was the thing"'.[80] Less obscurely, Greet was equally admired by America's first generation of university teachers of drama, among them Frederick Koch, founder of the Carolina Playmakers (and hence onlie begetter of his protégé Paul Green's Tudor pageant-play *The Lost Colony*, performed annually at Roanoke since 1937).[81] When Koch supplied a list of plays suitable for the groups of 'community players' and 'neighborhood players' which he saw forming 'on every side' in the years immediately following the First World War, he recommended three Shakespeares (*The Merchant of Venice, The Merry Wives of Windsor* and *A Midsummer Night's Dream*), and he particularly specified that performers of *A Midsummer Night's Dream* should use Greet's edition. ('The play is especially suited to out-of-doors. Costumes of Shakespeare's time.')[82] Koch's own Greet-style outdoor productions at Chapel Hill included one *Dream* which literalized Greet's suggestion that even Oberon and Titania should be child-like by casting all the fairies, including their king and queen, as children;[83] these shows are richly documented in the Folger Shakespeare Library and in the pages of a number of theatre studies journals of the inter-war years.[84]

With the outbreak of the First World War, however, Greet returned to England, where he joined Lilian Baylis in the management of the Old Vic. Although his career as a Shakespearean had begun in aristocratic gardens, by now he was visibly committed to a view of Shakespeare as accessible to all classes of Britons, more in keeping with the social ideals of the civic amateur movement than with those of the Pastoral Players. Though he continued to mount North American tours, he spent most of the 1920s running what would now be called the Old Vic's educational outreach department, setting up special matinée performances for schools in cavernous East End music halls.[85] (It was this work which resulted in his knighthood, and in the naming of Greet Street in Southwark.) He spent the last five years of his life, however, back in his signature mode. In 1932 the Royal Botanical Society's lease expired on Greet's favourite patch of Regent's Park, and a younger actor-manager, Robert Atkins, inevitably sought Greet's help when he set out to establish the Open-Air Theatre as a permanent summer venue for the performance of Shakespeare.[86] Quaintly designated 'Master of the Green-sward', Greet was employed as a consultant, a player of minor roles and a speaker of impromptu prologues, presiding genially over what his bio-grapher terms 'the result of the pioneer work to which he had devoted the best part of his life – the presentation of Shakespeare's plays out of doors in natural and neutral surroundings'.[87] The theatre, though now vastly remod-elled and extended, still mainly performs what Greet labelled the 'pastoral plays', with *A Midsummer Night's Dream* in its repertory in two seasons out of every three: and like the Woodland Players the New Shakespeare Com-pany still tend to play to audiences of contented picnickers who rarely see Shakespeare performed anywhere else.

The choice of repertory made by Greet's Woodland Players for their outdoor tours, substantially followed by Atkins and his successors at

Regent's Park, is every bit as striking as the Pastoral Players' choice of *As You Like It* for their performances at Coombe Woods. Despite these shows' affinities with stylized, unfamiliar modes of performance, whether borrowed from the Greeks or from the Elizabethans, their producers seem nonetheless to have understood outdoor performance primarily as the perfect consummation of Victorian and Edwardian naturalism. Even better than a wood near Athens consisting of extremely lifelike simulations of trees, apparently, was one consisting of real trees, and even better than having real tame rabbits on an indoor stage, *à la* Beerbohm Tree, was having real wild ones on an outdoor lawn. Similarly, the perfect solution to staging a play which includes both ancient Greek aristocrats and English rustics appears to be to perform it in a Greek auditorium which is in an English park, a strategy of which Peter Quince, with his anxious insistence that his players will need real moonlight and a real wall in order to enact 'Pyramus and Thisbe', would surely have approved. Greet would even sometimes state on posters for *Much Ado About Nothing* that 'the Church scene is omitted as not suitable for representation out of doors'.[88] (How much sense could *Much Ado About Nothing* make without the church scene, 4.1?) It as though outdoor performance was felt to be especially suitable for audiences completely lacking in imagination, but only so long as the plays involved depicted events all of which might have happened on wet grass.

ROWENA CADE AND THE MINACK

This underlying adherence to naturalism becomes most spectacularly visible around *The Tempest*, which Greet had claimed could only be performed adequately 'out of doors amidst the enchantment of nature', since it needed 'the idea of infinite space above and the mystery of the magic island beneath'.[89] In 1932, the same year that the picturesque open-air theatre at Regent's Park was inaugurated with a trial production of *Twelfth Night*, a positively sublime counterpart opened in distant Cornwall, with a production of the play for which it had been purpose-built (Figure 24). Here at Minack was something the West End had never managed to provide even in the heyday of the proto-cinematic special effect, *The Tempest* with a real sea – and, more often than not, a real tempest. Indeed the most famous of all Minack anecdotes concerns one fogbound matinée of this inaugural production, during which a two-masted barque actually ran aground on the rocks immediately behind the stage, among the waves ninety feet below – so that this historic show

Figure 24. *The Tempest*, Minack Theatre, 1932.

became a *Tempest* with a real shipwreck too. Certainly Minack has Regent's Park beaten hands down if what is required from open-air Shakespeare is sheer physical risk: a noticeboard now welcomes spectators with the words 'THE MINACK THEATRE IS BUILT INTO THE CLIFFSIDE. AS A RESULT THE WHOLE SITE IS POTENTIALLY HAZARDOUS. PLEASE TAKE PARTICULAR CARE OF YOUR OWN SAFETY AND THAT OF ANY CHILDREN FOR WHOM YOU ARE RESPONSIBLE. KEEP TO THE STEPS AND PATHS AT ALL TIMES.' But despite its perils and inconveniences, or perhaps because of them, Minack remains one of the most arresting of all modern Shakespearean theatres as well as the most famous to be devoted to amateur work, and it merits much more rigorous attention to its early history and its intellectual affiliations than it has yet received.

Accounts of Minack inevitably focus on its founder and indeed principal architect and builder, Dorothy Rowena Cade (1893–1983), and they typically marvel at how unlikely it should have been that this provincial spinster, already thirty-eight when she built Minack, should have become such a major figure in English outdoor Shakespeare. The souvenir booklet sold by the organization that now runs the theatre, The Minack Trust,

Figure 25. The cast of *A Midsummer Night's Dream*, the 1930 revival of the 1929 production, Crean, Cornwall, with costumes by Rowena Cade.

stresses that Cade's only experience of practical involvement in the theatre prior to her arrival in Cornwall in her thirties was being cast in the title role in a domestic production of *Alice in Wonderland* when she was eight, and it gives the impression that she drifted into dramatic activity in a wholly improvisatory manner, completely out of touch with any major currents in artistic thought. In fact, Cade had a great deal in common with E. W. Godwin, in that she was primarily a designer, and Minack, in the best modernist tradition, began as very much a designer's theatre (in its early seasons it even boasted some very fine modernist programme and poster designs by the artist Hilda Quick). Cade's greatest technical skills were in costume design, and she first became involved in local amateur dramatics in 1929, when she made the costumes and props for an outdoor production of *A Midsummer Night's Dream* at nearby Crean. As photographs of this show's 1930 revival reveal (Figures 25, 26), this was every bit as visually coordinated a piece of work as anything the Pastoral Players ever staged, and every bit as full of child-fairies as Ben Greet might have wished: look in particular at how the curls at the top of the disaffected fairies' hats match the curl on Titania's headdress. Cade's surviving costume drawing for Demetrius, moreover, preserved at the theatre's

Figure 26. *A Midsummer Night's Dream*, the 1930 revival of the 1929 production,
Crean, Cornwall, with costumes by Rowena Cade.

museum, not only provides him with Greek dress, in the approved manner, but also a Greek spelling, 'Demetrios'. But Cade had something in common with Lady Archibald Campbell too, namely, that she was a hostess. Cade's granite house on the cliffs near Porthcurno had already been the venue for a range of social and artistic activities before this, and after the success of the 1929–30 *Dream* Cade decided in effect to use amateur theatricals as a crowning social stunt. She more or less co-opted the company who had staged *A Midsummer Night's Dream* (essentially the works amateur dramatic society of the area's chief employer of educated technicians, the Eastern Telegraph Company, now part of Cable and Wireless) by buying the headland at the bottom of her garden for £100 specifically in order to turn it into an irresistibly spectacular venue for a follow-up production of *The Tempest*. Working over the winter of 1931–2 on the terracing, discreetly supplementing the cliffs' native granite with concrete, Cade constructed the most talked-about auditorium in the county, which remained an extension of the physical and social territory of her own Minack House. (At the same time she completely altered the nature of the society she had only recently joined by hiring professionals from London to direct and to play some leading roles.) It is hard not to see these manoeuvres as in part the expression of a social and artistic ambition worthy of E. F. Benson's Lucia: Fowey might have had Arthur

Quiller-Couch and Daphne du Maurier, St Ives all those potters and painters, but now, in artistic circles west of Penzance, Cade's word would be law.

Both the determination with which Cade pursued her theatrical project and its intellectual and ideological bases are clarified by knowledge of her educational background. As the theatre's booklet fails to point out, the young Cade had in the early 1900s attended Cheltenham Ladies' College. Cheltenham had been moulded by its greatest principal, Dorothea Beale (founder both of Girton in Cambridge and of St Hilda's in Oxford), specifically to produce women worthy to take their share in the management of Britain's imperial destiny. Its students were once described as 'The League of Empire Loyalists in gymslips', and to this day their most marked common trait is an invincible conviction of their own moral fitness to govern the world. During Cade's time at Cheltenham the school was very much in the forefront of the revival of classical drama: school and house plays included 'Scenes from Homer' (tableaux with dialogue, depicting the lives of Andromache, Nausicaa and Penelope), as well as Robert Bridges' neo-classical verse play *Achilles on Scyros*; and among many lavish outdoor pageants staged for successive Founder's Days there was a moralized, backbone-stiffening 'Pageant of Ancient Empires'. There were also school trips to see Frank Lascelles' Oxford pageant and an Oxford student production of Aristophanes' *The Frogs*, and, as the school's official history boasts, 'Free graceful expression was encouraged in various ways. The College was one of the first schools to use the Dalcroze system of Eurhythmics.'[90] Nor could Cade have complained of any lack of exposure to Shakespeare, indoors or out: there were visiting performances by Frank Benson's troupe and by the local branch of the British Empire Shakespeare Society; the girls of one house performed appropriate scenes from *Richard II* in the College garden; and there was also a visit from Rosamund Mayne Young's company with a Greet-style outdoor production of *Twelfth Night* (which was, incidentally, the second play to be performed at Minack, in 1933).[91] It is in this context that one has to look at the auditorium at Minack, as the brain-child of someone who had always seen outdoor Shakespeare in a classical context: fittingly, one spectator, looking at the theatre she had built, remarked that 'one can only think of Rowena Cade as one of the Olympians',[92] and one early performer there observed that 'There is a Greek or Elizabethan simplicity about it.'[93] As another commentator put it, accurately if bathetically conflating the theatre's major influences, 'Whether it be [at] the Minack, or Epidaurus, or the Regent's Park Theatre in London, the play's the thing.'[94]

Appropriately to this combination of the classical and the Shakespearean, Minack's most ambitious pre-war production was an epic *Antony and Cleopatra* in 1937, directed by Neil Porter from the Old Vic, a pageant of ancient empires indeed: Cade's notes as costume mistress record the purchase of no fewer than 100 pairs of sandals from the Penzance branch of Woolworth's. Fittingly if inaccurately, the script of the Stewart Granger film shot at Minack in 1944, *Love Story*, set against the backdrop of a production of *The Tempest*, unblushingly refers to Cade's auditorium as 'the old Roman amphitheatre up on the cliff'.

Minack, then, was founded as a direct heir of Bradfield and of Ben Greet, a stage where classicism and Elizabethan antiquarianism could be reconciled with naturalism, a suitable venue for hyper-real *Tempests* and gestures off out to sea towards Actium. The immediate appeal which this auditorium exerted in the 1930s, however, given its potential for discomfort and Cornwall's high all-year-round annual rainfall, still poses one key question: why perform or watch Shakespeare out of doors at all, in a climate like this? The answer probably has less to do with what outdoor performance in such locations does aesthetically for the plays than with what the plays do ideologically for the locations. Like Edwardian pageants, open-air productions of Shakespeare integrate specific places within a nostalgic vision of the nation, its history and its culture. Indeed the connection between the pageant and the pastoral performance of Shakespeare was drawn very early on, with characteristic acuity, by Rudyard Kipling, in *Puck of Pook's Hill* (1906). This enduringly popular piece of juvenile fiction depicts a pair of exemplary Ben Greet-style children who perform passages from *A Midsummer Night's Dream* so effectively in a Sussex field on Midsummer's Eve that they inadvertently summon Shakespeare's Puck in person. As the spirit of the place, Puck instructs them in their national past by magically allowing them to witness a pageant-like sequence of episodes from local history, most of them, as in Parker's historical spectaculars, dealing with the successive invasions by which the ethnic identity of the English was supposed to have been formed. As this elaborate piece of framing may suggest, in the late Victorian and Edwardian era, when the British Empire had proved that the national literature was eminently and perhaps worryingly exportable (as, for example, more and more Folios left England for new homes in the United States), the English literati had felt a need to identify Shakespeare's works with the soil of the homeland itself by whatever means were available. In an 1885 essay called *The Open Air*, for example, the patriotic Richard Jefferies tried to invoke Shakespeare as a male English Ceres, his texts merely a literary version of the fertile native landscape:

What part is there of the English year which has not been sung by the poets? all of whom are full of its loveliness; and our greatest of all, Shakespeare, carries, as it were, armfuls of violets, and scatters roses and golden wheat across his pages, which are simply fields written with human life.[95]

The trouble with this formulation is that the landscape and the arts seem to be rivals: indeed Jefferies goes on to claim that 'The lover of nature has the highest art in his soul.' Surely more convincing and efficacious than this solitary, introspective vision would be a collective ritual by which the inseparable bond between national poet and national landscape could actually be celebrated in the flesh. In 1769 Garrick had effectively tried to enact such a thing as a procession in the streets of Stratford, and it would be glimpsed again in the Shakespearean episodes of the Warwick and Kenilworth pageants: but it was the Pastoral Players' *As You Like It*, performed in the same year that Jefferies' essay was first published, which had succeeded in finding a better alternative, as many subsequent comments make clear. In 1919, for example, Roy Mitchell's *Shakespeare for Community Players* recommended outdoor productions for their 'native quality', on the grounds that, if an amateur actor-manager sets up his theatre somewhere suitable in the open air, 'Instead of having to say "This is coopered up to look as much as possible like Arden," he finds himself saying, "This *is* Arden."'[96] In fact, everywhere one looks under the surface of English outdoor Shakespeare one finds the desire to sit in an English field and say, 'This *is* Arden.' Compare the glee with which L. Du Garde Peach, celebrating the proliferation of village amateur dramatic societies in 1939, reports that 'today it is no unusual thing, somewhere in the quiet English countryside, to hear Sylvius apostrophizing his Phoebe or Orlando his Rosalind and, on looking over the hedge, to find a shepherd, script in hand, conning his part'.[97] Or compare Aidan Clarke, even closer to the perilous boundary between English whimsy and English mysticism, on the Richmond Shakespeare Society's 1935 *A Midsummer Night's Dream*, which for a spectator who had clearly been brought up on *Puck of Pook's Hill* simply released the innate, mutually reinforcing Englishness and Shakespeareanness of its Thameside location:

As I walked in, I saw a group of green fairies sitting in a corner of the field. Within the gates, in leafy dells and winding mossy ways, were lightly clad nymphs, creatures of the garden and the wood, nimble dancing forms, majestic personages crowned and garlanded. I felt that the figures I beheld were always

there, but [for whatever reason ...] I had failed to see the rightful regular
residents of Richmond's Terrace Gardens. From the moment in which I saw
my first fairy, onwards in the dusk, and all through the night, what men now call
reality became a dream; and the older dream, Shakespeare's dream, all men's
dream, the great old dream of Merrie England ... became the reality. The river
god claimed our allegiance and the garden deities our never quite forgotten
ancient love ... The fairies sang, and blessed the Terrace Gardens ... The Bard
of Avon will find no better stage than this green plot beside the silver Thames.
His servants, and our friends, the Richmond Shakespeare Society, have done
much towards the recovery of Merry England – for keeps.[98]

For 'Shakespeare's dream' here one might also read 'Bottom's dream': this
is a vision of Shakespeare as himself an artisan on perpetual, timeless
holiday, serving as his nation's embodiment and spokesman while identified, like his servants in the Richmond Shakespeare Society, as a fellow
amateur of Quince and Snug.

It is surely just such a desire as Clarke's to revive, recover and secure a
forever lost, forever threatened Merry England by playing Shakespeare all
over it which informs the early twentieth century's incongruous passion for
outdoor production. Only this, surely, can account for the fitness which
devotees continue to find in the location of Minack as 'England's first and
last theatre': looking out over the Western Approaches, it seems designed to
guarantee that, should a second Spanish Armada sail up the Channel, the
first thing its look-outs would see of the country they were trying to invade
would be an amateur production of *A Midsummer Night's Dream* or *The
Tempest*. In fact that 1932 opening production might have been expressly
designed to solicit the comment which it indeed widely received: 'Well
might this be Prospero's island.'[99] Minack labels the whole of the British
mainland as Shakespeare's, in a posture at once of beckoning lighthouse
and of defensive sentinel. It is only appropriate that soon after the end of
the 1939 summer season Minack was requisitioned by the Ministry of
Defence and fitted with a gun emplacement. It is a reminder, perhaps, that
England was not the only European country to have spent the 1930s
engaged in healthy outdoor pursuits by which strength might be achieved
through joy, building neo-classical concrete auditoriums, staging imperial-
ist pageants, and celebrating in the same breath an authentically native
culture and an identification with the imagined Apollos of ancient Athens.
Perhaps it is just as well that in inter-war England, as the likes of Ben Greet
and Robert Atkins never tired of demonstrating, the only ancient Athenian
anyone could really see themselves identifying with was that tireless star of
open-air rehearsals, Bottom the Weaver.

SHAKESPEARE AND THE SUMMER HOLIDAYS

Since the war, despite some difficult times, Minack has flourished. Like the Middlesbrough Little Theatre in the 1970s, it was taken into the subsidized sector in the 1950s, when it was managed for three years by the Cornish branch of the National Council for Social Services, but they were so appalled by the financial losses it was making at the time that they gave it back to Rowena Cade. Now run by a trust, and equipped with an impressive year-round visitor centre and souvenir-sales department, it has achieved both prosperity and independence. It receives productions from some of the best-regarded amateur societies in the country, including, since 1967, even the proud and once exclusively indoor Questors.[100] In fact its post-war history is one of attracting groups from ever further afield: Bristol (1958), Cambridge (1960), Nottingham (1962), Liverpool (1966), Ilkley (1977), even the Lake Worth Playhouse of Florida (1987). Digital cameras connected to its website now allow even the most distant enthusiasts to remind themselves of its architecture and setting, and to watch the successive weather-fronts approaching the stage from over the Atlantic horizon.[101] This facility enables devotees to obtain at least a diluted fix of Minack even during the winter, when there are no performances. The movement from indoor performance to outdoor which I have been describing marks a seasonal shift from amateur Shakespeare as a pastime for the winter to one for the summer, and one reason sometimes adduced for the relative post-war vigour of outdoor Shakespeare is that it allows societies increasingly dominated by the retired to import younger performers made available by the summer vacations of schools and colleges. If outdoor casts are sometimes enhanced by the presence of those on holiday, outdoor audiences, like those of the Edwardian pageant, always are. Although some resident theatregoers drive all the way down to Porthcurno and back to see performances from as far away as Exeter and even Bristol, the audiences at the Minack, like the casts, are composed very largely of people staying in western Cornwall for their summer holidays. For Britons as for those from overseas, both Shakespeare and a particular notion of Shakespeare's England have become tourist destinations.

The post-war hegemony of open-air performance among amateur Shakespeareans, and the cultural significance which it now carries for natives and visitors alike, are perhaps even better exemplified by the fate of a theatre and a theatre company in another holiday area, but one rather less remote from alternative sources of entertainment. At one of the first venues to imitate the Pastoral Players' outdoor Shakespeare at the end of the nineteenth century, adjoining a conurbation regularly visited by Greet and his Woodland Players,[102] the rivalry between indoor and open-air Shakespeare has been played out in recent decades with particular clarity. Bournemouth, the leading seaside resort of Hampshire until Edward Heath's county boundary reforms in the early 1970s declared it to be in Dorset (as the historic port of Poole immediately to the west had been all along), acquired a Little Theatre during the heyday of the amateur theatrical society, in 1919. (It was originally called the 'Bournemouth Dramatic and Orchestral Club', but became the Bournemouth Little Theatre Club in the 1920s.) By 1931, beating the Middlesbrough Little Theatre by twenty years, the society had raised enough money to open its own custom-designed 450-seat auditorium in the centre of the town, the Palace Court Theatre, a handsome playhouse with excellent acoustics and an Art Deco façade closely modelled on that of the Whitehall in London.[103] Soon after the National Trust took over Brownsea Island in Poole Harbour, opening it to the public in 1963 (after many years during which the island had been closed to visitors, a far cry from the sociable days of the by-then forgotten 1893 *As You Like It*), the island's new guardians decided to publicize their acquisition by hosting outdoor performances of a Shakespeare play there to mark the 400th anniversary of the dramatist's birth. The Trust naturally called on the Bournemouth Little Theatre Club, as the largest amateur theatrical organization in the area, to supply the personnel, and with just the sort of inspired literal-mindedness shown at the Minack three decades earlier the players decided that, given a venue which would involve ferrying both cast and audience to an island and stranding them there until the end of act 5, they should perform a play that is all about being stranded on an island until the end of act 5, namely *The Tempest*.

Potentially uncomfortable as the experience sounded – offering spectators the opportunity to get seasick en route to the auditorium, denying them the opportunity to go home during the interval, and subjecting them to the attentions of Brownsea's celebrated resident population of mosquitoes – this inconvenient venture nonetheless seems to have awakened or answered a very definite public desire. Demand for tickets was such that two extra performances had to be laid on to supplement the originally advertised three, so that this initial 1964 production was in the end seen by capacity audiences totalling 2,500.[104] An astonished *Bournemouth Daily Echo* reported that one holidaymaker had paid £2 each for four 10-shilling tickets,[105] and media excitement was not confined to the local area. The resonant symbolism of a historic island – the site of Baden Powell's first Boy Scout camp at that – being given over wholly to Shakespeare was not lost on journalists, and, like the Sherborne pageant or the first production at the Minack, the debut of the open-air theatre on Brownsea (admittedly, an event which took place during the August 'silly season', when news is scarce) attracted national publicity. A month before the show opened, *The Lady*, in the very spirit of 1893, was charmed in advance by a description of the setting: 'The acting area is a grassy clearing bounded by rhododendrons, a chestnut tree, and pines, and, should they not be scared away by the audience ranked on a gentle slope, there may be peacocks perched in the pine trees.'[106] (I can report from personal experience of the island's 1981 production of *As You Like It* that it would have taken a good deal more than an audience to scare away those peacocks or the successive generations of their descendants:[107] in 1964, as at every subsequent Brownsea show, they announced their intention of roosting with loud screams around the start of act 4. This isle is full of noises.) The *Daily Telegraph* reported on the unexpected popularity of the production; BBC television broadcast a feature in advance of the first night; and the *Guardian* sent Michael Frenchman to observe a rehearsal on the island and publish a substantial feature about it, complete with photograph.[108] What had appeared to be an immense and reckless financial risk for the Little Theatre Club instead fully covered its costs and made a substantial profit for the National Trust. Before the final performance was over, discussions were already under way about staging *A Midsummer Night's Dream* the following year. There has been an open-air production of a Shakespeare play on Brownsea every summer since then, now playing to 4,000 spectators annually and selling out months in advance of the first performance.

Perhaps inevitably, this annual outdoor Shakespearean fixture soon resulted in the Bournemouth Little Theatre ceasing to perform Shakespeare indoors. In fact while the society's outdoor, offshore Shakespeare prospered, all of its other activities fell on hard times. In 1970 the club had to sell its elegant auditorium in the town centre, which subsequently became a cinema and then an evangelical church,[109] and after using a series of temporary venues it moved in 1975 to a new home, the former upstairs staff canteen of a garage in the unfashionable suburb of Winton, now converted into an auditorium with less than a quarter of the capacity of its more glamorous predecessor. Meanwhile, the thriving Shakespearean enterprise on Brownsea Island abandoned the aegis of the Bournemouth Little Theatre, splitting off as an independent registered charity, the Brownsea Open-Air Theatre. Remarkably, exactly the same pattern of conventional amateur theatre being eclipsed by outdoor amateur Shakespeare was then repeated elsewhere in the same conurbation. In 1975 a new dramatic society was formed to rival the Bournemouth Little Theatre Club, known as the Bournemouth Players, who performed initially in the studio-sized theatre in the basement of the old Burlington Hotel in Boscombe. In the summer of 1979 this group performed *A Midsummer Night's Dream* in the garden of nearby Christchurch Priory, and this production was so successful that they have offered a Shakespeare play there every summer since then. In 1986 they gave up their non-Shakespearean, indoor activities altogether to concentrate solely on providing this mainland alternative to Brownsea, renaming themselves the Bournemouth Shakespeare Players. Whatever Bournemouth audiences want, it does not seem to be shelter. (Something of the same pattern has been visible even in colder, northerly Middlesbrough, where the most recent performances of Shakespeare on offer have been staged not at the Middlesbrough Little Theatre but in a temporary outdoor auditorium in the gardens of the Middlesbrough Institute of Modern Art.)[110]

In an area now otherwise notoriously indifferent to live drama, as the fate of the Palace Court Theatre suggests, indeed in a town which one of Ben Greet's successors as a visiting Shakespearean actor-manager, Sir Anthony Quayle, once described as 'the graveyard of the English theatre',[111] what can explain the continuing popularity of open-air amateur Shakespeare? It is true, granted, that the Brownsea Open Air Theatre usually achieves high production values. Carefully exploiting the ambiguity of the word 'professionally', for example, as ambitious amateur companies sometimes do, its website makes the paradoxical-sounding but lawyer-proof claim that 'The company is professionally run, but all those involved with BOAT, whether onstage, backstage or front-of-house, are unpaid volunteers.' But even some grander boasts, made by local journalists on the players' behalf, have sometimes been borne out by subsequent events. Reviewing Brownsea's 1999 *A Midsummer Night's Dream*, for example, the *Bournemouth Daily Echo* declared that 'the shining star of this production is Lisa Starwiaski's elegant, lyrical Titania. Who needs the Royal Shakespeare Company when we have talent like this on our own doorsteps?'[112] As if consciously determined to vindicate this remark, Lisa Starwiaski went straight from Brownsea to RADA, adopted the stage name of Dillon, and then proceeded rapidly to Stratford, appearing as a fine Desdemona in Gregory Doran's *Othello* in 2004–5, and making a welcome return to the Swan during the 2006–7 Complete Works Festival as an equally good Celia in Samuel West's Crucible production of *As You Like It*. But how many in the audiences for outdoor amateur productions of Shakespeare actually go there purely to savour dextrous stage-management or fine classical acting?

In practice, the main critical criterion applied to outdoor and indoor amateur productions alike, which is enforced with particular rigour in the open air, does not concern acting at all, but concentrates on the perceived appropriateness or otherwise of the costuming. It seems to be a constant, going back through the early work of the Stockport Garrick to the Kilkenny Theatrical Society, that the audiences for amateur productions of Shakespeare want to see Shakespeare performed in a conservative version of what for them constitutes 'proper' historical dress, whether that is armour for the battle scenes in *Henry IV*, doublet and hose for Hamlet *à la* Middlesbrough Little Theatre, or green tights and a short tunic for Rosalind-as-Ganymede.[113] Just as in amateur performance the audience sees not actors but people, so they see dressing-up clothes rather than costumes, and they want to like and to be impressed by what they see.[114] As we saw in the case of the Stockport Garrick's early Shakespeares in the 1900s, medieval and Renaissance costumes acquired a definite ideological valence in the early twentieth century, connoting fidelity to a particular version of the Middle Ages and the Renaissance as a lost golden world of voluntary craft labour. The irresistible extra factor which outdoor performance can supply to compound the perennial appeal of the Elizabethan couture which the English seem to treat as a sort of *de facto* national dress is a juxtaposition of old-style Shakespearean clothing with real locations, locations which ideally belong to an idyllic pastoral English landscape, or which incorporate historic buildings equally charged with associations of national heritage and continuity.[115] These include the college gardens of Oxford and Cambridge, as in the case of the Cambridge Shakespeare Festival; the grounds of stately homes, as at Stamford; the gardens of large medieval churches like Christchurch Priory; or, in the case of Brownsea, an island which is not only miraculously cut off from the modern world but which can offer a castle-cum-stately-home, a gothic church, and a flock of peacocks within the same field of vision as the green plot that is its stage. To watch Shakespearean comedy in these surroundings, as at Richmond, is to spend festive holiday time in Merry England itself.

For a large and otherwise under-represented middle-class and lower-middle-class audience, then, the open-air amateur performance of Shakespeare in Elizabethan dress continues the cultural work of the

Edwardian pageant by other means. The development of electric light and electric amplification which have made this possible, paradoxically, have freed the audiences for twentieth- and twenty-first century amateur Shakespeare to go on being unabashedly nostalgic for an innocently pre-industrial England, when costume was always authentic and so were the people who wore it. Open-air Shakespeare, the blank-verse Dunkirk Lite of every provincial summer, celebrates much the same 'Shakespeare's Kingdom' as was hymned at the British Empire Exhibition, or in the manifesto of Frank Benson as reported by H. V. Morton in Chapter 2. Its appeal to a Tudor *genius loci* is one which would be recognized immediately by Louis Napoleon Parker; and the stoicism on which its audiences never tire of congratulating themselves is a survival of the same patriotism voiced more militantly, in a cadence borrowed from *King John* (5.7.115–18), at the close of Arthur Bryant's Shakespearean pageant at Greenwich in 1933:

> All the past proclaims her future: Shakespeare's voice and Nelson's hand,
> Milton's faith and Wordsworth's trust in this our chosen, chainless land
> Bear us witness: Come the world against her, England yet shall stand.[116]

This predominantly amateur aesthetic finally and belatedly came to the notice of professional critics of Shakespearean performance in the late 1990s. In 1997, a new theatre opened in central London, most of the auditorium of which was open to the sky. Its half-timbered walls and thatched roof spoke of heritage and historical continuity, soon attracting impressive numbers of tourists both from Britain and from abroad. On a kind of stage with which the amateurs employed by William Poel and Nugent Monck earlier in the century would have been immediately familiar, actors in recreated clothing of the Elizabethan period performed under the supervision of people listed in its programmes as 'Master of Verse' and 'Master of Play', just as Ben Greet had once been 'Master of the Greensward' at Regent's Park. Whenever their lines mentioned the weather, the actors looked up at the grey sky, met an audience member's eyes and raised their eyebrows, to warm and indulgent laughter, and at the end of each performance they exhibited revels and dances of the olden times. It was, of course, Shakespeare's Globe on Bankside, and in its early seasons many academics and professional theatre critics accustomed to seeing Shakespeare only at venues like the Pit, the Olivier or the Donmar Warehouse were frankly baffled by what they found there.[117] Who were all these people prepared to stand around in the rain in anoraks, watching people in tights perpetrating what was often pretty coarse acting? Where had they learned to laugh so loudly at the jokes to show that they knew where they were? And from what constituency had this theatre been able to draw such a practised-looking team of middle-aged volunteer front-of-house staff? Above all, how were these people all managing to have such a good time? Minack may still be the most celebrated amateur theatre in the country, but in some respects Shakespeare's Globe now runs it a close second. Shakespeare has long been the most translated and transplanted of all playwrights, his world-wide currency now regularly discussed as if it were primarily a post-national phenomenon of the transcontinental cinema and the electronic mass media: but one thing which an enormous international audience evidently still wants from him is a globally recognizable, incipiently Luddite, perennially amateurish, deeply parochial Englishness. Complete with the weather.

Conclusion

CHUDLEIGH My dear father –

DUNSCOMBE (*working himself into a passion*) See what Shakespeare – himself a player – thinks of the amateur actor. Look at him in the *Midsummer Night's Dream* – the Weaver Bottom – a conceited, pragmatical, imbecile idiot!

CHUDLEIGH And see how Shakespeare rewards him! Who falls in love with this idiot and imbecile? Titania, Queen of the Fairies.

DUNSCOMBE Yes, sir. And do you know why? Because Puck, before he shows this broken-brained weaver to Titania, raises him in the scale of intellect from an amateur actor to a donkey. Shakespeare knew that as a donkey he was presentable at the fairy court – as an amateur actor the thing was too impossible.

(T. W. Robertson, M.P., 1870)[1]

For all the popularity of the contemporary outdoor productions chronicled in the previous chapter, the amateur performance of Shakespeare continues to inspire embarrassment, anxiety and derision – much of it, like that of Dunscombe Dunscombe, MP, claiming to take its cue from Shakespeare's own depiction of amateur performance in *A Midsummer Night's Dream*. For Dunscombe, acting is a socially degrading pursuit, inappropriate to the status of his son: public exposure to the stares and critical opinions of an audience is a humiliation which ought to be reserved for members of the untouchable caste of professional players. But the passing of the Victorian social attitudes which make Dunscombe oppose his son's favourite hobby with such vehemence seems to have done little to rehabilitate the pursuit among the literati. In the popular culture of the post-war period amateur Shakespeareans have usually served primarily as the butts of jokes. Non-professional productions of Shakespeare have sometimes made less satirical thematic and practical appearances in fiction – in Robertson Davies' *Tempest-Tost* (1951), for instance, set against the backdrop of a mishap-prone outdoor *Tempest* in Canada, or in Simon Brett's whodunnit *An Amateur Corpse* (1978), in which the suspects conveniently and repeatedly assemble in a London suburb to rehearse *The Winter's Tale*. Elsewhere, though, amateurs who enjoy acting Shakespeare are usually represented as suffering from a pitiable discrepancy between the scale of their vanity and the scale of their talent. It is true that the dying East Anglian village dramatic society depicted in Andy Cadiff's film *A Bunch of Amateurs* (2008), a group with which a has-been Hollywood star (played by Burt Reynolds) accidentally winds up playing King Lear, is inevitably granted the happy outcome which this transatlantic sub-genre of Ealingesque comedy requires: their production is a triumph, the society's finances are saved, and the Hollywood star hires the Old Vic for a sold-out one-off gala performance to celebrate, rather in the manner of Sir Francis Delaval. Most of the film's jokes about actors en route to this unlikely apotheosis, however, assume that the phrase 'a bunch of amateurs' is more usually synonymous with 'a bunch of losers'. The awful amateur production of *Romeo and Juliet* glimpsed in Edgar Wright's film *Hot Fuzz* (2007) is much more typical, and the emblematic amateur Shakespearean of recent times has been Patrick Barlow's comic alter ego, Desmond Olivier Dingle. Dingle is the 'Artistic Director and Chief Executive' of the catastrophically over-ambitious two-man troupe The National Theatre of Brent, a company whose self-important name mockingly remembers the British Drama League's insistence that the drive to encourage local amateur performance and the campaign to establish a national theatre should be inseparable. A self-appointed expert on almost everything, he is also the author of *Shakespeare: The Truth* (1993), described on its cover as 'Desmond Olivier Dingle's *controversial exposé*, including family tree, props list, complete history of the English language, handy acting tips, tourist guide to Stratford, glossary AND special feature: "Shakespeare's Unknown Wives".'[2] Like his Shakespearean avatars Bottom and Quince, Dingle is represented as ludicrous not because he is guilty of social derogation like Chudleigh Dunscombe but because he suffers from social and intellectual aspirations above his station. Just as artisans may look funny to the likes of Duke Theseus when attempting to imitate heroes from classical mythology, so lower-middle-class enthusiasts may look laughable if they adopt the name of a thespian peer as a middle name and wax serious about Shakespearean performance. Despite the broad social appeal celebrated by the amateurs of Cambridge in 1864, Shakespeare's plays are still felt to be socially inappropriate for certain classes of performer.

Even the independent producer and director Norman Marshall, who in the 1920s had been a regular and enthusiastic adjudicator for the British

Drama League Festival of Community Drama and a tutor on the League's summer schools for amateur actors and directors, came to believe after the war that amateur players were a bit too much like Bottom the Weaver for comfort. His important study *The Other Theatre* (1947), among chapters devoted to several broadly non-commercial playhouses of the preceding quarter-century such as the Gate, the Festival Theatre in Cambridge and the Old Vic, does include twenty pages on 'The Amateur Theatre', but beyond Marshall's warm tributes to the work of Nugent Monck at the Maddermarket, to that of Charles Smith at the Leeds Civic Playhouse, and to that of the Unity Players in Camden, this chapter mainly records disappointment. Once, he says, he believed that

the development of the amateur movement was bound to have an invigorating effect on the professional theatre by providing an audience of enthusiastic playgoers with a working knowledge of acting and production ... It was only gradually that I began to realise how seldom is the amateur interested in the theatre as a whole.

In support of his disillusioned view of non-professionals as incorrigibly small-minded and self-centred, he quotes a former editor of *The Amateur Stage*, John Bourne, to the effect that the amateurs' cause

is not that of the theatre as a whole, but the spontaneous and unconsidered desire to don the motley and have fun and games in doing so ... When the light evenings come, they throw off the motley and turn to tennis with that same spontaneity and simplicity that prevents them ever reaching Wimbledon.

After devoting several paragraphs to castigating his unpaid colleagues for being insufficiently committed to the progress of dramatic art, Marshall only reluctantly concedes that 'it is arguable that the main function of the amateur movement is simply to give as many people as possible opportunities for indulging in an extremely pleasant form of recreation'.[3]

In defiance of this familiar chorus of disdain and disapprobation, this conclusion will first of all recapitulate the narrative of this book by looking quickly at the performance history of *A Midsummer Night's Dream*, examining the ways in which Shakespeare's presentation of Quince's troupe of artisans has and has not corresponded to the different modes of amateur performance in which Shakespeare's plays have been offered over time. Secondly, it will recapitulate the argument of the book by considering which distinctive dramatic effects have been most enabled by non-professional performance, and why. Lastly, it will glance at amateur Shakespearean activity across the different categories outlined in the previous chapters, looking first at the current heirs of the expatriate players discussed in Chapter 3, before returning to Britain to consider some present-day instances of domestic, civic and outdoor performance.

RUDE MECHANICALS

To condense and oversimplify the history of amateur Shakespearean performance which this book has uncovered: in the seventeenth and eighteenth centuries aristocrats cast themselves as the heroes of Shakespeare's tragedies and histories, and their daughters as the heroines of she-tragedies (though preferably not Juliet); in the nineteenth, officers and gentlemen preferred to stage themselves in comedy drag versions of the tragedies, while the lower middle classes, their unexpected leisure pursuit in mixed company finding its image in the courting holiday time of Shakespeare's green worlds, turned to the comedies proper; and in the twentieth century everyone, even those imprisoned in Dartmoor as conscientious objectors, performed *A Midsummer Night's Dream*, ideally in the open air. With its balance of strong roles, its exquisitely actor-proof structure, and its unfailingly hilarious depiction of non-professional performance, *A Midsummer Night's Dream* now seems so obviously the Shakespeare play with which any amateur theatrical group would start that it is salutary to see both how recent its popularity with amateurs really is and how dependent its modern success has been, even in the professional theatre, on a widespread familiarity with the kinds of recreational performance established over the last century and a half.

The performance history of *Dream* from its own time to the present usefully encapsulates much of the narrative which this book has offered. Although it was appropriately played in shortened form by apprentices in the Interregnum and early Restoration in the form of Robert Cox's *The Merry Conceited Humours of Bottom the Weaver*, *A Midsummer Night's Dream* fell from favour as this sort of amateur performance faded from popular memory, and indeed once the newly established Theatres Royal had taken to casting actresses rather than boys as heroines its jokes surrounding Flute's impersonation of Thisbe looked and sounded obsolete. In the eighteenth century, when the non-professional performance of high tragedy was primarily an aristocratic pursuit rather than one available to artisans, 'Pyramus and Thisbe', which crucially provides *A Midsummer Night's Dream* with its finale even after the play's intrigues have been resolved and its lovers married, simply made no sense. The mechanicals, accordingly, were usually absent from the play's few, professional, eighteenth-century revivals; they never appeared in Garrick's unsuccessful musical version *The Fairies* (1755), and they never got to perform their play in George Colman's longer but even shorter-lived adaptation *A Fairy Tale* (1763). In the period's two separate afterpieces based on their sections of the play, Richard Leveridge's *Pyramus and Thisbe, a Comic Masque* (1716) and John Frederick Lampe's *Pyramus and Thisbe, a Mock Opera* (1745), Quince's troupe had to be rewritten as a bunch of professionals instead of a bunch of amateurs, translated from volunteer Athenian actors into hired Italian musicians so that their scenes could dwindle into close topical parodies of Italian *opera seria*. Romanticism's willingness to suspend disbelief in fairies, especially when assisted by Mendelssohn's musical score, helped *A Midsummer Night's Dream* back onto the professional stage in largely uncut form in the mid nineteenth century, but for the amateur stage 'Pyramus and Thisbe' was more important as a Shakespearean precedent for all-male burlesque than it was as a recommendation for reviving the whole play. (As we've seen, Quince's prologue was used independently of the rest of *Dream* by the Pic-Nic Club, and 'Pyramus and Thisbe' was excerpted for performance as a free-standing burlesque by genteel Victorian bachelors.) It was only after real-life amateur dramatic societies open to all classes began to proliferate in the early twentieth century that the mechanicals really came into their own.[4] Ben Greet may have claimed that this play owed its modern surge in popularity to the success with which companies like his own Woodland Players had shown it off in outdoor venues, but it would be equally possible to argue that even in professional productions such as his, *A Midsummer Night's Dream* rode to its current status as the most frequently performed work in the Shakespeare canon on the back of the Little Theatre Movement.

With the establishment of civic amateur drama, the mechanicals' sections of the play were transformed from the surreally whimsical speculation they represented in Shakespeare's own time (wouldn't it be funny if unqualified lower-class amateurs tried to act tragedy?) into a piece of observational comic satire (isn't it funny when unqualified lower-class amateurs try to act tragedy!). Professional productions (such as Adrian Noble's for the RSC in 1994, the basis for his 1996 film) have regularly treated Quince, Snug and their associates as honorary members of the British Drama League (just as did Geoffrey Whitworth in *The Theatre and Stage* in 1934), informing their social milieu with minutely nuanced present-day detail, and they have been the richer for being able to do so.[5] However they are styled, though, the effect of the mechanicals' scenes is always far more powerful in non-professional performance, where 'Pyramus and Thisbe' becomes an amateur-performance-within-an-amateur-performance rather than just an amateur-play-within-a-professional-one, and where the entire production becomes the willing object of these scenes' affectionate satire. Even professional directors have sometimes pursued this superior *mise-en-abyme* effect: in Jonathan Best's exquisite chamber production at the Barbican concert hall in 2001, for instance, for which the City of London Sinfonia performed Mendelssohn's incidental music, a small cast of players drawn from the RSC posed as genteel Victorian amateurs sociably putting on *A Midsummer Night's Dream* together as a spot of after-dinner private theatricals.[6]

THE AMATEUR EFFECT

In its depiction of the mechanicals and their performance, *A Midsummer Night's Dream* models not just an amateur dramatic society but the relationship between an amateur troupe and its audience. Or rather, it depicts a particular onstage attitude of aristocratic spectators to artisan performers which implies a much more mutually supportive relationship between the audience of *A Midsummer Night's Dream* and its own players, whether they are amateur or professional: if we were to interrupt a performance of *A Midsummer Night's Dream* with jokes as continually as the aristocrats interrupt 'Pyramus and Thisbe', obviously, many of the play's pleasures would be denied us. To put it another way, the identification of Demetrius' snobbish and mocking view of the mechanicals as Shakespeare's (essentially the strategy employed by Dunscombe Dunscombe in this conclusion's epigraph) is not borne out by the play proper, any more than the disruptive behaviour of the lordly audience of the Pageant of the Nine Worthies is endorsed in the last act of *Love's Labour's Lost*. ('This is not generous, not gentle, not humble,' as the schoolmaster Holofernes is allowed to point out, reproaching his king to his face, 5.2.623.) Although Philostrate speaks of 'Pyramus and Thisbe' as work, a show offered by artisans 'Which never laboured in their minds till now' (5.1.73), it is clear that the troupe's dramatic offering is made voluntarily, as a gift, by people who have acted before and who now take delight in having their play selected for performance before the Duke (4.2.30–40). In the fifth act, the three pairs of newlyweds watch a play for pleasure which is being performed for pleasure: for this special portion of this one special evening, at least, these hard-handed men are participating, however ineptly, in the cultured leisure of their social superiors. Even in the stratified onstage mortal world that this play depicts, the effect is distinctly levelling: Theseus, for example, does not get anything like the tongue-tied, deferential performance he expects (5.1.89–105), since Bottom keeps dropping out of character to contradict his interjections about the play. ('No, in truth sir, he should not . . .', 'No, I assure you, the wall is down that parted their fathers . . .', 5.1.182, 345–6).

It is just this mutually recreational aspect of amateur performance which has enabled it to have such a re-creative effect on the plays of Shakespeare – whether by allowing act 4 of *The Winter's Tale* to metamorphose into a cross-dressed masquerade about female friendship, or by letting *The Tempest* become the pretext for a spell of collective national self-contemplation on an island. Whereas in the professional theatre the actors are at work while the audience are at play, enforcing a fundamental distinction between the two groups regardless of the shape of the auditorium, in the amateur theatre both cast and spectators are at play together. (An unkinder version of this formulation would suggest that while in the professional theatre the audience are enjoying themselves while the actors are toiling, in the amateur theatre the opposite is the case.) It is true that in the amateur theatre the players and their audiences are usually of the same social class (if not actually members of the same families, as in the case of many of the instances of private theatricals discussed in my first chapter), but even when this has not been the case the producers and consumers of the theatrical event have met as equals under conditions of shared leisure. In these circumstances, the customary frameworks by which the relative authority of play, performer and spectator are understood in the conventional theatre of any period are drastically altered, generating and releasing quite different meanings.

If it is the case that one of the special conditions of amateur performance is that actors are not merely actors but people known to the audience, and indeed, the audience is not merely an audience but composed in part at least of people known to the actors, other special conditions also apply. The actors' clothes, for instance, are not solely perceived as costumes functionally revealing some inner essence of their fictitious characters, but remain, vividly, real dressing-up clothes; and the venue is not simply a functional structure in which actors can be seen and heard by an audience, but remains meaningful in itself, in ways which may resonate powerfully with the play. On the non-professional stage, Shakespeare's plays have been populated by casts actively living through their scripts, trying out and projecting multiple and expanded relations with their acquaintances, families and wider societies both as fellow actors and as audiences. The amateur performance of Shakespeare has permitted an immense social and international range of different casts and audiences to participate in the making of theatrical meaning in their own immediate surroundings. While the contexts of amateur performance have at different times and in different places imposed limits on what Shakespeare's plays can do or mean (as have those of the professional stage), the opportunities for the deepening and elaboration of their characteristic effects, whether comical, tragical or historical, have been extraordinary. Always as interested in the present tense and immediate situation of their performance as they are in the fictitious past time of their plots, Shakespeare's plays are uncannily responsive to the local circumstances of their production, and in those provided by amateur performers they have found perennially fruitful ground.

In fact, wherever Shakespeare's plays have got out of ordinary commercial playhouses and into different social situations courtesy of amateur enthusiasts, some aspect of their action or thematics has usually been powerfully intensified. For the aristocrats of Chapter 1, for instance, for whom theatrical performance was an important means of asserting status within and beyond the family, it was often the plays' own interests in family dynamics, rank and hereditary right which came to the fore, along with more local concerns with particular pieces of territory. (Just as *Henry IV part 1* must have carried special significance when performed at Berkeley Castle, for instance, so the depictions of Wales in both this play and *Cymbeline* must have seemed especially pertinent at Wynnstay in the Marches.) For the civic-minded amateurs of Chapter 2, it was the inclusiveness of the comedies, with their promises of lasting companionship and social renewal – aspects of the plays which the Stockport Garrick Society deliberately sought to foster even off the stage, with the institution, for instance, of 'Benedict's Party'. For the military officers of Chapter 3, by contrast, it was often the plays' depictions of courage, cowardice and authority which came dramatically into focus. There must have been all the difference in the world between watching a professional actor such as Stephen Kemble making Falstaff's speech against honour and in favour of survival on the stage of Covent Garden and watching Colonel Braddyll making the same speech at the Duke of Wellington's headquarters in Portugal, where the performance itself, for both cast and spectators, constituted a means of savouring an interlude between real battles.[7] In a comparable but different way, for the outdoor performers of Chapter 4 the pastoral comedies came vividly to life as opportunities for the consecration of different real places as temporary corners of

Shakespeare's imaginary world, allowing particular copses, fields and sea-cliffs briefly and poignantly to become a wood near Athens, the forest of Arden or the edges of Prospero's island.

The Shakespeare canon's recurrent interest in cross-dressing, meanwhile, is something which amateur performance has taken up and run with throughout its history. Some amateurs have availed themselves of the burlesque style of Flute-as-Thisbe, by which dressing up as the opposite sex might remain socially acceptable in drawing-room and barrack-room performance because signalled as comic and anomalous: as Chapter 2 showed, in the hands of some nineteenth-century amateur performers this mode escaped from 'Pyramus and Thisbe' to take over even the traumatically indecorous Shakespearean tragedy at which the mechanicals' performance appears to glance, *Romeo and Juliet*. But amateur performance has also taken up the more mimetically committed manner of Viola-as-Cesario, by which, translating from the comparatively straightforward female-to-male disguise such scenes had become in the mainstream modern theatre back to the male-to-female-to-male dynamics of the Elizabethan stage, all-male prisoner-of-war casts were able tantalizingly to simulate the sorts of performances by actresses which their audiences would far rather have been at liberty to enjoy. In amateur performance, Shakespeare's depictions of gender and its metamorphoses have served variously to enforce and playfully to subvert sexual norms, even in the bosoms of families, in church halls and in the armed forces. The costuming used in amateur performance has also regularly enabled not just the actors but the audiences of amateur Shakespeare to pretend to be in other places or other times: whether at home in England while watching *The Merry Wives of Windsor* on St Vincent, or in an imagined timeless Merry England while watching *A Midsummer Night's Dream* at Richmond, or already in a democratic, egalitarian future of shared civic culture while watching a modern-dress *Merchant of Venice* at the Bolton Little Theatre.

The tendency of amateurs, consciously or not, to choose plays which chime dramatically with the circumstances of their production partly explains some striking divergences between amateur and professional repertories across time. Few readers of orthodox reception histories of the Shakespeare canon, for instance, would have suspected the prominence enjoyed by *Henry IV part 1* on the amateur stage from the seventeenth century through the nineteenth. In the conventional theatre of the time the play was adequately popular with character actors willing to pad-up as Falstaff, but since it did not offer the sort of single, dominating 'straight' role which appealed to actor-managers it was under-represented in the commercial repertory. (Garrick, for instance, only appeared in this play on six occasions, in the heroic but for him disappointingly small part of Hotspur.) Nor, I suspect, would such readers have anticipated the extraordinary predilection shown by amateur groups of all kinds and periods for choosing *The Merchant of Venice* as their first Shakespeare play, from the Kilkenny Theatrical Society to the Great Hucklow Village Players and well beyond. This again must in part be a practical matter to do with casting: the play has an especially lucid scenic structure, articulating its principal ideas via plot rather than through soliloquy, and it offers a range of equally prominent leading roles and some attractive supporting ones. (Although Morocco appears in only two scenes and Aragon in only one, for example, each is compensated by a conveniently light rehearsal schedule and the possibility of a terrific costume.) But thematically, too, *The Merchant of Venice* has special potential appeal to amateurs. For any voluntary theatre group this play's dramatic interest in defining insiders (such as the essentially amateur, not-for-profit moneylender Antonio) against outsiders (the mercenary, professional Shylock) is always to the point, while its explicit articulation of a nominally Christian ideology in opposition to Old Testament Judaism has made it especially attractive to civic groups operating, like the Unitarian society in Stockport which became the Garrick, as offshoots of particular churches (or simply performing, like the early Middlesbrough Little Theatre and many others, in hired or borrowed church halls). The recurrent popularity of this play with amateur players also makes visible the importance of *The Merchant of Venice*, for better and for worse, within the reception of Shakespeare more generally, again something which cultural histories centred solely on professional criticism and the professional stage have tended to underestimate. This was, after all, among the first Shakespeare plays to be either translated or acted in several countries (including India, China, Romania and Bulgaria), and given that the social issues surrounding capitalism, usury and debt have become only more prominent since Shakespeare's time, while emergent nations have regularly sought to define themselves in ethnic and religious terms, it has rarely been less than topical, even if few of its performances can have been as anxiously and disturbingly so as that at Stalag 383.[8]

AMATEUR SHAKESPEARE ABROAD

How, though, are the different traditions of non-professional Shakespeare bearing up in the early twenty-first century? To start with the successors to Chapter 3's diplomats and military officers, expatriate theatre continues to thrive, although military personnel appear to have largely abandoned Shakespeare since the days of Michael Goodliffe and Frank Twiss. The navy remains the most theatrical of the armed services, boasting a central Royal Naval Theatrical Association, based at HMS Collingwood in Hampshire (which makes grants to drama groups dispersed throughout the navy in order to keep their theatrical equipment up to standard), and a Royal Navy Drama Festival (complete with guest adjudicator and awards ceremony) which takes place every spring. The central RNTA also mounts a production of its own every alternate summer, and it is an index of how times have changed since the days when Captain Keeling stocked up on Shakespearean quartos in 1607 that since 2002 these have all been of plays adapted from the works of Terry Pratchett.[9]

This neglect of Shakespeare among the uniformed services, however, is more than compensated by his importance among post-war diplomats. On the Continent in the early twenty-first century, for instance, the uncertainty as to whether Shakespeare is to be performed as British or as part of a common European cultural heritage which perplexed Samuel Egerton Brydges still puzzles some of the organizations currently doing Shakespeare in front of mixed expatriate and native audiences, albeit with different inflections according to the demographics and the levels of linguistic proficiency found in different groups. Much of this activity is of the same double nature as that of the 1830 *Henry IV* in Geneva – whereby a club of Anglophones forms in order to perform a sort of voluntary cultural diplomacy addressed to the host culture as well as to one another – but it offers Britons in its audiences one experience also available at Stratford, at the Globe or in many outdoor theatres back home, namely that of seeing part of their national culture through the eyes, and over the shoulders, of non-Britons. This sort of amateur Shakespeare thrives with particular vigour alongside more official, state-sponsored activities designed to represent Britain to its neighbours. The higher the concentration of Britons lying abroad for their country, it appears, the more Shakespeare gets produced, with the most ambitious productions clustered around cities with a substantial diplomatic presence. It would be interesting to speculate as to whether the career of diplomacy attracts an unusually high percentage of frustrated classical actors, or whether it simply offers a particularly undemanding workload, but to date no reliable surveys are extant.[10]

A resurgence of non-professional Shakespeare in continental Europe, for example, followed Britain's entry into the entity formerly known as the Common Market in 1973, with particularly striking activity in

Strasbourg and in Brussels. At the former, the Council of Europe's staff theatre group (known as 'Tagora') performs Shakespeare in a spirit comparable to that of Samuel Egerton Brydges, playing to core audiences of expatriate Anglophones swelled by local Francophone school and college groups. In 1991, outdoing Charles Michel Lullin in cosmopolitan outreach, they performed a bilingual *A Midsummer Night's Dream* in which the fairies spoke French. (Lord, what fools these [English] mortals be.)[11] The largest concentration of designated amateur Shakespeareans in Europe, however – producing the Bard's works on a scale comparable to the annual amateur Shakespeare festivals back home in Stamford and Cambridge – is provided by the Brussels Shakespeare Society, which, after a series of tentative workshops and readings, was formally established in 1976. Its founder was Ian Flintoff, at the time an ex-actor working as a *porte-parole* for the European Commission (though he subsequently returned to Britain and to his original calling, acting both with the Royal Shakespeare Company and at the National Theatre). Like the English theatricals in Florence in the 1820s it boasts a lord as its figurehead – its honorary president is Lord Kinnock, the former British commissioner at the European Union who now chairs the British Council. In keeping with the more aristocratic traditions of the practice, too, the BSS now performs every summer in the grounds of the castle at Corroy-le-Château, thanks to the support and hospitality of Monsieur le Marquis de Trazegnies, as well as mounting one or two indoor productions per year. Complying with the long-established British expatriate enthusiasm for Falstaff which this study has already recorded, their impressive portfolio of past productions includes both parts of *Henry IV* and two productions of *The Merry Wives of Windsor*.[12] Elsewhere in modern Europe too, Brydges' sense that thespian Britons abroad ought to turn to Shakespeare's magic page, and that foreigners ought to take note, seems to prevail: in Helsinki the repertory of the Finn-Brit Players, founded in 1981, has to date included only three Shakespeare plays (*Twelfth Night, Macbeth* and *The Winter's Tale*) out of approximately forty full-scale shows, but these have always attracted unusual interest, and in 2006 *The Winter's Tale*, chosen as the group's silver jubilee production, drew audiences double those attracted by other plays.[13] This is similar to the experience of the New World Theatre Club in Luxembourg – originally founded in 1968 with, as its name implies, an emphasis on American plays, but subsequently dabbling in Shakespearean compilations (*An Evening With Shakespeare* and *The Hollow Crown*) and eventually mounting successful full-scale productions (*The Taming of the Shrew, Macbeth, The Merry Wives of Windsor*).[14]

Back in Charles Michel Lullin's native city, however, Shakespeare's popularity with expatriate amateur players has been less overwhelming, even though Geneva – long the home of international organizations such as the League of Nations, the International Labour Organization and the World Health Authority – has continued to play host to a large English-speaking population. The Geneva English Drama Society was formally established in 1933, drawing on earlier theatrical activities associated with British delegates and staff members at the International Labour Organization, and it has produced between four and six productions every year since then, but remarkably this group performed no Shakespearean plays at all for the first forty years of its existence, unless one counts George Bernard Shaw's jeu d'esprit *The Dark Lady of the Sonnets*. With its early ties to the labour movement, the GEDS at first decisively took the Shav side in the Shaks vs Shav debate, producing Shaw's plays on a regular basis (including, naturally enough, his controversial *Geneva*, first produced soon after its composition in 1938 and revived in 2008), but eschewing his Elizabethan *bête noire*. This is one expatriate repertory from which Shakespeare has been largely squeezed out by more topical serious drama and more modern comedy: the other playwrights patronized by the society in the years leading up to a fortieth anniversary production of Aristophanes' *Lysistrata* included Thornton Wilder, Noël Coward, Peter Shaffer, John Osborne, Harold Pinter, Joe Orton and Ray Cooney. It was only in 1973–4 that the society finally succumbed to *Twelfth Night*, and since then Shakespeare has accounted for only six productions (one of them a compilation) out of 150.[15]

One explanation for Shakespeare's similarly limited presence in another Swiss centre, Basel, is supplied by the same demographic factor which for James Fenimore Cooper characterized the 1829 *Henry IV* in Florence, namely a superiority in numbers and ability of its female performers. Unwilling to adopt Harris-like cross-gender casting, The Semi-Circle in Basel, founded in 1965, have to date staged no full-length Shakespeare at all, but only an evening of excerpts called 'Will Power', precisely because of the natural facility in acting enjoyed by its women: 'We have a lot of excellent female actors and rather few good male actors,' explains one candid member of their governing committee, unconsciously concurring with Frank Humpherson. 'Shakespeare needs mainly stronger actors.'[16] In Germany, the Frankfurt English-Speaking Theatre actually evolved in the 1970s from the British Women's Club of the Taunus, but they have since recruited sufficient males to mount full-scale conventionally gendered productions of *A Midsummer Night's Dream* and *Twelfth Night*.[17]

Further to the north, however, as far as expatriate amateur Shakespeare is concerned, something is rotten in the state of Denmark. The Copenhagen Theatre Circle, founded in the late 1960s under the patronage of the British ambassador to Denmark (where should he have his thanks?), has never yet produced a full-scale Shakespeare play, largely because this society too has a preponderance of women among its membership.[18] Among the merry English wives of Copenhagen, *Hamlet*'s two female roles simply aren't enough to make the play worth reviving in its usual form (even this close to Elsinore), and so the Copenhagen Theatre Circle, instead of performing the tragedy in its entirety, adapted parts of it early in 2007 as the framework for a compilation which imported a whole gallery of female characters from Shakespeare's other plays. This was called 'Frailty, Thy Name Is Woman', and it combined elements of the structure of *Hamlet* ('a young man, the Hamlet figure, his mother and stepfather were the threads that held the various scenes together') with a throwback, potentially every bit as misogynistic as the Prince in the nunnery scene, to the medieval morality drama which the Shakespearean stage once displaced: these cut-and-pasted women were each supposed to personify one of the Seven Deadly Sins. They included 'Lady Macbeth, Beatrice, Queen Margaret ... and so on, each representing one of the sins ... We felt that it was cheating a bit to use Juliet as Lust!'[19] Just as the Harris sisters stayed at home and acted an adapted *Winter's Tale* while their brother negotiated treaties abroad, female-dominated amateur Shakespeare in this instance still seems to be confined to a semi-private space rather than participating fully in the international arena.

AMATEUR SHAKESPEARE AT HOME

Back in Britain, too, there is still a semi-private amateur Shakespeare as well as a public one, and some of the traditions of domestic performance outlined in my first chapter are alive and well. It is true that the aristocracy has taken far less interest in performing Shakespeare in the twentieth and twenty-first centuries than it did in the eighteenth: as far as I have been able to discover, the last nobleman to follow the career trajectory of the Earl of Barrymore was Henry Paget, 5th Marquess of Anglesey (the notorious 'Dancing Marquess'), who died in debt in 1904, at the age of twenty-nine, after squandering much of his inheritance on mounting a lavish production of *Henry V* in which he played the King. But although the best-known instance of private Shakespeare since that

Figure 27. *As You Like It*, Dressing-Up Box Theatre Company, Oxford, 2007: William Franklin (Orlando, 13), Charis Taplin (Hymen, 7), Hannah Tillmann-Morris (Rosalind, 10).

time is a fictitious one, the *Hamlet* staged at the Blenheim-like stately home Scamnum Ducis in Michael Innes' crime novel *Hamlet, Revenge!* (1937),[20] in some humbler houses the traditions of private performance live on. The originally aristocratic practice of casting children in adult roles, for example, which dates all the way back to Surrenden and was actively recommended by Ben Greet's acting editions, persists, and not just in schools. Some theatrically inclined families, just like the Harrises and their Salisbury connections, continue to cooperate on their own Shakespearean productions: every summer in a suburb of Oxford, for example, a select invited coterie enjoys the annual offering of the Dressing-Up Box Theatre Company, no member of which is over fourteen, and who perform just as Greet would wish them to, outdoors in a garden (Figure 27).

Commentators on the health of the mainstream, civic tradition, meanwhile, divide between the quietly pessimistic and the exuberantly visionary. In the post-war period, television and the internet have joined the cinema among a much-cited catalogue of enemies to live theatre in all its forms, but the most serious threat to the non-professional sector has come not from rival forms of recreation but from the erosion of free time. Many civic amateur dramatic groups were only able to come into existence at all because in the years following the First World War the lower and middle classes were allowed to spend more of their lives out of the workplace (hence the appropriateness of the Shakespearean slogan which Billy Butlin adopted for the chain of holiday camps which he founded in 1936, 'Our true intent is all for your delight'), and they have correspondingly suffered from recent changes in working patterns. 'Increased work commitments and less leisure time, which have become the hallmarks of many professions, have affected active members' ability to devote effort to The Questors at all levels,' lamented Gwenan Lloyd Evans in 1989.[21] Increasingly, only the very young or the much older are able to dedicate themselves to amateur theatricals, contributing further to a widespread sense of the non-professional stage as a theatrical rearguard rather than an artistic vanguard. While in the summer, outdoor productions during school and college holidays prosper, in the winter, presumably, cross-age casting – always prevalent in amateur societies, where the role of young Hamlet may only be available to those with twenty years' proven service – may become as important as the cross-gender casting, in one direction or the other, which this study has illustrated within most periods of amateur theatrical history.

Despite Evans' anxiety, however, in the early twenty-first century, just as in the early nineteenth and again in the early twentieth, the balance of power between the professional and the non-professional performance of the Shakespeare canon is shifting once more. Ever since the days when the Amateurs of Cambridge campaigned for the erection of a statue of Shakespeare, the fate of the non-professional stage and the destiny of the National Theatre project have been intimately linked, and in the years before subsidized theatres were established it was local amateur companies who took the responsibility for mounting those classical plays which the commercial playhouses would not touch. At a time when the British government is making vague noises about a 'big society' in which the voluntary sector is to take over services formerly provided by the state, a time when threatened budget cuts are calling the very survival of the subsidized theatre into question, it may be that the amateurs will have to step into the breach once more. In retrospect, it is quite possible that the most important landmark in Shakespearean performance in the first years of this century will prove not to be the Royal Shakespeare Company's professional Complete Works Festival of 2006–7, but the same company's incorporation of amateur performers into its World Shakespeare Festival of 2012, part of the 'Cultural Olympiad' to be staged alongside the London Olympic Games.[22]

Alternatively, it may well be that the real historic milestone in early twenty-first-century Shakespearean performance will turn out have been the all-amateur rival to Stratford's Complete Works Festival, the great York Shakespeare Project. This was first planned in 2000 by participants in a millennial production of the York mystery plays, the very plays in which another local performer, the young Judi Dench, made her own first public, amateur stage appearances, as the Virgin Mary, in 1957.[23] The begetters of the York Shakespeare Project decided that as an encore to the mysteries the city ought to stage each of Shakespeare's plays in turn across two whole decades – approximating to the period over which they were composed – and across a range of different venues, both indoor and outdoor. A passionately voluble description of this undertaking, issued by its founder, Frank Brogan, as the first performances began in 2002, implicitly urged the volunteer thespians of York to start preparing for its planned culminating production by throwing themselves into the task of conceiving an amateur starlet worthy of the Bard:

All the plays in twenty years, in roughly chronological order, the last being *The Tempest* which will be performed in 2022 or thereabouts. Now there's a thought – because Miranda, Prospero's daughter, well, she's only a young lass, isn't she? Thirteen or so? [*sic – Brogan appears to have confused Miranda's age with Juliet's*]. So ideally she will be played by someone a few years older – sixteen or seventeen perhaps, certainly someone no more than eighteen years old. Now that person, the person who will play Miranda, hasn't been born yet! The person who plays Miranda could literally be any aspiring female actor born between 2006 and 2008 who is living in York during the period of the production of *The Tempest*. You could say we will be looking for someone of the calibre of Dame Judi Dench at that age to play that part . . . But so that our Miranda becomes a reality, The York Shakespeare Project has to create such an enthusiasm and support within the York community . . . that people will be queuing up to play not only Miranda but Prospero and Caliban and Ariel and Ferdinand and every other character, not only in *The Tempest* but in all the plays from *Richard III* [*chosen as the project's first production because of its local associations*] onwards. And to work backstage, sell tickets, fundraising, publicity and yes, make cups of tea too! And let's not forget the all-important role of our audience, to sit and see and be transported by this twenty year act of theatre. This is what The York Shakespeare Project is all about. A whole community involving itself in productions of excellence and innovation. A whole community showing itself, through the work of Shakespeare, to the world.[24]

It seems that the artistic and civic ambitions which drove Edwin T. Heys a century earlier, here leavened with national and international ambitions too, have not deserted the provincial cities of England yet.

It would be a mistake in emphasis, however, to end this concluding account of the state of present-day amateur Shakespeare, or indeed this entire cultural history of amateur Shakespearean performance, with a quotation so eminently vulnerable to ridicule as the self-aggrandizing dream of a northerly Desmond Olivier Dingle. The chief impulse which continues to draw people to perform the plays of Shakespeare themselves instead of solely paying others to perform them, I suspect, and which continues to reward their audiences, is something more modest than this, and possibly more complex. It was certainly visible in one non-professional production which I watched during the summer of 2009, a production which conveniently brought together many of the themes of this book. Featuring a programme bearing a prominent endorsement from a knight, Sir Geoffrey Cass, and donating its proceeds to charity, this show recognizably belonged to the same tradition as the Kilkenny Theatrical Society, but its demographics tied it more closely to the civic traditions of the later nineteenth and early twentieth centuries. Although its cast, like those at the Minack in its early days, included a few professional and semi-professional actors (here offering their services for free *à la* Eliza O'Neill), the majority of them, just as in an earlier fund-raising Shakespearean production in the same city, were amateurs of Cambridge. In fact, this was a *de facto* works amateur dramatic society, since the production was staged to mark the 475th birthday of Cambridge University Press, predominantly by volunteers from among its employees. It took place in a field at the bottom of the institution's sports ground, in front of just the sort of small copse of trees which Ben Greet would have recommended. The play, it is perhaps needless to say, was *A Midsummer Night's Dream*.

There was much about this attractive and inventive show, however, directed by Susan Painter as 'an excitingly dark, refreshing and modern interpretation of this much-loved tale', which Greet would not have recognized. At the opening and closing of each half, for instance, the acting area was eerily stalked by silent black-clad dryads in expressionless white masks, and indeed the supernatural beings in general were considerably more sinister than the winsome children favoured by the Edwardians. A coarse, cruel, slightly slobbering Puck (Nik White) deliberately gave an impression of partial autism, while Titania's fairy train were positively gnome-like. Arrestingly, whenever Cobweb, Mustardseed and Peaseblossom were present, they were accompanied by an additional, non-speaking fairy wearing a woollen hat with ear-flaps, who sat towards the rear of the stage gloating over her mistress's

Figure 28. *A Midsummer Night's Dream*, Cambridge University Press, 2009. Titania
(Tricia Peroni), Bottom (James Stuart), Knotgrass (Sarah Stanton).

humiliation, all the while knitting like a fairy Madame Defarge: in the
programme she was listed as 'Knotgrass' (Sarah Stanton) (Figure 28).
The mechanicals, meanwhile, had seized the opportunity to parody the
incipiently bureaucratized workings of the present-day non-professional
theatre: Quince (Declan Lynch), explicitly described in the programme
as the 'leader of an amateur dramatic group', was perpetually attended
by an over-busy non-speaking young woman with a clipboard who
might have been on a work-experience scheme, listed as 'P.A. to Peter
Quince' (Danièle Gibney).

At the matinee I saw, it rained during much of the first half, driving those members of the audience who had sat themselves on blankets immediately in front of the actors back onto the canvas-sheltered rows of plastic seats further back, but during the interval many crept companionably back onto the sodden grass regardless, angling to be as close to the actors as possible. It was perfectly clear that, despite or as a result of the production's unassimilated compilation of miscellaneous design ideas, styles of speech and levels of basic acting ability, these people were all finding the play both immensely touching and immensely funny. It was not just the play they were finding touching and funny, moreover, but the fact of who was in it: I overheard a number of conversations in which people commented on the appropriateness or otherwise of the roles assigned to their friends. From looking through a programme in which the cast and crew had offered brief descriptions of themselves and their reasons for being in the show, I could look up and glimpse the same cast and crew members bustling about making ready for the second half: an arbitrary and potentially ill-assorted group of people happily convened, along with their audience, by a great play. For each of them, it was evident, simply reading or even watching *A Midsummer Night's Dream* had not been enough: they had wanted to get it without book, to feel its words in their own mouths and pace out its action with their own limbs, and in the process to make it central to a chapter of their own biographies. Like the participants in an Edwardian pageant, they were each transforming something which belongs to collective national history into part of their own personal, local, bodily memories. Just as the adult Harris girls must have been reminded every time they saw or read *The Winter's Tale* of the friendships of their youth, so for every member of that cast *A Midsummer Night's Dream* would forever be not just a text but a particular remembered summer, a particular network of acquaintanceships, a particular green plot in Cambridge. In the same way, for my grandfather *Hamlet* always recalled the days when, building a new theatre for Middlesbrough, he had personified the authority of his amateur society's rightful founders, and for me part of the charm of *As You Like It* will always be its association with the experience of carrying a borrowed guitar to a midge-infested island and singing to the accompaniment of screeching peacocks. There are many things to do by way of interpreting, understanding and sharing a Shakespeare play that are completely beside the point compared to actually living in it for a while.

The second half got under way. A broken-brained weaver (James Stuart) continued to enjoy his unexpected intimacy with the Queen of the Fairies (Tricia Peroni). Knotgrass got on with her knitting. The sole mortal in the story allowed to share our knowledge that the fairies even exist, the weaver eventually woke from what he only half-believed had been a dream, and reflected with joy that this experience might be transformed into a ballad to adorn the amateur performance for which he had been rehearsing earlier on. The clouds briefly cleared above Cambridge, though there was a cold breeze. When everything less important in the play had at last been settled – who would have the changeling boy, which young aristocratic man would marry which young aristocratic woman, whether one of them would be sent to a nunnery by her father, whether the Duke's bride would go on sulking about it – both we on the grass and they in the play on the grass finally got to see what we had been waiting for, the artisans' performance of 'Pyramus and Thisbe'. The aristocrats affected to be much cleverer than the weaver and his colleagues, despite being much less funny and much less well-meaning: but even so, they were held together as an audience by the mechanicals' play, identified as a society at last capable of renewing itself, and, whether they noticed the fact or not, the amateur play resonated with just the issues they had been contending with so incompetently for the previous four acts – forbidden courtship, a wild wood, parental prohibition, dying for love. We others on the grass, the cast's friends and families and well-wishers, were held as members of that audience too. When the weaver ceased pretending to be the dead Pyramus and leapt to his feet to contradict the Duke again and offer the choice of an epilogue or a bergamask dance, he could have had a standing ovation if had he not been too good an ensemble member to angle for it. For four hundred years Shakespeare has suited and indulged such amateur actors and their audiences with endless generosity. Chudleigh Dunscombe was right. Bottom may be a conceited, pragmatical, imbecile idiot, but Titania loves him: and the play loves him, and its audiences love him, and if you have never felt that you too wanted to be in his place, even if only for one week of one summer, you must be a complete ass.

Notes

INTRODUCTION: SHAKESPEARE IN CULTURE

1 Samuel Egerton Brydges, 'Prologue III. For Shakespeare's Henry IV. Written 13 Jan. 1830.', in *The Anglo-Genevan Critical Journal for 1831* (2 vols., Geneva, 1831), vol. 1, 303–5.

2 See Norman Marshall, *The Other Theatre* (London: Lehmann, 1947), 86–7.

3 From Captain Keeling's journal, ed. Gary Taylor, in Ivo Kamps and Jyotsna Singh, eds., *Travel Knowledge: European 'Discoveries' in the Early Modern Period* (New York and Houndmills: Palgrave, 2001), 219–20. For the most thorough reconstruction of this event to date, see Gary Taylor, '*Hamlet* in Africa 1607', in *ibid.*, 223–48.

4 *Ibid.*, 220.

5 All references to Shakespeare are to the Oxford edition, ed. Stanley Wells and Gary Taylor (2nd edn, Oxford: Oxford University Press, 2005).

6 See Park Honan, *Shakespeare: A Life* (Oxford: Oxford University Press, 1999).

7 Marshall, 86.

8 The term 'community theatre', which in Britain tends to be used of broadly political shows often dramatizing contentious incidents from local history (such as the work of Ann Jellicoe, radical successor to the pageant-makers I discuss in Chapter 4), has a more inclusive sense in the United States, where it is sometimes used to refer to productions which in Britain would simply be termed 'amateur'. See, for example, Robert E. Gard and Gertrude S. Burley, *Community Theatre: Idea and Achievement* (1959: Westport: Greenwood, 1975); Jan Cohen-Cruz, *Local Acts: Community-based Performance in the United States* (Rutgers: Rutgers University Press, 2005), and Leah Hager Cohen, *The Stuff of Dreams: Behind the Scenes of an American Community Theater* (New York: Viking, 2001).

9 See Adrian Rendle, *Everyman and His Theatre* (London: Pitman, 1968). On a closely related but distinct phenomenon, see John Lowerson, *Amateur Operatics: A Social and Cultural History* (Manchester: Manchester University Press, 2005).

10 Such is this writer's symbolic importance, however, that even a decision *not* to perform Shakespeare becomes a significant fact of any theatre company's history and identity, and if a grand *longue durée* history of all

non-professional performance *were* to be written, revivals of Shakespeare would make as reasonable a starting point as any.

11 On non-professional theatre elsewhere in Europe, for instance, see Marie Madeleine Mervant-Roux, ed., *Du théâtre amateur: approche historique et anthropologique* (Paris: CNRS Editions, collections 'Arts du Spectacles/ Spectacles, Histoires, Société', March 2004); on Shakespeare, now the most frequently performed playwright in France, see especially Isabelle Schwartz-Gastine, 'Le Songe d'Une Nuit d'Eté: une troupe emblematique', in *ibid.*, 32–45.

12 See especially Robert Shaughnessy, *The Shakespeare Effect: A History of Twentieth Century Performance* (Houndmills: Palgrave, 2002).

13 On the Shakespearean events of 1932, see especially Terence Hawkes, *That Shakespeherian Rag: Essays on a Critical Process* (London: Routledge, 1986); also Graham Holderness, *The Shakespeare Myth* (Manchester: Manchester University Press, 1988), 'Introduction'.

14 I am ruling out William Hawkins' *Praelectiones Poeticae* (Oxford, 1758) as a contender for the title of first proper academic monograph on Shakespeare on the grounds that this was merely the text of some lectures given on the subject, and given entirely in Latin (right down to the quotations, which Hawkins translated) at that.

15 See especially Nicola Watson, 'Kemble, Scott, and the Mantle of the Bard', in Jean Marsden, ed., *The Appropriation of Shakespeare: Post-Renaissance Appropriations of the Works and the Myth* (Hemel Hempstead: Harvester, 1991), 73–92.

16 For Bradley's importance to analysts of the Shakespeare phenomenon, see especially Hawkes' *That Shakespeherian Rag*. The verdict on Bradley's influence is quoted from Tom Matheson, 'Bradley, A(ndrew) C(ecil)', in Michael Dobson and Stanley Wells, eds., *The Oxford Companion to Shakespeare* (Oxford: Oxford University Press, 2001), 53. On Bradley's importance see also Katharine Cooke, *A. C. Bradley and His Influence in Twentieth-Century Shakespeare Criticism* (Oxford: Oxford University Press, 1972), and, the latest of many reprints, A. C. Bradley, *Shakespearean Tragedy*, ed. Robert Shaughnessy (Basingstoke: Palgrave, 2006). On the continuing use of Bradley by performers, see e.g. Sîan Thomas, 'Lady Macbeth', in Michael Dobson, ed., *Performing Shakespeare's Tragedies Today* (Cambridge: Cambridge University Press, 2006), 94–105.

17 On the Folger's Folio acquisitions see especially Anthony James West, *The First Folio: The History of the Book: An Account of the First Folio Based on Its Sales and Prices, 1623–2000* (Oxford: Oxford University Press, 2001).

18 T. S. Eliot, review of Herbert Grierson's edition of *Metaphysical Lyrics and Poems of the Seventeenth Century*, *Times Literary Supplement*, 20 October 1921.

19 The Folger, famously, both literalizes and trumps the feudal-relic-lurking-at-the-heart-of-bourgeois-democracy view of Bardolatry by enshrining its relics of the superseded Old World at the very nerve-centre of the New, in the middle of Washington, DC.

20 See Conclusion, below.

21 The description of amateur acting as a case of 'members of the audience getting up on stage' comes from Bertolt Brecht: see John Willett, ed., *Brecht on Theatre* (London: Methuen, 1964), 'Is it worth speaking about the amateur theatre?' (*c.* 1940), 149–50.

22 I owe my information about this extraordinary theatrical event, if it exactly counts as one, to Peter Holland.

23 See, for example, Martin Blocksidge, ed., *Shakespeare in Education* (London: Continuum, 2005); Sharon Beehler and Holger Michael Klein, *Shakespeare and Higher Education: A Global Perspective* (New York: Edwin Mellen, 2000).

24 See especially Humphrey Carpenter, *O.U.D.S.: A Centenary History of the Oxford University Dramatic Society, 1885–1985* (Oxford: Oxford University Press, 1985).

25 See e.g. Hank Rogerson's television documentary *Shakespeare Behind Bars* (2005); the London Shakespeare Workout Prison Project (www.londonshakespeare.org.uk/Mission/prisonmission2.htm); Murray Cox, *Shakespeare Comes to Broadmoor* (London: Kingsley, 1992).

26 I am thinking in particular here of Abigail Rokison, president of the British Shakespeare Association, whose parents met when cast as Bottom and Titania.

CHAPTER 1: SHAKESPEARE IN PRIVATE: DOMESTIC
PERFORMANCE

1 For an overview of the phenomenon during its Georgian heyday, see Gillian Russell, 'Private Theatricals', in Iain McCalman and Jon Mee, eds., *The Oxford Companion to the Romantic Age* (Oxford: Oxford University Press, 2001), 726.

2 See Sybil Rosenfeld, *Temples of Thespis: Some Private Theatres and Theatricals in England and Wales, 1700–1820* (London: Society for Theatre Research, 1978), 85, 91, 169; *The Private Theatre of Kilkenny* ([Kilkenny], 1825), 2; Lord William Lennox, *Drafts on My Memory* (2 vols., London, 1866), vol. II, 72–3. For further examples staged outside Britain see Chapter 3. At the Berkeley Castle performances, the exchange between Hotspur and Northumberland in 1.3 must have stood out:

> HOTSPUR ... In Richard's time,—what do you call the place?—
>   A plague upon it, it is in Gloucestershire;
>   'Twas where the madcap duke his uncle kept,
>   His uncle York; where I first bow'd my knee
>   Unto this king of smiles, this Bolingbroke,—
>   'Sblood!
>   When you and he came back from Ravenspurgh.
> NORTHUMBERLAND At Berkeley castle.
> HOTSPUR You say true.

3 *The Miniature, a Periodical Paper*, 21 (1804: 2 vols., Windsor, 1806), vol. I, 280.

4 See [Robert Cox], *The Merry Conceited Humours of Bottom the Weaver* (London, 1661), 'lately, privately, presented, by several APPRENTICES for their harmless recreation'. An introductory letter from the Stationer to the Reader offers this text's ability to generate non-professional theatre as one of its chief recommendations: 'this . . . we know may be easily acted, and may be now as fit for a private recreation as it hath formerly been for a public'.

5 See, for example, Colin Franklin, *Shakespeare Domesticated: The Eighteenth-century Editions* (Aldershot: Scolar Press, 1991); Michael Dobson, *The Making of the National Poet: Shakespeare, Adaptation and Authorship, 1660–1769* (Oxford: Oxford University Press, 1992), 146–58, 224–5.

6 Laetitia Yeandle, *Sir Edward Dering, 1st Bart., of Surrenden Dering and His 'Booke of Expences' – 1617–1628* (Kent Archaeological Society papers no. 20, www.kentarchaeology.ac/authors/020.pdf, accessed 12 March 2006), 54–5, 58, 62–3. See also her 'The Dating of Sir Edward Dering's Copy of "The History of King Henry the Fourth"', *Shakespeare Quarterly* 37 (1986), 224–6. On the political situation at this time see especially Paul Salzman, *Literary Culture in Jacobean England: Reading 1621* (Houndmills: Palgrave, 2002), esp. 142.

7 Yeandle, *Booke of Expences*, 118, 137, 156.

8 *Ibid.*, 138.

9 See George Walton Williams and Gwynne Blakemore Evans, eds., *The History of King Henry the Fourth, as Revised by Sir Edward Dering, Bart.* (Charlottesville: University of Virginia Press, for the Folger Shakespeare Library, 1974). On Dering as a play collector see T. S. Lennam, 'Sir Edward Dering's Collection of Playbooks, 1619–1624', *Shakespeare Quarterly* 16 (1965), 145–53.

10 Yeandle, *Booke of Expences*, 146.

11 *Ibid.*, 146–7. The last part of this entry is difficult to discern: Yeandle wavers between 'given himore' and 'given him< >?'

12 Williams and Evans, 75.

13 *Ibid.*, 2–3.

14 *Ibid.*, 168–9.

15 'France being ours we'll bend it to our awe, / Or break it all to pieces.'

16 Williams and Evans, 222–3.

17 Peter Holland, 'Shakespeare Abbreviated', in Robert Shaughnessy, ed., *The Cambridge Companion to Shakespeare in Popular Culture* (Cambridge: Cambridge University Press, 2007), 26–45; 28.

18 *The Spanish Curat*, in *Comedies and Tragedies Written by Francis Beaumont and Iohn Fletcher* (London, 1647), 49–50.

19 Joseph Roach, 'Public Intimacy: The Prior History of "It"', in Mary Luckhurst and Jane Moody, eds., *Theatre and Celebrity in Britain, 1600–2000* (Basingstoke: Palgrave, 2005), 15–30.

20 On toy theatres, see George Speaight, *Juvenile Drama: The History of the English Toy Theatre* (London: Macdonald, 1946); George Speaight *et al.*, *William West and the Regency Toy Theatre* (London: Sir John Soane's Museum, 2004); on Greet, see Chapter 4, below.

21 In 1667–8 the Duke of Monmouth appeared at court in an amateur production of *The Indian Emperor* at the age of seventeen, while in 1681 the future Queen Anne appeared at Holyrood in an amateur production of Nathaniel Lee's *Mithridates*, at the age of sixteen. Rosenfeld, 10.

22 William Coxe, *Memoirs of John, Duke of Marlborough* (6 vols., London, 1819), vol. III, 643. Cf. the bowdlerizing cuts made to the text of the Fletcher/Shakespeare/Theobald play *Double Falsehood* when it was performed by the Noel family in Exton, Rutland, *c.* 1750: Brean Hammond, ed., *Double Falsehood* (Arden 3rd edition, London: Black, 2010), 117. The promptbook survives as Folger Prompt D36.

23 Hogarth, incidentally, was still producing variants of his *Beggar's Opera* painting when he began work on this one.

24 *Daily Journal*, 17 February 1728.

25 Mrs Pendarves is now better known under her second married name of Delany. For her account of this production, see Lady Llanover, ed., *The Autobiography and Correspondence of Mary Granville, Mrs. Delany: with Interesting Reminiscences of King George the Third and Queen Charlotte* (3 vols., London, 1861), I, 158.

26 *London Magazine*, January 1749. See Harry William Pedicord, *'By Their Majesties' Command': The House of Hanover at the London Theatres, 1714–1800* (London: Society for Theatre Research, 1991), 29–30.

27 William Pitt, Lord Lennox, *Celebrities I Have Known* (2 vols., London, 1876), I, 218–22.

28 On domestic productions of she-tragedy as 'vehicles for the negotiation of sexuality within the family and the definition of the gendered roles of boys and girls', see Gillian Russell, *The Theatres of War: Performance, Politics, and Society, 1793–1815* (Oxford: Clarendon Press, 1995), 129–30.

29 The disgraced couple were packed off to the American colonies, and were only gradually rehabilitated into English society, via posts obtained for O'Brien as Barrack-Master of Quebec and Secretary and Provost-Master-General of the Bermudas: eventually they were allowed to live in one of the family houses at Stinsford, near Dorchester, and O'Brien was made Receiver General for Dorset. See Susan Rands, '"Publicity perpetuates the mortification": The Marriage of William O'Brien and Lady Susan Fox-Strangways', *Studies in Theatre and Performance* 21:1 (2001), 52–6; Stella Tillyard, *Aristocrats* (London: Chatto and Windus, 1994), 183–8; Joanna Martin, *Wives and Daughters: Women and Children in the Georgian Country House* (Hambledon and London: Continuum, 2004), 35–48.

30 *Salisbury Journal*, 20 June 1774.

31 Although the Harris papers refer to this play simply as *Florizel and Perdita* it is clear that they were using Morgan's abbreviation of *The Winter's Tale*

rather than Garrick's *Florizel and Perdita*, since the cast list for their production includes neither Leontes nor Paulina, who both appear in Garrick's version. Donald Burrows and Rosemary Dunhill, eds., *Music and Theatre in Handel's World: The Family Papers of James Harris* (Oxford: Oxford University Press, 2002), 780 (Burrows and Dunhill themselves, however, miss this point, misidentifying the play as Garrick's). The Harrises' use of Morgan's adaptation is confirmed by references in their correspondence to its location, since Morgan, unlike Garrick, places his afterpiece in 'Bithynia' rather than Bohemia.

32 *Ibid.*

33 On Elizabeth Harris' social activities in London around this time, where she was a member of the 'Ladies Club' or 'Coterie', see Gillian Russell, *Women, Sociability and Theatre in Georgian London* (Cambridge: Cambridge University Press, 2007), 68–73.

34 On Harris and his milieu see Clive T. Probyn, *The Sociable Humanist: The Life and Works of James Harris, 1709–1780* (Oxford: Clarendon Press, 1991). For Harris' interest in Shakespeare see, for example, *Miscellanies by James Harris* (4 vols., London, n.d. [1787]), vol. I, 110–11.

35 This building is still extant, as is the Harrises' adjoining house, now called Malmesbury House. The Chapel Room was mainly used for musical performances: Handel had attended a recital there when he stayed with James Harris in 1739.

36 Elizabeth Harris to James Harris Jr, 6 January 1770: Burrows and Dunhill, 575.

37 *Ibid.*

38 *Ibid.*

39 *Ibid.*

40 *Ibid.*, 579.

41 *Salisbury Journal*, 20 June 1774.

42 Burrows and Dunhill, 775.

43 *Ibid.*, 777–8.

44 See Dobson, *Making of the National Poet*, 49–52, 54–7.

45 Burrows and Dunhill, 778.

46 Coxe, 643.

47 'Gertrude is a kind of *impresario* and has all the torment of planning the scenes, describing the dresses, and hearing the complaints besides the trouble of getting up the part of Almeyda in the tragedy and that of the Clown in the farce – poor little thing', wrote Louisa on 30 October 1774: Burrows and Dunhill, 774.

48 *Ibid.*, 778.

49 *Ibid.*, 777–82.

50 Macnamara Morgan, *Florizel and Perdita, or, The Sheep-Shearing* (London, 1762), 13.

51 *Ibid.*, 22.

52 Burrows and Dunhill, 777–82.

53 Morgan, 1.
54 See Dobson, *Making of the National Poet*, 146–9; Harris, *Miscellanies*, vol. III, 24–5.
55 *The Correspondents, an Original Novel, in a Series of Letters* (London, 1775), 27–8; see also 175–80. Peach's remarks on Shakespeare as the poet of female friendship were excerpted in the *Gentleman's Magazine* and the *Monthly Review*.
56 Burrows and Dunhill, 782.
57 *Ibid.*, 818.
58 Arnold Hare, *The Georgian Theatre in Wessex* (London: Phoenix, 1958), 122.
59 *Bath Journal*, 17 November 1774.
60 *Bath Journal*, 1 December 1774.
61 She was said, however, to have been slighted by a Mr Bowles: see Probyn, 238.
62 *Salisbury Journal*, 28 November 1774.
63 In Morgan's adaptation, even the Old Shepherd, 'Alcon', turns out to be only dressed up as a rustic too, since at the end of the play he reveals that he is really Antigonus who, unmolested by any bear, has stayed in Bithynia to look after Perdita under an alias while awaiting news from home of Leontes' change of heart.
64 *Salisbury Journal*, 27 March 1775. This conclusion echoes that of Mr Tobin's 'On seeing Miss Wyndham in the part of Creusa' five years earlier: 'No more sweet Girl, attempt to play / Such cold ambitious parts / While you possess a milder sway / And reign the Queen of Hearts[.]' Burrows and Dunhill, 579.
65 See Robert Benson and Henry Hatcher, *Old and New Sarum, or Salisbury* (Salisbury, 1843), 582.
66 One further such warm piece of verse is preserved among the Harris papers. It was written by one Dr Lillington after seeing the Duchess of Queensbery congratulate the performers of *Elvira* and *The Sheep-Shearing* with kisses after the show:

> When Sarums kings and queens and nymphs and swains
> Their mimick arts rehearsed and love sick strains
> The Duchess saw and praised and kiss'd them too
> Which every man in raptures wish'd to do
> With heart and lips to give them all their due. (Burrows and Dunhill, 782)

67 21 March 1775; Burrows and Dunhill, 817. There must have been some sort of reconciliation between performers and press, however, as in 1776 the *Salisbury Journal* was enthusiastically reporting another production by the young ladies of the Close, this time of Thomas Franklin's *The Earl of Warwick* and David Garrick's operatic afterpiece *Cymon*.
68 *Salisbury Journal*, 27 March 1775.
69 It is worth recalling here that another amateur actress, Lady Stanhope, who appeared in Nicholas Rowe's *The Fair Penitent* opposite the Duke of York's

Lothario in the raffish Delaval theatricals in St James's in the previous decade, actually had herself painted in the role of Calista by Benjamin Wilson, surrounded by the mourning props from act 5 scene 1, and the resulting picture (later engraved) looks very like one of the fancy-portraits for which other fashionable women of the time would sit in their favourite masquerade outfits. See Rosenfeld, plate 3.

70 Benson and Hatcher, 582.

71 4 December 1774: Burrows and Dunhill, 783–4.

72 Thomas Gisborne, *An Enquiry into the Duties of the Female Sex* (London, 1797), 173–5; 174.

73 Thomas Otway had largely developed his influential style of pathos-rich, feminocentric tragedy while adapting *Romeo and Juliet* as his own *Caius Marius* in 1680.

74 See Rosenfeld, 76–94. For Miss Wynne's costume, which resembles that worn by Dorothea Jordan on the professional stage, see Figure 11c; also Elisabeth J. Heard, 'The Theatre at Wynnstay: Eighteenth-Century Private Theatricals at their Finest', *Theatre Notebook* 58: 1 (2004), 18–34.

75 Most eighteenth-century acting texts, going further than Dering (who simply cut its second half), cut the single scene, 3.1, in which Lady Mortimer and her father Glendower appear, leaving Lady Percy and Mistress Quickly as the sole female roles.

76 James Powell, *The Narcotic and Private Theatricals* (London, 1787), 35.

77 Appropriately, Powell's play has never been given either a professional production or a semi-professional one, but has only been performed once, by a disinterested local amateur group (in that former hotbed of Augustan amateur drama, Lymington, in 2000).

78 David Garrick, *A Peep Behind the Curtain, or the New Rehearsal* (London, 1767), 21–3.

79 'Epilogue, written by Captain Topham', in Thomas Morton, *The Way to Get Married* (London, 1796), 91–2.

80 See Frederick Reynolds, *The Dramatist; or, Stop Him Who Can*, in Elizabeth Inchbald, ed., *The British Theatre* (25 vols., London, 1808), vol. xx, 25.

81 Frederick Reynolds, *The Life and Times of Frederick Reynolds* (2 vols., London, 1827), vol. ii, 6.

82 *European Magazine*, August 1788, 115–18.

83 Cumberland's essay ends with a plea that well-born amateur players should instead, effectively, reinvent the court masque – ceasing to imitate the stages and repertoire of the patent houses, commissioning site-specific occasional plays to be performed in their grand houses as parts of whole multi-media fetes and generally staying away from his chosen profession altogether. 117–18.

84 James Thomas Kirkman, *Memoirs of the Life of Charles Macklin Esq.* (2 vols., London, 1799), vol. i, 340. On the Delavals' theatrical activities see Rosenfeld, 95–108.

85 *Ibid.*, 138.

86 Quoted in *ibid.*, 137.

87 An engraving of Barrymore's opulent theatre during its brief heyday is reproduced in the *General Magazine*, March 1792.

88 I.e. without every Romeo knowing how much his Juliet's virtue was worth. These remarks were widely quoted: see e.g. the *Annual Register* 34 (1799), 5. On the career of the Earl of Barrymore see Anthony Pasquin [John Williams], *The Life of the Late Earl of Barrymore, Including a History of the Wargrave Theatricals* (3rd edn, London, 1793); Rosenfeld, 17–33.

89 See *ibid.*, 147–52. Hartopp-Wigley's productions also included *Richard III* and *Macbeth*.

90 *European Magazine*, 1788, 103–4.

91 These were *As You Like It, Coriolanus, Cymbeline, Hamlet, Henry IV part 1, Julius Caesar, King John, King Lear, Macbeth, The Merchant of Venice, Othello, Richard III, Romeo and Juliet, The Taming of the Shrew* (in the form of Garrick's abbreviation *Catherine and Petruchio*) and *Twelfth Night.*

92 See *A Collection of the Playbills of the Kilkenny Theatre* ([Kilkenny], 1811), 82.

93 *Ibid.*

94 See, for example, an anonymous 1817 tribute to the actor who at the time occupied the role in London, John Philip Kemble: 'His Hamlet shows the Gentleman compleat, / His easy manners – Oh heavenly Treat.' Harvard Theatre Collection, 'Kembleiana' vol. 7, TS 990 480.20.

95 Deirdre le Faye, ed., *The Letters of Jane Austen* (1995: London: Folio Society, 2003), 283. 'She is an elegant creature,' reported Austen afterwards, 'and hugs Mr Younge delightfully.' *Ibid.*

96 See *The Private Theatre of Kilkenny*, 121–2; *Gentleman's Magazine*, 1819, 635. For a vivid eyewitness account of O'Neill's Juliet at Kilkenny, and of the 1819 final season in general, see *Ierne; or Anecdotes and Incidents of a Life Chiefly in Ireland . . . by a Retired Civil Engineer* (London, 1861), 161–8.

97 *Christian Observer* 42 (1843), 99.

98 Samuel Madden, *Memoir of the life of Peter Roe* (Dublin, 1842), 323; on Roe's campaign against the theatricals and the players' responses in prologues and epilogues, see 319–35.

99 *Ibid.*, 329.

100 *Christian Observer* 42 (1843), 99. Reviewing Madden's biography of Roe (quoted above), the *Christian Observer* lamented that such had been the degeneracy of the time that the Kilkenny theatricals, despite Roe's opposition, had been attended by six bishops, six deans, seven archdeacons and fifty other clergymen, all accompanied by their families. *Ibid.*, 98.

101 Sir John Carr, *The Stranger in Ireland; or, a Tour in the Southern and Western Parts in the Year 1805* (Stamford, 1806), 251.

102 The Dublin playhouses generally derived their acting texts and stage business from the prominent London players who would come over to perform

there every summer. After 1808, as a result, the Kilkenny company generally learned the lines of its mainpieces from the relevant volumes of Elizabeth Inchbald's compilation *The British Theatre; or, A Collection of Plays, which Are Acted at the Theatres Royal, Drury Lane, Covent Garden, and Haymarket. Printed under the Authority of the Managers from the Prompt Books* (25 vols., London, 1808), to which they made only minor adjustments: since the appearance of Bell's edition of Shakespeare in the 1770s, such conveniently pre-cut editions of popular plays had been saving many amateurs from the kinds of dramaturgical and scribal work undertaken by Dering and Carrington.

103 *The Private Theatre of Kilkenny*, 28.
104 *Ibid.*, 54–5.
105 *Ibid.*, 5.
106 *Dublin Evening Post*, 28 November 1809.
107 *Kilkenny Paper*, 30 October 1805.
108 Mr Bushe's prologue to the opening night of the 1805 season, spoken by Richard Power: *Private Theatre of Kilkenny*, 19.
109 Carr, 251–2.
110 *Private Theatre of Kilkenny*, 9. The same point had been made by the *Dublin Evening Post*'s correspondent on 28 November 1809.
111 *Ierne*, 161.
112 See e.g. *A Collection of the Playbills of the Kilkenny Theatre*, 14, 18, 22, 27. It is worth noting here, though, that several of the Kilkenny plays could have been construed as articulating non-Unionist perspectives on the post-1798 world: as well as playing Hamlet, for instance, a nephew who agonizes about opposing his tyrannous uncle, Power also played Jaffeir in *Venice Preserved*, a son-in-law who agonizes about opposing his tyrannous father-in-law. Power's portrait as Hamlet was painted by an artist who later painted Daniel O'Connell.
113 See Lionel Pilkington, *Theatre and the State in Twentieth-Century Ireland* (London: Routledge, 2001), 17.
114 Quoted in *The Private Theatre of Kilkenny*, 102.
115 Carr, 251.
116 On both this point and the casting of children, cf. the account by 'Thespianus' of the private performance of Home's *The Douglas* mounted by 'Lady Fiddlestick', in 'Solomon Grildrig', ed., *The Miniature: A Periodical Paper* (Windsor, 1805), 317–20: 'But no one can conceive the plaudits bestowed on the Honourable Master Marmozet, her ladyship's only son, on his appearance in the character of the Peasant Norval; who was decorated with every splendour that fashion could devise, and the simple plaid could hardly be distinguished through a profusion of jewels' (319).
117 This is a copy of Mrs Inchbald's edition of the play, from the *British Theatre* series: Vet A5 e.1847.
118 *Ibid.*, 41. For the armchair, see 33.
119 *Ibid.*, 14.

CHAPTER 2: SHAKESPEARE IN PUBLIC: THE RESISTED RISE
OF THE AMATEUR DRAMATIC SOCIETY

1 Carr, 250. The official records of the Society published as *A Collection of the Play-bills of the Kilkenny Theatre* and *The Private Theatre of Kilkenny* make it clear that the theatre was only leased, but Carr's mistake is nonetheless instructive, tying this venture more closely at once to older systems of private theatre (in which the aristocratic performers would invariably own their own theatres) and to the future model pioneered by the Stockport Garrick Society.

2 Rosenfeld, 12.

3 *A Memorial of the Tercentenary of Shakspere, at Cambridge* (Cambridge, [1864]), 12. Prices ranged from 3s (Lower Boxes) to 6d (Gallery).

4 *Ibid.*, 3.

5 See Sidney Lee, *Shakespeare and the Modern Stage* (London: Constable, 1907), 176–7; Richard Foulkes, *The Shakespeare Tercentenary of 1864* (Bath: Society for Theatre Research, 1984), 9.

6 Dobson, *Making of the National Poet*, 137–41ff.

7 In [Pierre Bayle *et al.*], *A General Dictionary, Historical and Critical* (10 vols., London, 1734–41), vol. IX, 189.

8 *London Daily Post and General Advertiser*, 9 April 1741.

9 This tableau stands in for the original Stratford performance of Garrick's *Ode upon dedicating a building, and erecting a statue, to Shakespeare, at Stratford-upon-Avon*, performed in front of the similar copy of the Scheemakers statue which Garrick presented to Stratford and which now stands in a niche in the façade of the town hall.

10 Maria Julia Young, *Memoirs of Mrs Crouch* (2 vols., London, 1806), vol. II, 210–11; unidentified press cutting, 22 April 1794, in Folger W.b.577, item 12.

11 Quoted in Valerie L. Gager, *Shakespeare and Dickens: The Dynamics of Influence* (Cambridge: Cambridge University Press, 1996), 268.

12 Lawrence Huston Houtchens and Carolyn Washburn Houtchens, eds., *Leigh Hunt's Dramatic Criticism, 1808–1831* (New York: Columbia University Press, 1949), 26–7.

13 *London Daily Post and General Advertiser*, 12 April 1739.

14 This was borrowed so that it might preside over the farewell dinner of London's latest true-begotten Hamlet, Kemble, in 1817: *An Authentic Narrative of Mr Kemble's Retirement from the Stage* (London, 1817), 68.

15 Charles Dickens, speech to the General Theatrical Fund, quoted in Gager, 41.

16 On Garrick's visit to Wynnstay see John Askew Roberts, *Wynnstay and the Wynns: A Volume of Varieties* (London, 1876), 15–16.

17 *Private Theatre of Kilkenny*, 62–3.

18 Quoted in Jane Moody, 'Writing for the Metropolis: Illegitimate Performances of Shakespeare in Early Nineteenth-century London', *Shakespeare Survey* 47 (1994), 61–9; 61; *The Illegitimate Theatre in London, 1770–1840*

(Cambridge: Cambridge University Press, 2007), 129. See also *Report from a Select Committee on Dramatic Literature, with Minutes of Evidence* (London, 1832), 142, 216. This debate closely foreshadows more recent ones about the monopoly on broadcasting once held by the BBC, and continuing discussions about the place of the BBC in an otherwise commercial marketplace in which rival channels have proliferated.

19 Rosenfeld, 95–108.
20 On the Margravine's theatricals, and her guest appearance at the Earl of Barrymore's in 1792, see A. M. Broadley and Lewis Melville, eds., *The Beautiful Lady Craven: The Original Memoirs of Elizabeth, Baroness Craven, Afterwards Margravine of Anspach and Bayreuth and Princess Berkeley of the Holy Roman Empire (1750–1828)* (2 vols., London: John Lane, 1914), vol. I, lxxix–cv; Rosenfeld, 53–75.
21 See Annibel Jenkins, *I'll Tell You What: The Life of Elizabeth Inchbald* (Lexington: University Press of Kentucky, 2003), esp. 241–3, 259–60.
22 Rosenfeld, 64–7.
23 *The Beautiful Lady Craven*, vol. II, 138.
24 These included Marsollier's *Camille, où le souterrain*, Nicolas-Thomas Barthe's *Les Fausses Infidélités* and Rousseau's *Pygmalion*, together with readings of *Robert, chef des brigands* (La Martelière's translation of Schiller's *Die Räuber*) and Beaumarchais' *La Mère coupable* (which de Brécy found repugnant). See le Vicomte Gauthier de Brécy, *Mémoires véridiques et ingénus de la vie privée, morale et politique d'un homme de bien* (Paris, 1834), 265–91.
25 *Ibid.*, 284–5. On Lullin's other theatrical activities see Chapter 3, below.
26 *The Beautiful Lady Craven*, vol. I, xciii. Gillray's print is *Enter Cowslip, with a Bowl of Cream. Vide Brandenburg Theatricals* (13 June 1795).
27 *The Times*, 7 November 1792. The theatre opened in 1793, originally with a capacity of 150; it was later enlarged to double this size. The Margravine gave up amateur drama after the death of the Margrave in 1806, and the theatre was eventually demolished in 1822. Its site is now occupied by another haunt of avant-garde theatre, the Riverside Studios.
28 See *The Morning Herald*, 19 July 1802: the higher subscription and entry charges for men reflect their higher consumption of wine. See also 'Opening and Proceedings of the Dilettannti, or Pic-Nic Society', *Sporting Magazine*, vol. 20 (London, 1802), 31–2.
29 This playhouse had been built as the New Theatre in 1772, and was finally demolished in 1903, to be replaced by the Scala.
30 This is a regular theme of the short-lived magazine which was initially founded in the interests of vindicating Greville's club, *The Pic-Nic* (1802–3); cf. the letter from 'X' on the subject in issue 1, 4–5.
31 See, for example, the memoirs of one avowed member of the Pic-Nics, Henry Angelo: Henry Angelo, *The Reminiscences of Henry Angelo* (2 vols., London, 1828), 288–97. On the Pic-Nics and their struggle with the patent theatres, see especially Russell, *The Theatres of War*, 126–8.

32 Angelo, 290.

33 *Ibid.*, 290, 294.

34 Quoted in Jenkins, 446.

35 *The Beautiful Lady Craven*, civ.

36 *Morning Herald*, 23 February 1803.

37 *The Pic-Nic* 2 (15 January 1803).

38 *The Spirit of the Public Journals for 1802* (London, 1803), 181–204.

39 Quoted in *ibid.*, 203.

40 *Morning Herald*, 23 February 1803; in Folger scrapbook A.16.3 (Lysons vol. iii), 168–9, together with much other contemporary satire on the Pic-Nics.

41 See Russell, *The Theatres of War*, 134.

42 It is striking that Henry Angelo, one of its members, had been a witness to the destruction of the Pantheon in 1792, itself the locus of an earlier, comparable experiment in feminocentric public culture: see Russell, *Women, Sociability and Theatre*, Chapter 5.

43 Lord William Lennox, *Celebrities I Have Known* (4 vols., London, 1876–7), vol. ii, 72–3. On Berkeley's theatricals outside London see also Samuel Young Griffith, *Griffith's New Historical Description of Cheltenham and Its Vicinity* (2 vols., Cheltenham, 1826), vol. i, 68–9; John Goding, *Norman's History of Cheltenham* (London and Cheltenham, 1863), 348.

44 In a series of speeches against the Dramatic Licenses Bill in 1833–4; see especially Hansard HL Deb June 1834 vol. 24 cc. 908–12 (as Lord Seagrave).

45 See, for example, Joseph Grimaldi *et al.*, *Memoirs of Joseph Grimaldi* (London, 1846), 161.

46 Lennox, vol. i, 242–6. This speech was made in 1827. Despite his pretensions to public virtue, Fitzhardinge was described after his death as 'a sort of tenth-rate Rochester' (*Morning Leader*, 17 October 1857). He is sometimes cited as the original for the Marquis of Steyne in Thackeray's *Vanity Fair*.

47 On these riots see especially Marc Baer, *Theatre and Disorder in Late Georgian London* (Oxford: Clarendon Press, 1992); also Michael Dobson, 'John Philip Kemble', in Peter Holland, ed., *Great Shakespeareans Volume ii: Garrick, Kemble, Siddons, Kean* (London: Continuum, 2010), 55–104; 92–5.

48 See, for example, Harvard Theatre Collection HTC 401; Folger PROMPT Wint. T 28.

49 Folger W.b.67, 13a.

50 This took place in January 1882. See the album of playbills from these performances, the earliest dating from 1849, in Twickenham Library. I am grateful to Tom Betteridge for this reference.

51 Adrian Rendle, *Everyman and His Theatre: A Study of the Purpose and Function of the Amateur Society Today* (London: Pitman, 1968), 4, Figure 3.

52 See George Winchester Stone, Jr, and George M. Kahrl, *David Garrick: A Critical Biography* (Carbondale: Southern Illinois University Press, 1979), 100–1.

53 It's a sign of how far theatre historians have often assumed that the Theatres Royal really did have a monopoly on cultural significance that in the early

1980s the editors of Garrick's collected plays, although they published its text in a journal article, excluded *Ragandjaw* from their edition. Harry William Pedciord, '"Ragandjaw": Garrick's Shakespearean Parody for a Private Theatre', *Philological Quarterly* 60:2 (spring 1981), 197. I am grateful to Robert D. Hume for this point.

54 On Shakespearean burlesque in general, see especially Richard W. Schoch, *Not Shakespeare: Bardolatry and Burlesque in the Nineteenth Century* (Cambridge: Cambridge University Press, 2002).

55 Rosenfeld, 8.

56 See Stanley Wells, ed., *Nineteenth Century Shakespeare Burlesques* (5 vols., Osaka: Eureka, 2004), vol. 1, xxi.

57 Charles William Smith, *Family Theatricals, Selected from Standard Authors* (London, 1860), 'Preface' (np).

58 *The Book of Drawing-Room Plays and Evening Amusements* (London, [1860]), by 'Henry Dalton', similarly offers shortened versions of the trial scene from *The Merchant of Venice* and the first scene of *The Tempest* to use as a charade for 'courtship', together with a drastically abbreviated *A Midsummer Night's Dream*, 47–57.

59 W. J. Sorrell, *The Amateur's Hand-book and Guide to Home or Drawing Room Theatricals. How to Get Them Up and How to Act in Them: and How to 'Get Up' Theatricals in a Country House; and a Supplement Containing a List of Suitable Plays, with the Number of Male and Female Characters* (London, 1866).

60 George Hodder, *Memories of My Time, Including Personal Reminiscences of Eminent Men* (London, 1870), 180–95. The Ghost was played by Henry Mayhew.

61 www.oldstagers.com; George Taylor, *A History of the Amateur Theatre* (Melksham: Colin Venton, 1972), 37–8.

62 Neville Lynn, *The Thespian Papers* (London, 1887), 102–3.

63 *Ibid.*, 89.

64 *Romeo and Juliet, or, The Shaming of the True* (Oxford, 1868).

65 Ruth Bourne, diary for 1889, Herefordshire Record Office: quoted in Robin Haig, *A History of Theatres and Performers in Herefordshire* (Little Logaston: Logaston Press, 2002), 87–8.

66 Louisa M. Alcott, *Little Women* (1868: ed. Valerie Alderson, Oxford: Oxford University Press, 1994), 10. Lacking a trapdoor in the drawing room, Jo has to content herself with staging *The Witch's Curse, An Operatic Tragedy*.

67 George M. Baker, *The Mimic Stage* (Boston, 1869), 102–4.

68 *The Bombay Miscellany* vol. IV (Bombay, 1862), 723, 585.

69 *Ibid.*, 723.

70 *Ibid.*

71 See Wells, III, ix. On this production and its proto-*Charley's Aunt* social milieu see especially Carpenter, 11–13.

72 *Hamlet Travestie* (Oxford, 1849). Stanley Wells attributes this script to Reynolds Hole: Wells, vol. III, xi.

73 See Wells, vol. IV, X, and, for the play itself, 75–140. On further amateur burlesques, see xiii–xiv, xix, xxi, xxii.

74 John Bernard, *Retrospections of the Stage* (2 vols., Boston, 1832), vol. I, 25, 38, 50.

75 Francis Grose, *Grose's Classical Dictionary of the Vulgar Tongue* [1811] ... *Revised and Corrected by Pierce Egan* (London, 1823), np. I am grateful to Catherine Robinson for this reference.

76 See John A. Thieme, 'Spouting, Spouting Clubs and Spouting Companions', *Theatre Notebook* 29 (1975), 9–16.

77 The title *The Spouter's Companion* had been used in 1770 for an anthology of prologues and epilogues: the undated 1820s publication includes famous passages from Shakespeare among other 'favourite Recitations, Comic and Serious'.

78 Leman Thomas Reade, *The Modern Speaker* (London, 1826), esp. 57, 163, 168, 170, 192, 240.

79 Andrew Murphy, *Shakespeare for the People: Working-class Readers, 1800–1900* (Cambridge: Cambridge University Press, 2008), 137–57. See also Antony Taylor, 'Shakespeare and Radicalism: The Uses and Abuses of Shakespeare in Nineteenth-Century Popular Politics', *The Historical Journal* 45 (2002), 357–79.

80 Murphy, 148.

81 *Proceedings of the Sheffield Shakespeare Club, from Its Commencement, in 1819, to January, 1829. By a Member of the Club* (Sheffield, 1829). This club was originally spurred into existence as a resistance group determined to ignore the anti-theatrical sermons being preached by the local vicar.

82 See, for example, the silk playbill from the 1851 benefit of *Much Ado About Nothing* preserved among the Combermere papers in the National Army Museum, Chelsea, NAM 1995–06–61–9.

83 See Nita A. Dawson, *One Hundred Years of Amateur Acting* (Manchester: Jesse Broad, 1947). George Taylor reports that a female amateur had originally planned to appear in 1861, but backed out at the last moment; 'lady members' only appeared regularly on the stage from the 1880s onwards. See George Taylor, 38–9.

84 See Dawson, 12–13. Women were only admitted to full membership of this society in the late 1870s.

85 *A Memorial of the Tercentenary*, 5–6.

86 *Ibid.*, 4.

87 *Ibid.*, 5.

88 *Ibid.*, 12. See Foulkes and Werner Habicht, 'Shakespeare Celebrations in Times of War', *Shakespeare Quarterly* 52 (2001), 441–55. Habicht reproduces a protesters' handbill addressed to the people of Stratford complaining of this class exclusion.

89 *A Memorial of the Tercentenary*, 4.

90 In this Britain fell behind the US, where the Booths' 1864 benefit per-formances of *Julius Caesar*, despite the fact that President Lincoln was

subsequently assassinated after one of their revivals, did ultimately help to pay for the statue of Shakespeare in Central Park. See e.g. New York, Winter Garden, *Julius Caesar*, Playbill, Booth Benefit for the Shakespeare Statue Fund, 25 November 1864, Shelfmark BILL Box U4 W78 1864–65 no. 2a. Folger Shakespeare Library.

91 Foulkes, 20–1, 42–3.

92 From the inscription on the statue's pedestal: cf. Mark Antony in *Julius Caesar* on Caesar's walks and gardens, 3.2.240–4: 'He hath left them you, / And to your heirs for ever'. The inscription refers to Grant as 'Baron Albert Grant, MP', since he had been given the title 'Baron' for financial services rendered by Victor Emmanuel II of Italy in 1868, and in 1874 had just been re-elected as MP for Kidderminster. By the time the statue was unveiled, however, the election had been declared null and void due to corrupt practices. Grant has often been identified as the principal model for the speculator Melmotte in Anthony Trollope's novel *The Way We Live Now* (1874–5).

93 *Twelfth Night*, 4.2.43–4.

94 Geoffrey Whitworth, *Theatres of My Heart* (London: Gollancz, 1930), 77.

95 Foulkes, 48–9.

96 See e.g. John Elsom and Nicholas Tomalin, *The History of the National Theatre* (London: Cape, 1978), 52. I am grateful to Russell Jackson for this reference. The site is now occupied by the School of Tropical Medicine. On the YMCA and the encouragement of Shakespearean recitations during the First World War, the most important text remains William Hargreaves, *The Night I Appeared as Macbeth*, still one of the finest depictions of early twentieth-century amateur Shakespeare (London: Lawrence Wright, 1922):

> 'Twas through a Y.M.C.A. concert, I craved a desire for the stage.
> In Flanders one night I was asked to recite; Gadzooks, I was quickly the rage.
> They said I was better than Irving, and gave me some biscuits and tea
> (I know it's not union wages, but that was the usual fee).
> Home I came; bought a dress;
> Appeared in your Theatre, and what a success –
> CHORUS
> I acted so tragic the house rose like magic,
> The audience yelled 'You're sublime!'
> They made me a present of Mornington Crescent,
> They threw it a brick at a time.
> Someone threw a fender, which caught me a bender,
> I hoisted a white flag and tried to surrender.
> They jeered me; they queered me,
> And half of them stoned me to death;
> They threw nuts and sultanas, fried eggs and bananas,
> The night I appeared as Macbeth . . .

97 James Woodfield, for instance, cites in London alone the Stage Society (which survives as the English Stage Company at the Royal Court) (1899);

the Mermaid Society (1903); the New Stage Club (*c.* 1905); the Pioneers (1905); the English Drama Society (1905); the Literary Theatre Club (1906); the Play Actors Society (1907); the Oncomers Society (1911); the New Players Society (1911); the Drama Society (1911); the Adelphi Play Society (1912); the Religious Drama Society (1913); and the People's Theatre Society (1914). James Woodfield, *English Theatre in Transition, 1881–1914* (Beckenham: Croom Helm, 1984), 69–70. On this trend see especially Allardyce Nicoll, *English Drama 1900–1930: The Beginnings of the Modern Period* (Cambridge: Cambridge University Press, 1973), 78–87.

  98 Edwin T. Heys, letter on 'Amateur Dramatic Work in Stockport', unidentified press cutting *c.* 1 November 1901, in Stockport Garrick Society archive, album 1.

  99 For the most recent developments, see www.stockportgarrick.co.uk.

100 See, for example, Anna I. Miller, *The Independent Theatre in Europe, 1887 to the Present* (New York: Long and Smith, 1931), 217: 'Imbued with the best of the repertory spirit, the Stockport Garrick Society prepared the way for the first true modern repertory theatre in the English-speaking world, Miss Horniman's Manchester Repertory Theatre Company, which opened in the autumn of 1907.' See also Rendle, 8–10; Woodfield, 70.

101 In this it would be emulated, for instance, by the spin-off Altrincham Garrick Society, established by a founder member of the Stockport Garrick, W. S. Nixon, in 1914. See Pamela Knox, *The Flame Still Burns: The Story of Altrincham Garrick Theatre* (Altrincham: Altrincham Garrick Society, 1993), 1. It would also be emulated by the Bury Garrick Society and the Marple Garrick Society. Granville-Barker visited the Stockport Garrick as a lecturer; for his comments on the society see 'The Theatre: The Next Phase', *English Review*, April–July 1910, 631–48; 632.

102 Edwin T. Heys, letter on 'Amateur Dramatic Work in Stockport', unidentified press cutting, October 1901, in Stockport Garrick Society archive, album 1.

103 On the unprecedented significance and connotations of Anne Hathaway's Cottage for the late Victorians and Edwardians, see especially Nicola Watson, *The Literary Tourist: Readers and Places in Romantic and Victorian Britain* (Houndmills: Palgrave, 2006), 86–9.

104 'Constitution and Syllabus, 1902', in Stockport Garrick Society archive, album 1.

105 *Ibid.*

106 *City and County News*, 18 July 1902, *ibid.*

107 'Stockport Garrick Society,' reprinted from *The Stockport Advertiser*, 20 June 1902, *ibid.*

108 'While other amateur dramatic clubs trifle with *Caste* and *Captain Swift* and mechanical penny toys like these, [the Stockport Garrick Society] is this week tackling Ibsen's *Pillars of Society*, no less, and tackling it in a way that is at any rate immeasurably better than leaving it alone.' *Manchester Guardian* 26 February 1904, *ibid.*

109 'Stockport Garrick Society: The Mayor on the Drama', unidentified press cutting, January 1902, *ibid.*

110 Unidentified press cutting, *c.* 2 March 1902, *ibid.*

111 Unidentified press cutting, 5 March 1902, *ibid.*

112 7 March 1902, *ibid.*

113 *Stockport Express*, 8 April 1904, *ibid.* Charrington would remain a correspondent and advisor of the Society on Ibsenite matters: see George Taylor, 49.

114 *Ibid.*

115 *County News*, 23 March 1906, *ibid.* The Society's archive provides no clue as to why this single piece of cross-gender casting was adopted on this occasion.

116 Letter from 'A Garrick Member', *County News*, 2 March 1906, *ibid.*

117 Rendle, 10.

118 H. V. Morton, *In Search of England* (1927: London: Everyman, 1949), 250.

119 On Jackson, see especially J. C. Trewin, *The Birmingham Repertory Theatre, 1913–1963* (London: Barrie and Rockcliff, 1963).

120 G. W. Bishop, ed., *Amateur Dramatic Yearbook and Community Theatre Handbook, 1928–9* (London: A and C Black, 1928), 209.

121 On Poel, see especially William Poel, *Shakespeare in the Theatre* (London: Sidgwick and Jackson, 1913); Robert Speaight, *William Poel and the Elizabethan Revival* (London: Heinemann, 1954); Lewis Casson, 'William Poel and the Modern Theatre', *The Listener*, 10 January 1952, 56–8; Marion O'Connor, '"Useful in the Year 1999": William Poel and Shakespeare's "Build of Stage"', *Shakespeare Survey* 52 (1999), 17–32.

122 See also www.maddermarket.co.uk/.

123 Charles Rigby, *Maddermarket Mondays* (Norwich: Roberts, 1933), 4.

124 On Monck's work and its influence, see especially Nugent Monck, 'The Maddermarket Theatre and the Playing of Shakespeare', *Shakespeare Survey* 12 (1959), 71–5; Franklin J. Hildy, 'Playing Places for Shakespeare: The Maddermarket Theatre, Norwich', *Shakespeare Survey* 47 (1994), 81–90, and *Shakespeare at the Maddermarket: Nugent Monck and the Norwich Players* (Ann Arbor: UMI Research Press, 1986).

125 *Sunday Chronicle*, 16 November 1919, cutting in Stockport Garrick archive, album 2.

126 In Harold Downs, ed., *The Theatre and Stage* (2 vols., London: Pitman, 1934), vol. 1, 60.

127 Patrick Carleton, 'The Revolt Against Hollywood', in Patrick Carleton, ed., *The Amateur Stage: A Symposium* (London: Bles, 1939), 1–43; 17, 19.

128 Downs, ed., vol. 1, vi.

129 See e.g. Janet Dunbar, *Flora Robson* (London: Harrap, 1960), 72–5.

130 L. Du Garde Peach, *The Village Players Great Hucklow Present Twenty-Five Years of Play Producing, 1927–1952: A Record, Compiled by L. Du Garde Peach* (Great Hucklow: The Village Players, 1952), 3.

131 See Nora Ratcliff, *Rude Mechanicals: A Short Review of Village Drama* (London: Nelson, 1938); Mick Wallis, 'Drama in the Villages: Three Pioneers', in Paul Brassley, Jeremy Burchardt and Lynne Thompson, eds., *The*

English Countryside Between the Wars: Regeneration or Decline? (Woodbridge: Boydell, 2006), 102–15.

132 Whitworth, 13–14. For the proposed National Theatre's constitutional requirement to perform Shakespeare, see the appendix, 'Report of the Drafting Committee as Presented to H.M. Government', 77–9; 77, section 2, para. ii.

133 Marshall, 86.

134 Downs, ed., vol. i, vi.

135 Frank Humpherson, *Shakespeare for Amateurs: A Handbook for the Amateur Actor and Producer* (1935: London, Samuel French, 1936), 136. He goes on to offer tips on how best to train schoolboys.

136 'The Little Theatre is presenting a Shakespearian play for the first time. This is an interesting experiment, and before we started work we asked ourselves why so many amateur productions of Shakespeare are such dreary affairs. The answer is this: the producer is invariably weighed down by tradition, the cast is generally awed by a masterpiece, and the audience is only driven to the theatre by a stern sense of duty. Our rehearsals have **not** been conducted in a dim religious light, or beneath the shadow of a great genius. We have approached this play as Philistines – intelligent Philistines – and we hope that the audience will join us in this happy state.' Programme note by the producer, Marie Jeaffreson. Middlesbrough Little Theatre archive. The production was one of the most successful the company had yet offered.

137 See Gwenan Evans *et al.*, *A Few Drops of Water: The Story of the Questors Theatre, 1929–1989* (Ealing: Mattock Press, 1989), 7.

138 Michael Shipley *et al.*, *Bolton Little Theatre: 75 Years of Drama* (Bolton: Bolton Little Theatre, 2006), 5.

139 In Downs, ed., vol. i, 2. On this view, its context and its accuracy, see also Michael Dobson, 'Shakespeare as a Joke: The English Comic Tradition, *A Midsummer Night's Dream* and Amateur Performance', *Shakespeare Survey* 56 (2003), 117–25.

CHAPTER 3: SHAKESPEARE IN EXILE: EXPATRIATE PERFORMANCE

1 On the spread of Anglophone theatrical activity through the empire, particularly in the case of one popular she-tragedy, see Kathleen Wilson, 'Rowe's *Fair Penitent* as Global History: Or, a Diversionary Voyage to New South Wales', *Eighteenth-Century Studies* 41:2 (winter 2008), 231–51.

2 'Ode to Shakespeare', in Bodleian MS Mus d 14. The poem has accompanying music, attributed to William Boyce. The first couplet quoted here derives from the play *Harlequin Student* (1741); see Dobson, *Making of the National Poet*, 227.

3 Benjamin Stillingfleet, *Literary Life and Select Works of Benjamin Stillingfleet* (2 vols., London, 1811), vol. i, 80–1; J. S. Rowlinson, '"Our Common Room

in Geneva" and the Early Exploration of the Alps of Savoy', *Notes and Records of the Royal Society of London* 52:2 (July 1998), 221–35.
4 Stillingfleet, vol. I, 73–81.
5 *Ibid.*, 75.
6 *Ibid.*, 77.
7 *Ibid.*, 77. On objections to the eighteenth-century tradition of playing the witches as 'beggarly Gammers', see Dobson, 'John Philip Kemble', 80.
8 See Claire-Eliane Engel, 'Shakespeare in Switzerland in the XVIIIth Century', *Comparative Literary Studies* 17–18 (1945), 2–9; J. A. Galiffe *et al.*, *Notices généalogiques sur les familles genevoises* (6 vols., Geneva, 1830–92), vol. II (1831), 557: 'IX. No. François Calandrini, né le 3 juillet 1677, conseiller 1728, syndic 1738, premier syndic, †1750, ép. le 23 mars 1717, Susanne, f. de Charles Barnouin, B.G., dont il eut: 1. Madelaine, fem. de Richard *Nevill Aldworth*, tige des lords Braybroke, pairs d'Angleterre'.
9 See Thomas Medwin, *Journal of the Conversations of Lord Byron* (New York, 1824), 89–90. Byron had to abandon this production because his mistress Teresa Guiccioli, who did not wish to perform herself, would not trust him to rehearse with any other Desdemona or Emilia in her absence.
10 See H. C. G. Matthew and Brian Harrison, eds., *The Oxford Dictionary of National Biography* (60 vols., Oxford: Oxford University Press, 2004), vol. XLI, 834 (on O'Neill), vol. XLIV, 176–7 (on Normanby).
11 Charles Dickens, ed., *The Life of Charles J. Mathews, Chiefly Autobiographical, with Selections from His Correspondence and Speeches* (2 vols., London, 1879), vol. II, 12.
12 Unidentified contemporary press cutting, New York Public Library for the Performing Arts, MWEZ+nc.8748.
13 'I do not scruple to say that Lady Normanby is the sweetest actress I have ever seen, and I am backed by the opinion of everyone that her Juliet has never been more beautifully done ... The Masquerade Scene in "Romeo and Juliet" was quite enchanting; all the lovely English girls here of high fashion, dressed in most beautiful fancy costumes, performed the dance in a manner that captivated everybody.' Mathews, in Dickens, ed., vol. II, 12–13.
14 *Ibid.*, 11–12.
15 See James Fenimore Cooper, *Gleanings in Europe: Italy* (1838), ed. John Conron and Constance Ayers Denne (Albany: SUNY, 1981), 24: 'Then we have, beside the regular exhibitions of the town, rival houses in two English theatres, with amateur-performers; at the head of one of which is Lord B–, and at the head of the other Lord N–. At the latter only, however, can one be said to see the legitimate drama; the other running rather into music, – an experiment not to be idly attempted in Italy.'
16 *Ibid.*, 24–5. On Cooper's relations with Burghersh and Normanby, see James Franklin Beard, ed., *The Letters and Journals of James Fenimore Cooper*, vol. I (Cambridge, MA: Harvard, 1960), 346. On Normanby's theatricals see also Clara L. Dentler, *Famous Foreigners in Florence, 1400–1900*

(Florence: Bemporad Marzocco, 1964), 188; Aubrey S. Garlington, *Society, Culture and Opera in Florence, 1814–1830: Dilettantes in an 'Earthly Paradise'* (Aldershot: Ashgate, 2005), 87.

17 Galiffe *et al.*, vol. 1 (1830), 110: 'Charles-Michel, chef du bureau des étrangers, soit *alien office*, en Angleterre, où il s'est marié'; William Wickham, *The Correspondence of the Right Honourable William Wickham, from the Year 1794 ...*, *Edited, with Notes, by His Grandson, William Wickham MA* (2 vols., London, 1870), vol. 11, 145.

18 Mistrustful of d'Arblay, who proposed to leave England to accept a position in Napoleon's army during the peace of Amiens, Lullin imposed a condition that d'Arblay should not return for at least a year – a condition which, when the appointment ran into difficulties and d'Arblay found it impossible to reclaim the property his family had lost at the revolution, left him stranded in Paris without his wife and son: 'Sans cesse j'avais devant les yeux le Sieur Lullin, de l'Alien Office,' wrote d'Arblay, recalling the depths of his initial despair,

et la promesse que j'ai été contraint de faire, pour obtenir mon passeport, d'être au moins *un an* avant de retourner en Angleterre. L'insolence de ce Lullin me fait encore bouillir le sang. Quelques personnes en font cependant l'éloge. En ce cas l'exception dont il m'a honoré est flatteuse!

[I had perpetually before my mind's eye Mr Lullin of the Aliens Office, and the promise I was forced to make, in order to obtain my passport, that it would be at least *one year* before I returned to England. The insolence of this Lullin still makes my blood boil. Some people, nonetheless, praise him. In that case the exception with which he has honoured me is flattering!]

In the event Burney and her son joined d'Arblay in France, and, when the war resumed soon afterwards, the family found themselves confined there for the next decade. *Diary and Letters of Madame d'Arblay*, ed. Charlotte Barrett. New edition with portraits (7 vols., London, [nd]), vol. IV, 137 (8 March 1802).

19 On Lullin's friendship with Kemble, see W. Powell Jones, 'Sir Egerton Brydges on Lord Byron', *Huntington Library Quarterly* 13:3 (May 1950), 325–37.

20 Lullin repeated this play with his sister and her circle back in Switzerland, playing Richard with a degree of naturalism, including the blacking of his teeth, which shocked his compatriots: see Alville [Alix de Watteville], *Anna Eynard-Lullin et l'époque des congrés et des revolutions* (Lausanne: Feissly, 1955), 89–103. Lullin's doings in London, and his marriages to two Englishwomen in succession (Maria, and then Nancy, successors to his first, Genevan, wife Sara Natron), are occasionally glimpsed in the correspondence of his scientist uncle Marc-Auguste Pictet, who frequently used Lullin as a courier to his London contacts such as Sir Joseph Banks. See Marc-Auguste Pictet, *Correspondance science et techniques* (4 vols., Geneva: Slatkine, 1996), vol. I: *Les Correspondants genevois*, 170; vol. III: *Les Correspondants britanniques*, 373, 375, 552, 570.

21 Augustus John Cuthbert Hare, *The Story of Two Noble Lives* (3 vols., London, 1893), vol. III, 385.

22 Lady Theresa Lewis, ed., *Extracts of the Journals and Correspondence of Miss Berry* (3 vols., London, 1866), vol. II, 476–7.

23 Valerie Offord, 'The Welcoming City', exhibition catalogue, State Archives of Geneva, 2003: www.geneva-heritage.com/ArchExhib/EngCat.pdf, 5–6. Lullin's expatriate performances are also mentioned in William Maginn's article about Samuel Egerton Brydges, 'Gallery of Literary Characters: Sir Egerton Brydges', *Fraser's Magazine* 9 (February 1834), 146.

24 Roger de Candolle, ed., *L'Europe de 1830: vue à travers la correspondance de Augustin Pyramus de Candolle et Madame de Circourt.* (Geneva: A. Jullien, 1966), 14.

25 Hailing Geneva as 'Dear spot of Freedom!', the prologue to *Venice Preserved* offers Otway's pathos-rich tragedy as an appropriate gift to the city which gave the world Rousseau, evidence that Britain too 'Nurses the fervid soul and melting breast'. Samuel Egerton Brydges, 'Prologue II', in *The Anglo-Genevan Critical Journal for 1831* (2 vols., Geneva, 1831), 302–3.

26 *Monthly Mirror* 13 (1802), 219; Ian Fletcher, ed., *For King and Country: The Letters and Diaries of John Mills, Coldstream Guards, 1811–14* (Staplehurst: Spellmont, 1995), 88: 'They have got a private theatre there [at Wellington's headquarters] too. Colonel Braddyll is going over to act Falstaff, which I here he does inimitably.' John Mills, letter home to his mother from Val dos Ayres, Portugal, 13 November 1811.

27 Alville, 98–103.

28 Samuel Egerton Brydges, *The Autobiography, Times, Opinions, and Contemporaries, of Sir Egerton Brydges, Bart.* (2 vols., Geneva, 1834), vol. II, 102–3.

29 Samuel Egerton Brydges, *The Lake of Geneva* (2 vols., Geneva, 1832), vol. I, 129.

30 Powell Jones, 328–9. For Austen's view of Brydges, see le Faye, ed., 22.

31 Samuel Egerton Brydges, *The Anglo-Genevan Critical Journal for 1831* (2 vols., Geneva, 1831), vol. I, 303–5.

32 On the national resonances of the figure of Falstaff, see Michael Dobson, 'Falstaff after John Bull: Shakespearean History, Britishness, and the Former United Kingdom', *Shakespeare Jahrbuch* 136 (2000), 40–55.

33 Brydges, *The Anglo-Genevan Critical Journal for 1831*, I, 302–3.

34 *Ibid.*, 306–8.

35 *Dublin Literary Gazette, or Weekly Chronicle of Criticism, Belles Lettres, and Fine Arts* (February 1830) no. 6, 140: 'I see by the Geneva papers, that an English theatre has been established in that town. The actors, however, are amateurs, and their scenery and decorations are spoken of more highly than their acting.'

36 For example, Christoph Martin Wieland, Johann Jakob Bodmer and Johann Joachim Eschenburg. Zurich was also the birthplace of Henry Fuseli, a man who certainly did not need any prologue by Brydges to introduce him to Falstaff.

37 Russell, *The Theatres of War*, 130–5. On the impact of the experience of foreign warfare on eighteenth- and nineteenth-century culture more generally, which informs the contemporary press's interest in reporting 'Bon Ton Theatricals' staged by officers, see Mary Favret, *War at a Distance: Romanticism and the Making of Modern Wartime* (Princeton: Princeton University Press, 2010).

38 At Philadelphia all the roles seem to have been played by British officers. When Philadelphia fell to the rebel army American officers took over the theatre until Congress banned stage performances on 16 October 1778, ruining George Washington's plans for that evening. See Felicia H. Londre and Daniel J. Watermeier, *The History of North American Theater* (New York: Continuum, 1998), 74.

39 Quoted in Esther Cloudman Dunn, *Shakespeare in America* (New York: Macmillan, 1939), 112.

40 'Prologue, spoken at the opening of the John Street theatre, New York, 1777': quoted in George O. Seilhamer, *History of the American Theatre Before the Revolution, During the Revolution and After* (3 vols., Philadelphia, 1888–91), vol. II, 27–8; on this prologue, see Russell, *The Theatres of War*, 164–6.

41 New York Historical Society: *Receipts of the 'Theatre Royal' John Street New York AD 1779*, nos. 74 and 197. On these productions, see also Frances Teague, *Shakespeare and the American Popular Stage* (Cambridge: Cambridge University Press, 2006), 20–2; Jared Brown, *The Theatre in America During the Revolution* (Cambridge: Cambridge University Press, 1995); Russell, *The Theatres of War*, 160–7.

42 Although Esther Cloudman Dunn's account of these seasons, in *Shakespeare in America*, 114–19 (substantially followed by Frances Teague), claims that all the profits were pocketed by the officers themselves, see *New York, Theatre, 1782. General Account of Receipts and Disbursements for the two last Seasons* (New York, 1782), in the New York Historical Society. On the evidence of this document the theatre genuinely paid out more than a thousand pounds during 1782 'in CHARITY to the Widows and Children of the ... Regiments', as well as to 'Refugees' and 'Inhabitants of N. York and its Environs'.

43 Seilhamer, vol. II, 28.

44 *Receipts of the 'Theatre Royal' John Street*, no. 148.

45 The propaganda importance of theatre as an emblem of loyalty and traditional culture during the conflict was most fully expressed by the soldier-playwright General Burgoyne: see e.g. his prologue to the performance of Aaron Hill's *Zara* given in Boston in 1775. John Burgoyne, *The Dramatic and Poetical Works of the Late Lieut. Gen. J. Burgoyne* (2 vols., London, 1808), vol. II, 238.

46 On the state of Kingstown a decade earlier, see Charles Shephard, *A Historical Account of the Island of St Vincent* (London, 1831), 6–7; on the court house, see Virginia Heyer Young, *Becoming West Indian: Culture, Self and Nation in St Vincent* (Washington, DC: Smithsonian Institution Press, 1991), 47.

47 NAM 1984–09–31–26.

48 *Ibid.*
49 *Ibid.*
50 *Ibid.*
51 Gillian Russell, in her study of different forms of theatre and theatricality during the Napoleonic wars, *The Theatres of War*, similarly distinguishes between military performances of burlettas, musicals and farces, in which comic transvestite performances in female roles were welcomed, and military performances, usually by higher-ranking officers, of serious full-length plays, in which female performers were preferred. See Russell, *The Theatres of War*, Chapter 6, 'Mars and the Muses', esp. 137.
52 Lieutenant-Colonel Newnham, 'Amateurs in Foreign Parts', in W. G. Elliott, ed., *Amateur Clubs and Actors* (London, 1898), 220–46; 246. On British theatres around the Atlantic empire in general, and in the Caribbean in particular, see Kathleen Wilson, *The Island Race: Englishness, Empire and Gender in the Eighteenth Century* (London: Routledge, 2002).
53 Lord William Lennox, *Fashion Then and Now* (2 vols., London, 1878), vol. II, 100–1.
54 *Ibid.*, 78.
55 *Ibid.*, 101. Lennox continues as follows: 'A few untoward instances attended our winter campaign, among them the following ...'
56 See William S. McFeely, *Grant: A Biography* (1981: New York: Norton, 1982), 29. This production was directed by James Longstreet, who described it in an interview conducted by Hamlin Garland in around 1890; the typescript of the interview is now in the Doheny Library at the University of Southern California. In his own memoirs, Grant kept quiet about this performance.
57 For this epilogue, see Jonathan Mitchell Sewall, *Miscellaneous Poems* (Portsmouth, NH, 1801), 123–5. The comparison between the American rebel army and a warrior who fights against his own country is riskier than Sewall appears fully to recognize.
58 See Nathaniel Hawthorne, ed., 'Papers of an Old Dartmoor Prisoner', *US Democratic Review* (New York, January–September 1846); also W. Jeffrey Bolster, *Black Jacks: African-American Seamen in the Age of Sail* (Cambridge, MA: Harvard University Press, 1998), Chapter 4. I am grateful to Joyce MacDonald for this reference.
59 On early American appropriations of Shakespeare, see Michael Dobson, 'Fairly Brave New World: Shakespeare, the American Colonies and the American Revolution', *Renaissance Drama* n.s. 23 (1992), 189–207; Teague, ch. 1, *passim*.
60 The bills for these performances are preserved by the New York Historical Society: 7th Regiment Records Box 36 folder 6. John H. Bird was billed as stage-manager for all of them; as well as casting himself as Portia and as Bombastes he played Iago and Brutus, along with Dazzle in *London Assurance*.
61 Newnham, 230, 221.

62 *Ibid.*, 229–30. On the participation of British officers' wives in garrison amateur theatricals in India, see also Annabel Venning, *Following the Drum: The Lives of Army Wives and Daughters* (London: Headline, 2005), 225.

63 Cf. Newnham's account of the Hong Kong Amateur Dramatic Club, which remained all-male until 1879, and in which all the members – following the example of the Canterbury Old Stagers – appeared only pseudonymously, for fear of local disapproval (p. 234).

64 See Captain George Nugent, 'The Guards' Burlesque', in Elliott, ed., 9–21. This organization had evolved from 'The Grenadier Guards' Nigger Minstrel Troupe'.

65 See, for example, the repertories of the 'Corps Dramatique of Soldiers, 56th Regiment, Deesai, 1864', NAM 7 907–28, of the 'Theatre Royal, Royal Scots Fusiliers' ('The Ladies and Gentlemen Amateurs of Toungoora'), NAM 86 11–30, and that of the 'Royal Bijou Theatre, Gavelior' in 1877, NAM 1989 09–55–3.

66 On cross-dressing in shipboard performances of the Napoleonic period, particularly the double bill of Rowe's *The Fair Penitent* and Inchbald's *Who's the Dupe?* given on HMS *Bedford* in 1791, see Russell, *The Theatres of War*, 146–56. The finest hour of Royal Navy light comedy and pantomime was probably represented by the whole winter season produced during one of the expeditions sent in search of the explorer Franklin through the Canadian Arctic in 1850–1, when the crews of three Royal Navy ships, HMS *Lady Franklin*, HMS *Assistance* and HMS *Resolute*, detained on Griffith Island for the winter, declared themselves 'The Royal Arctic Theatre' and produced a season of historical dramas, harlequinades, afterpieces and farces so diverting that no crew members were lost through scurvy or other disease during the entire stay. The extensive repertory included no Shakespeare whatsoever.

67 *Ruhleben Camp Magazine* 6 (29 August 1915), 45. Quoted in Ton Hoenselaars, 'ShakesPOW', *Linguaculture* 2 (2010), 67–82.

68 *Ibid.* See Israel Cohen, *The Ruhleben Prison Camp: A Record of Nineteen Months' Internment* (London: Methuen, 1917).

69 Clara Calvo, 'Work of National Importance: Shakespeare in Dartmoor', unpublished paper, European Shakespeare Research Association conference, Pisa, October 2009, 8–9. On Shakespearean performances given by refugees from Nazi Germany while interned on the Isle of Man during the Second World War, see Ton Hoenselaars, 'A Tongue in Every Wound of Caesar: Performing *Julius Caesar* behind Barbed Wire during World War II', unpublished paper, ESRA, Pisa, October 2009.

70 Letter from Bombardier George H. Good, 15 July 1943: NAM 2001–06–224–73.

71 John Mansel, *The Mansel Diaries*, ed. E. G. C. Beckwith (London: Wildwood House, 1977), 67. Mansel was himself invited to play the centurion in a production of Masefield's *Good Friday*, but he restricted himself to designing and painting scenery for shows such as *Dick Whittington*, *Captain*

Brassbound's Conversion and *The Dover Road*, since so much of his time was already taken up with forging identity papers for escapers. He was the original for the character played by Donald Pleasence in *The Great Escape*.

72 M. N. McKibbin, *Barbed Wire: Memories of Stalag 383* (London: Staples, 1947), 85.

73 W. Wynne Mason, *Prisoners of War* (Wellington, New Zealand: Historical Publications Branch, 1954), 251–2. On the economics of these productions, which varied from camp to camp, see also *ibid.*, 251–2.

74 For this and other surviving images, see Michael Goodliffe, memoir, on www.mgoodliffe.co.uk, consulted June 2006.

75 *Ibid.*

76 McKibbin, 84; R. J. Duncan, album of theatrical records and photographs from Stalag 383, NAM 1999–03–45.

77 S. P. Mackenzie, *The Colditz Myth: British and Commonwealth Prisoners of War in Nazi Germany* (Oxford: Oxford University Press, 2004), 210.

78 See Goodliffe; Mansel, 136.

79 *Ibid.*

80 Stephen Orgel, *Impersonations: The Performance of Gender in Shakespeare's England* (Cambridge: Cambridge University Press, 1996).

81 Mansel, 68.

82 Graham Palmer, *Prisoner of Death* (Wellingborough: Stephens, 1990), 179.

83 Letter from Bombardier George H. Good, 15 July 1943: NAM 2001–06–224–73.

84 George Moreton, *Doctor in Chains* (London: Corgi, 1980), 96. Cf. James Delingpole's meticulously researched historical novel *Coward at the Bridge* (2009: London: Pocket, 2010), 324: 'You don't know the true meaning of lust till you've sat in a prison-camp concert hall with five hundred captured officers, some of whom have been behind the wire since Dunkirk, all gazing rapt as a trio of heavily made-up ephebes barely out of public school sashay, trill and pout their way through "Three Little Maids".'

85 Susan Elliott, with Barry Turner, *Denholm Elliott: Quest for Love* (1994: London: Headline, 1995), 44–5.

86 Mackenzie, 212.

87 Platt's diary is preserved in the archives of the Imperial War Museum.

88 Marjorie Garber, *Vested Interests: Cross-Dressing and Cultural Anxiety* (New York: Routledge, 1992), ch. 10.

89 See Duncan.

90 See the papers of Brigadier Robert Loder, preserved in the King's College Archive Centre, Cambridge (GBR/0272/P/Misc22), which include programmes from these productions and even the catalogue of a Munich theatrical costumier, F & A Diringer; also Sandy Hernu, *Q: The Biography of Desmond Llewelyn* (Seaford: S B Publications, 1999), 57–61, which includes contemporary drawings of some of these actors in female roles.

91 Goodliffe.

92 Hernu, 60; Mansel, 67. For further evidence of such well-resourced productions, see the theatrical reports in the camp magazine of Stalag XXA, *Prisoners' Pie*, NAM 9307–223.

93 Mansel, 67.

94 *Ibid.*, 68. Cf. Goodliffe: '[A]fter the first year we became highly organised so that we managed to get most of our requirements sent into the camp by the Germans.'

95 Mason, 237.

96 On arrangements for seating Germans, see the 'Minute Book for the Brigade Entertainments Committee, Theatre Committee, Music Committee' among the Loder papers, Misc 22/7.

97 Hernu, 60.

98 The skills and facilities developed in the costume department of the theatre at Eichstätt, for example, enabled Major-General William Broomhall and four colleagues briefly to escape disguised as a Nazi general, his batman, an adjutant and two Red Cross officials. The authorities became circumspect accordingly: 'The modern day costumes were civilian clothes sent from the UK to individuals and confiscated by the Germans. They were brought into the camp only for each performance, as also were the tools for scene making. There was always a German Guard with them.' Loder papers, Misc 22/4.

99 According to McKibbin, the authorities at Stalag 383 at first impeded the prisoners' attempts to produce their own drama but later, 'when the Theatre proved a great success despite them, they realized that entertainment was necessary and that photographs in Red Cross magazines of prisoners enjoying themselves made good propaganda'. Eventually the prison had two theatres, the 'Ofladium' and the 'National Theatre of Hohenfels'; thanks to the commandant's enthusiasm for operetta the Ofladium was even provided, at his insistence, with an orchestra pit, shovels being imprudently issued to prisoners for its construction, 'some of which were no doubt returned after use'. McKibbin, 85.

100 Brigadier Robert Loder, papers, in the King's College Archive Centre, Cambridge (GBR/0272/P/Misc22): manuscript note, Misc 22/4. The same distinction between those interested in escaping and those interested in theatre occurs in Michael Gilbert's semi-autobiographical detective-novel-cum-war-thriller *Death in Captivity* (London: Hodder and Stoughton, 1952), which was based on Gilbert's experiences as a prisoner in Italy.

101 A 'Shakespearean Reading Society' at Oflag VIB was, however, permitted to hold Sunday readings of *Richard III*, *Richard II* and *Henry IV part I* in 1941–2. Loder papers, manuscript notes by Lieutenant W. Andrew Biggar, Misc 22/6. This society also gave readings of *A Midsummer Night's Dream*, *Much Ado About Nothing* and *Coriolanus*.

102 See Carl Schmitt, *Hamlet oder Hekuba: Der Einbruch der Zeit in das Spiel*, 1956, translated and edited by Jennifer Rust and David Pan as *Hamlet or Hecuba: The Intrusion of the Time into the Play* (New York: Telos, 2009).

103 Reginald R. Buckly, *The Shakespeare Revival and the Stratford-upon-Avon Monument* (London: Allen and Son, 1911), viii.

104 Hermann Burte, *Sieben Reden von Burte* (Strasbourg: Hunenburg, 1943), 20; and see George Mosse, *Nazi Culture* (1966: Madison: University of Wisconsin, 2003), 141–4; Rodney Symington, *The Nazi Appropriation of Shakespeare: Cultural Politics in the Third Reich* (Lewiston, NY: Edwin Mellen, 2005), 244; Anselm Heinrich, *Entertainment, Propaganda, Education: Regional Theatre in Germany and Britain between 1918 and 1945* (Hatfield: University of Hertfordshire, 2007), 192–4.

105 See Zoltan Markús, 'Der *Merchant von Velence*. The *Merchant of Venice* in London, Berlin, and Budapest during World War II', in Dirk Delabastita, Jozef de Vos and Paul Franssen, eds., *Shakespeare and European Politics* (Cranbury: Associated University Presses, 2008), 143–57.

106 McKibbin, 85.

107 *Ibid.*, 85–6.

108 Frank Twiss, *Social Change in the Royal Navy, 1924–1970: The Life and Times of Admiral Sir Frank Twiss, KCB, KCVO, DSC*, compiled and edited by Chris Howard Bailey (Sutton Publishing: Stroud, 1996), 88.

109 *Ibid.*, 89.

110 *Ibid.*, 88–9.

111 See the private papers of Lieutenant Colonel E. J. Hazell, Imperial War Museum, IWM 85/42/1.

112 Twiss, 89–90. At another Japanese camp, Shakespeare's complete works were popular solely because the thin paper on which they were printed was so well-suited to rolling cigarettes. See Gavan Daws, *Prisoners of the Japanese: POWs of World War II in the Pacific* (New York: Harper Perennial, 1996); Hoenselaars, 'ShakesPoW', 3.

113 Twiss, 89.

114 See e.g. his *The Image of the Poet: British Poets and their Portraits* (Oxford: Clarendon Press, 1982).

115 Piper's journals and other miscellaneous PoW papers are catalogued as NAM 1994–06–110–8.

116 David Piper, *I Am Well, Who Are You?* (Exeter: Brightsea, 1998), 54–6.

117 It is catalogued with the journal, as NAM 1994–06–110–8.

118 David Piper, PoW journal, 6 June 1944.

119 *Ibid.*

CHAPTER 4: SHAKESPEARE IN THE OPEN: OUTDOOR
PERFORMANCE

1 Shipley *et al.*, 49.

2 The rest of the 2002–3 Bolton season might serve as a representative specimen of the repertory of a solid post-war British amateur dramatic society. Untypically, the group staged one new play (*Wakes* by Roger Spencer), but the rest of the season was entirely characteristic: an Alan

Bennett double bill, *Corpse!* by Gerald Moon, J. B. Priestley's *When We Are Married*, a youth production of Willy Russell's *Our Day Out*, Harold Pinter's *Betrayal*, a P. G. Wodehouse (*Good Morning Bill!*), and an Oscar Wilde (*Lord Arthur Saville's Crime*). *Ibid.*, 18.

3 This production won a prize for its costumes, and the society now intends to return to the regular performance of Shakespeare.

4 Michael Green, 'The Questors and Coarse Acting', in Evans *et al.*, 94–101.

5 See K. Edmonds Gateley, *To Play At Will* (Stratford: Herald Press, 1988).

6 David Conville, *The Park: The Story of the Open Air Theatre, Regent's Park* (London: Oberon, 2007), 13.

7 www.villagers.hampshire.org.uk/, consulted summer 2004–summer 2010.

8 See www.illyria.uk.com/, www.chapterhouse.org/. The best academic study dealing with this sort of company is Stephen Purcell, *Popular Shakespeare: Simulation and Subversion on the Modern Stage* (Houndmills: Palgrave, 2009).

9 www.cambridgeshakespeare.com/.

10 Both the Bolton Little Theatre and the Questors, incidentally, also remember the later 1940s as a golden age, when in particular their membership included BBC personnel trying out scripts and ideas.

11 Programme note to *Our Town*, 1948: Middlesbrough Little Theatre archive.

12 'Our toil shall strive to mend', programme note for *Romeo and Juliet*, 1946, *ibid.*

13 See J. L. Styan, *The Shakespeare Revolution* (1977: Cambridge: Cambridge University Press, 1983).

14 The foyer was slightly remodelled and enlarged at around this time, in such a way that the box named after Gielgud, which used to be in the centre rear of the stalls, now dispenses programmes and confectionery in the lobby.

15 Denys Val Baker, *The Minack Theatre* (Penzance: G. Ronald, 1960), 24.

16 See e.g. Watson, *The Literary Tourist*, 56–68.

17 On this episode and its significance, see Nicola J. Watson, 'Sir Walter Scott', in Adrian Poole, ed., *Great Shakespeareans: Scott, Dickens, Eliot, Hardy* (London: Continuum, 2011). Lady Penelope's choice of what would not be a popular play with either professionals or amateurs for many years to come was ahead of its time; it is her discovery that her fellow players are not very familiar with the script which eventually results in the play being reduced to tableaux.

18 These are now in the theatrical archives of the Victoria and Albert Museum: a selection are reproduced in John Stokes, *Resistible Theatres: Enterprise and Experiment in the Late Nineteenth Century* (London: Elek, 1972).

19 *The Dramatic Review*, 6 June 1885, 297. Quoted in Stokes, 48.

20 *Ibid.*, 47–50.

21 *Poole Guardian*, August 1893: quoted in the *Bournemouth Daily Echo*, undated cutting in the Brownsea Open-Air Theatre archive, summer 1972. Cf. the charitable outdoor *Midsummer Night's Dream* rehearsed at Simla at just this time, Chapter 3, above.

22 Godwin published these in *The Architect* in 1875: see Michael Walsh, 'Craig and the Greeks', in *Drama Forum*: www.cssd.ac.uk/dramforum/journal/craig2/html, accessed June 2006.

23 Quoted in *ibid.*

24 See Carpenter, 26–34. True to amateur precedent, the first two Shakespeares offered were *The Merchant of Venice*, 1883, and *Henry IV part 1*, 1884.

25 See Fiona MacIntosh and Edith Hall, *Greek Tragedy and the British Theatre* (Oxford: Oxford University Press, 2005), Chapter 15, 'Page versus Stage: Greek Tragedy, the Academy, and the Popular Theatre', *passim*.

26 I am grateful to Lepper's son, Charles Lepper, for showing me this auditorium in the summer of 2004. As if to demonstrate the connections between this classical revival and Shakespeare, Lepper junior, who practically grew up in the Bradfield theatre, went on to become a Shakespearean actor, later understudying Claudio in Peter Brook's famous Stratford *Much Ado About Nothing* in 1950.

27 For fuller accounts of the Edwardian pageant, see Ayiko Yoshino, *The Edwardian Historical Pageant: Local History and Consumerism* (Tokyo: Waseda University Press, 2010); Michael Dobson, 'The Pageant of History: Staging the Local Past, 1905–39', in Mark Thornton Burnett and Adrian Streete, eds., *Filming and Performing Renaissance History* (Houndmills: Palgrave, 2010).

28 See Cecil B. Gooden, *The Story of the Sherborne Pageant* (Sherborne: Bennett, 1905); Louis Napoleon Parker, *The Sherborne Pageant* (Sherborne: Bennett, 1905).

29 See Louis Napoleon Parker, *The Warwick Pageant* (Warwick: Evans, 1906), *The Dover Pageant* (Dover: Grigg and Sons, 1908).

30 See Robert Withington, *English Pageantry: An Historical Outline* (Cambridge, MA: Harvard University Press, 1918); Deborah Sugg Ryan, '"Pageantitis": Frank Lascelles' Oxford Historical Pageant, Visual Spectacle, and Popular Memory', *Visual Culture in Britain* 8:2 (2007), 63–82.

31 [Gilbert Hudson *et al.*], *The Pickering Pageant* (Pickering: Boak and Sons, 1910).

32 See Jed Esty, *A Shrinking Island: Modernism and National Culture in England* (Princeton: Princeton University Press, 2003), 46–54; Ayako Yoshino, '*Between the Acts* and Louis Napoleon Parker – the Creator of the Modern English Pageant', *Critical Survey* 15.2 (2003), 49–60.

33 Roger Simpson, 'Arthurian Pageants in Twentieth-Century Britain', *Arthuriana* 18:1 (2008), 63–88; 63. The closest recent literary descendant of the Edwardian pageant in this respect is perhaps Adam Thorpe's novel *Ulverton* (1992).

34 [Frank Lascelles *et al.*], *The Oxford Pageant, June 27–July 1, 1907: Book of Words* (Oxford: Oxford University Press, 1907), 6.

35 Mick Wallis, 'Delving the Levels of Memory and Dressing up in the Past', in Clive Barker and Maggie Gale, eds., *British Theatre Between the Wars, 1918–1939* (Cambridge: Cambridge University Press, 2000), 190–214; 200.

36 Mary Kelly, 'Pageants', in Harold C. Downs, ed., *The Theatre and Stage* (2 vols., London: Pitman, 1934), vol. II, 689–92, 735–8, 783–6, 833–6, 881–4, 929–32, 981–4, 1,035–8; 1,035.

37 Hudson *et al.*, preliminary pages.

38 For a case-study in the local politics of all this, see Michael Woods, 'Performing Power: Local Politics and the Taunton Pageant of 1928', *Journal of Historical Geography* 25:1 (1999), 57–74. Woods sees these events as potentially progressive, though Mick Wallis is more sceptical: according to him, the institutions which sponsored and participated in pageants, unlike the medieval guilds responsible for the mystery plays, were 'typically peripheral to the economic and social life of the town, not centres of mercantile and craft power but bolt-holes for petit-bourgeois worthiness and pretended influence'. Wallis, 195.

39 Kelly, 689.

40 *Ibid.*, 691–2.

41 Percy Mackaye, *Caliban By the Yellow Sands* (New York, 1916), xviii.

42 Parker, *The Warwick Pageant*, 3.

43 [Hudson *et al.*], 39–44.

44 Berenice de Bergerac, *The Oxford Pageant of Victory* (Oxford: Vincent Works, 1919), 21–3.

45 Photographs of this event are preserved in the National Army Museum library in Chelsea; see NAM 1990–07–31.

46 See Wallis, 191–3.

47 Kelly, 930–1.

48 On Elizabethan pageants and Shakespeare, see also Michael Dobson and Nicola Watson, *England's Elizabeth: An Afterlife in Fame and Fantasy* (Oxford, 2002), 138–46.

49 See Franklin J. Hildy, 'Reviving Shakespeare's Stagecraft: Nugent Monck and the Maddermarket Theatre, Norwich, England' (PhD, Northwestern University, Evanston, 1980), 103–5, 277–9, 312–17. 'He is the most successful pageant producer in England, and can handle a huge crowd with tremendous effect,' observes Norman Marshall in *The Other Theatre* (London: Lehmann, 1947), 95.

50 *New York Times*, 19 May 1936.

51 Also quick off the imitative block, incidentally, was Dulwich College, which mounted an all-male outdoor school production of *As You Like It* in the same year.

52 Greet even gave public lectures about the Oberammergau passion plays, for example at the London School of Economics on 3 October 1930 (New York Public Library for the Performing Arts: Greet scrapbooks, MWEZ 10,007).

53 *Toledo Daily Blade*, 18 April 1908.

54 *New York Times*, 19 May 1936.

55 Roy Mitchell, *Shakespeare for Community Players* (Toronto and London: Dent, 1919), 57.

56 *The Ben Greet Shakespeare for Young Readers and Amateur Players: A Midsummer Night's Dream* (New York: Doubleday, 1912), 108.

57 *Ibid.*, 46.
58 'Shakespeare himself played this part [Adam] at Wilton, Salisbury, where the play was written, in 1599' – Ben Greet, *The Ben Greet Shakespeare for Young People and Amateur Players: As You Like It* (New York: Doubleday, 1912), 48.
59 Winifred Isaac, *Ben Greet and the Old Vic* (London: published by the author, 1963), 38, 33.
60 *Ibid.*, 49–52.
61 Greet, *Dream*, 3.
62 Greet was, however, willing to compromise with popular taste in some respects: when staging *A Midsummer Night's Dream* he would often employ a small local orchestra to play the Mendelssohn incidental music ('If music be used in this play it is difficult to find anything so appropriate as that of Mendelssohn'; *ibid.*, 22 and *passim*).
63 *New York Times*, 19 May 1936.
64 Richmond Shakespeare Society archive: unmarked press cutting, album 1.
65 Isaac, 35.
66 *Ibid.*, 34–5. The persistence of this patrician-garden-party model of outdoor performance into the post-war period is attested by Prunella Scales, who when still a drama student in 1950 was hired, along with her peers, by one of the patronesses of the Richmond Shakespeare Society to perform *Romeo and Juliet* at a social function in a private garden. Alan Bates was Romeo: Scales played his page, Balthasar, and particularly recalls the stage direction 'Enter Balthasar, booted' in relation to the problem of keeping the costumes unsullied by the mud. She has avoided open-air work since. Private conversation, summer 2004.
67 Isaac, 39.
68 *Ibid.*, 216.
69 See e.g. the surviving playbill from a Greet production in Hartford, Connecticut, 16 May 1908: 'In the evening the grove will be lighted with apparatus brought by the Ben Greet Players and especially designed for such occasions' (NYPLPA, Woodland Players scrapbook, MWEZ 23,659).
70 Greet, *Dream*, 58.
71 *Ibid.*, viii.
72 Rev. S. N. Sedgwick, *With Shakespeare's Fairies* (London: Sheldon, 1912), ii.
73 Greet, *As You Like It*, v–viii, 16.
74 *Ibid.*, 108.
75 Greet, *Dream*, 138.
76 *Ibid.*, xi.
77 Programme note from *A Midsummer Night's* Dream, 1925, preserved in the personal scrapbook of Ruth Vivian, a former leading light of the Smith College Dramatic Society who toured in Greet's company throughout the 1920s: NYPLPA, MWEZ n.c.18,835.
78 See e.g. Montrose J. Moses, 'Pastoral Players', *The Theatre*, December 1908.

79 My own copy of Greet's acting edition of *A Midsummer Night's Dream* was autographed by him for Anita Damrosch, daughter of the American conductor Walter.

80 Patty Lee Clark, *The Admirable Miranda* (Westfield, MA: Times and Newsletter, 1905), np.

81 On *The Lost Colony*, which originally had Shakespeare among its cast of characters, see Dobson and Watson, 284.

82 Frederick Koch and Elizabeth Lay, 'Plays for Amateurs', *University of South Carolina Record* 172 (January 1920), 1–24.

83 'Their innocent, important babble about nothing, and their little dignified quarrels making them appear so self-satisfied, is like our modern unconscious child,' runs Greet's note to Oberon and Titania's confrontation at 2.1.60. Greet, *Dream*, 32.

84 See especially Ann Preston Bridgers, 'Shakespeare in the Forest', *The Carolina Play-Book* 14:2 (June 1941), 50–3; Folger Art File c291.8, especially number 15. In the years immediately preceding the First World War Greet even lobbied for the establishment of an American national theatre for Shakespeare, to be located in Washington, DC, but the American Shakespearean theatre which finally was built under his influence, albeit after his death, is in New York. Heir to the many outdoor performances Greet staged in and around the city, this is the Delacorte in Central Park, established by Joseph Papp in 1962, and now home of the New York Shakespeare Festival.

85 See e.g. *The London Graphic*, 11 December 1920.

86 See J. C. Trewin, 'Robert Atkins and the Open Air Theatre, Regent's Park', in *Robert Atkins: An Unfinished Autobiography*, ed. George Rowell (London: Society for Theatre Research, 1994), 113–19; Conville, 13–14.

87 Isaac, 228.

88 *Ibid.*, 218.

89 *Ibid.*, 66–7.

90 A. K. Clarke, *A History of the Cheltenham Ladies College, 1853–1953* (1953: London: Faber, 1954), 134–5.

91 E-mail from Rachel Roberts, school archivist, 18 October 2004.

92 Averil Demuth, *The Minack Open-Air Theatre: A Symposium* (Newton Abbot: David and Charles, 1968), 14.

93 Tim Cribb, in *ibid.*, 67.

94 Demuth, 23.

95 Richard Jefferies, 'Outside London', from *The Open Air* (1885), in S. J. Looker, ed., *Jefferies' England* (London: Constable, 1937), 327.

96 Mitchell, 57.

97 L. Du Garde Peach, 'Village Drama', in Patrick Carleton, ed., *The Amateur Stage* (London: Bles, 1939), 155.

98 Richmond Shakespeare Society archive: *Richmond and Twickenham Times*, (11?) May 1935.

99 Demuth, 26.

100 Evans *et al.*, 120–2.

101 See www.minack.com/.
102 See the interview with Greet in *The Bournemouth Graphic*, 25 September 1902, in which he boasts of having brought theatre to the town over a period of 'fifteen or sixteen years'. Pressed on the subject by the journalist's first question, Greet tactfully insisted that Bournemouth, so far from being boring, had 'many splendid facilities'.
103 See www.bournemouthlittletheatre.co.uk/, last consulted August 2010.
104 See www.brownsea-theatre.co.uk/, last consulted August 2010.
105 *Bournemouth Daily Echo*, 12 August 1964.
106 *The Lady*, 9 July 1964.
107 'Michael Dobson plays Amiens who sings the famous air Under the Greenwood Tree. Michael is a member of a local punk band.' Unidentified press cutting, August 1981, Brownsea Open-Air Theatre archive.
108 See *Daily Telegraph*, 11 August 1964; 'Prospero's Cabin', article by Michael Frenchman from the *Guardian*, August 1964, and other undated cuttings from local newspapers, Brownsea Open Air Theatre archive, scrapbook 1.
109 The Palace Court Theatre, subsequently the Playhouse, was run as a repertory theatre and receiving house for a while (in the mid-1970s I saw Evelyn Laye and Dulcie Gray perform there in a production of Edward Percy and Reginald Denham's *Ladies in Retirement*), and the small cinema, the Galaxy, in what had originally been a luxurious green-room in the basement briefly survived these shows upstairs, but Bournemouth's only venue suitable for unamplified spoken-word drama is now used as a church by the Pentecostal group the Assemblies of God. See www.theatrestrust.org.uk/resources/theatres/show/558-playhouse-bournemouth.
110 These were visiting performances by Illyria (*A Midsummer Night's Dream*, 2009) and the touring company from Shakespeare's Globe (*The Comedy of Errors*, 2010). The one instance I know of an amateur theatre successfully bucking this trend is provided by the formidable Richmond Shakespeare Society, who came in from the cold with the inauguration of their indoor Mary Wallace Theatre in Twickenham in 1981; but having been founded to offer outdoor productions, they continue to do so every summer.
111 This remark was made during an interview with the *Bournemouth Daily Echo* while Quayle's Compass company were visiting the draughty and overlarge Pavilion with their touring production of *The Tempest* in 1986.
112 *Bournemouth Daily Echo*, 27 July 1999.
113 This observation is based on years of overhearing conversations at amateur Shakespeare productions, years of meeting amateur exponents of Shakespeare and the study over the last few years of unreasonable numbers of reviews of amateur productions of Shakespeare: see, for example, the *Bournemouth Daily Echo* on Wendy Williams' 1981 Brownsea *As You Like It*, which was unusually played in Edwardian costumes: 'young Mr Dobson resembles an undergrad from the Charley's Aunt cast ... [but] given the warmth and gaiety of the piece we swallow all the absurdities'. Undated cutting, August 1981, Brownsea archive.

114 On the distinction in the theatre between clothes and costumes, see especially Aoife Monks, *The Actor in Costume* (Houndmills: Palgrave, 2010).

115 For a closer analysis of an outdoor production in relation to heritage and the conventions of costume, namely the Oxford Theatre Guild's 2004 *Merchant of Venice*, see Michael Dobson, 'Writing about [Shakespearean] Performance', *Shakespeare Survey* 58 (2005), 160–8.

116 [Arthur Bryant], *Book of the Pageant, Greenwich, 1933* (London: Fleetway, 1933), n.p.

117 For early critical responses to Shakespeare's Globe, see 'Shakespeare and the Globe', *Shakespeare Survey* 52 (1999); Christie Carson and Farah Karim-Cooper, eds., *Shakespeare's Globe: A Theatrical Experiment* (Cambridge: Cambridge University Press, 2008).

CONCLUSION

1 T. W. Robertson, *M.P.* (1870), in *The Principal Dramatic Works of T. W. Robertson* (London, 1889), 327.

2 Patrick Barlow, *Shakespeare: The Truth* (London: Methuen, 1993).

3 Marshall, 85, 87.

4 I have developed this argument at more length in 'Shakespeare as a Joke: *A Midsummer Night's Dream*, the English Comic Tradition, and Amateur Performance', *Shakespeare Survey* 55 (2003), 117–25.

5 On Noble's production, see especially Peter Holland, *English Shakespeares* (Cambridge: Cambridge University Press, 1997), 187–91.

6 On this production, see Michael Dobson, 'Shakespeare Performances in England, 2001', *Shakespeare Survey* 55 (2002), 256–86; 280.

7 The depiction of the corrupt pressing of recruits in *Henry IV*, similarly, made it an appropriate companion, in a number of garrison theatrical repertories, of George Farquhar's *The Recruiting Officer*.

8 On the importance of this play since Shakespeare's time, as well as on its contexts within it, see James Shapiro, *Shakespeare and the Jews* (New York: Columbia University Press, 1997).

9 Correspondence with Stephen 'Johno' Johns, RNTA, summer 2007 et seq.

10 Cf. the instance of English diplomatic amateur theatre immortalized by Tom Stoppard in *Travesties*, the production of *The Importance of Being Earnest* in which James Joyce became peripherally involved in Zurich in 1916.

11 E-mail correspondence with the director of *A Midsummer Night's Dream*, 1991, and *Twelfth Night*, 2001, Louise Palmer, April 2007.

12 E-mail correspondence with Jonathan Goldsmith, chair, and with long-standing member and director Catriona White, May–June 2007; see also www.shaksoc.com/pastproductions.htm.

13 E-mail correspondence with the chair, Jack C. Leo, April 2007.

14 See www.nwtc/lu.

15 E-mail correspondence with Mark Clayton, website manager, and Neil-Jon Morphy, archivist and seventy-fifth anniversary coordinator,

April–May 2007; conversation with former member Lara Feigel, 2009; see also www.geds.ch.

16 E-mail correspondence with their publicity officer, Michael Clarke, April 2007.

17 See www.festfrankfurt.org.

18 'In our more than forty years of existence we have never produced a full-scale Shakespeare play. The main reason for this is that the plays require such large casts and there are so many male roles. As is the case with most amateur companies, we are always short of men!' E-mail correspondence with the secretary and vice-chair, Maureen Egerup, May 2007.

19 *Ibid.*

20 On this novel, see Marjorie Garber, 'A Tale of Three *Hamlets*, or, Repetition and Revenge', *Shakespeare Quarterly* 61:1 (spring 2010), 28–55.

21 Evans *et al.*, 157. Just in anecdotal support of this point I might mention that the members of both the university English departments within which I have taught since returning to Britain fifteen years ago used to mount impressive productions of Shakespeare during their summer terms, but had ceased to do so by the mid-1990s: the days when a distinguished professor of English literature could ask to be cast as Gertrude as a retirement present (as did Barbara Hardy at Birkbeck; the request was granted, too) have gone.

22 The first preliminary working weekend, involving talks between the RSC and sixty-five representatives of amateur arts bodies, took place in Stratford at Halloween 2009. According to Robin Simpson, chief executive of the Voluntary Arts Network,

> There was a fantastic mood and genuine learning in both directions. RSC Artistic Director, Michael Boyd, gave an opening speech in which he said 'the World Shakespeare Festival, at the very least, will be a great project we can all enjoy but, at best, could be quite culture-changing: something very radical is happening in theatre in this country.' He stayed with us all weekend and genuinely listened and learned from the umbrella bodies. He was really excited about what we might do together and has asked for a follow-up meeting with us as soon as possible. (www.centralcouncilforamateurtheatre.org.uk/newsletters.htm, consulted spring 2010).

In this connection it is striking, too, that the site in Shoreditch occupied by The Theatre before it was transplanted to Southwark to become the Globe (a site which still preserves some of the foundations of this former headquarters of Shakespeare's company the Lord Chamberlain's Men) is at the time of writing being transformed into the home venue of central London's leading amateur company, Tower Theatre.

23 On some other amateur theatrical celebrations of 2000, see Michael Dobson, 'British Personality of the Millennium: English Shakespeares, Amateur and Professional, in the New Century', in Balz Engler and Ladina Bezzola Lambert, eds., *Shifting the Scene: Shakespeare in European Culture* (Newark: University of Delaware Press, 2004), 51–69.

24 'A few words from Frank Brogan, Project Founder', http://yorkshakespeareproject. org, consulted summer 2006.

Index

Lightning Source UK Ltd.
Milton Keynes UK
UKOW06f1146070216

267861UK00008B/271/P